AVIATION WEATHER

For Pilots and Flight Operations Personnel

Revised 1975

DEPARTMENT OF TRANSPORTATION
FEDERAL AVIATION ADMINISTRATION
Flight Standards Service

DEPARTMENT OF COMMERCE
NATIONAL OCEANIC AND ATMOSPHERIC ADMINISTRATION
National Weather Service

Washington, D.C.

Reprinted by **asa** PUBLICATIONS

Editorial Note:

Figures 137 through 139 and 142 on pages 160,
161, and 165 have been rearranged to align with
their proper legends. Corresponding corrections
have been made in the Contents, page XII.

Editorial Note: (9/82)

Figures 137 through 139 on pages 160 and 161
have been rearranged in order to flow in
proper sequence with the text. Corresponding
corrections have been made in the Contents,
page XII.

Preface

AVIATION WEATHER is published jointly by the FAA Flight Standards Service and the National Weather Service (NWS). The publication began in 1943 as CAA Bulletin No. 25, "Meteorology for Pilots," which at the time contained weather knowledge considered essential for most pilots. But as aircraft flew farther, faster, and higher and as meteorological knowledge grew, the bulletin became obsolete. It was revised in 1954 as "Pilots' Weather Handbook" and again in 1965 under its present title.

All these former editions suffered from one common problem. They dealt in part with weather services which change continually in keeping with current techniques and service demands. Therefore, each edition became somewhat outdated almost as soon as published; and its obsolescence grew throughout the period it remained in print.

To alleviate this problem, the new authors have completely rewritten this edition streamlining it into a clear, concise, and readable book and omitting all reference to specific weather services. Thus, the text will remain valid and adequate for many years. A companion manual, AVIATION WEATHER SERVICES, Advisory Circular 00-45, supplements AVIATION WEATHER. This supplement (AC 00-45) periodically is updated to reflect changes brought about by latest techniques, capabilities, and service demands. It explains current weather services and the formats and uses of weather charts and printed weather messages. The two manuals are sold separately; so at a nominal cost, a pilot can purchase a copy of the supplement (AC 00-45) periodically and keep current in aviation weather services.

C. Hugh Snyder, National Weather Service Coordinator and Training Consultant at the FAA Academy, directed the preparation of AVIATION WEATHER and AVIATION WEATHER SERVICES. He and his assistant, John W. Zimmerman, Jr., did much of the writing and edited the final manuscripts. Recognition is given to these meteorologists on the NWS Coordinator's staff who helped write the original manuscript, organize the contents, and plan illustrations: Milton Lee Harrison, Edward A. Jessup, Joe L. Kendall, and Richard A. Mitchem. Beatrice Emery deserves special recognition for her relentless effort in typing, retyping, proofing, correcting, and assembling page after page of manuscript. Many other offices and individuals have contributed to the preparation, editing, and publication of the two volumes.

Contents

PART II. OVER AND BEYOND

Illustrations

Introduction

Weather is perpetual in the state of the atmosphere. All flying takes place in the atmosphere, so flying and weather are inseparable. Therefore, we cannot treat aviation weather purely as an academic subject. Throughout the book, we discuss each aspect of weather as it relates to aircraft operation and flight safety. However, this book is in no way an aircraft operating manual. Each pilot must apply the knowledge gained here to his own aircraft and flight capabilities.

The authors have devoted much of the book to marginal, hazardous, and violent weather which becomes a vital concern. Do not let this disproportionate time devoted to hazardous weather discourage you from flying. By and large, weather is generally good and places little restriction on flying. Less frequently, it becomes a threat to the VFR pilot but is good for IFR flight. On some occasions it becomes too violent even for the IFR pilot.

It behooves every pilot to learn to appreciate good weather, to recognize and respect marginal or hazardous weather, and to avoid violent weather when the atmosphere is on its most cantankerous behavior. For your safety and the safety of those with you, learn to recognize potential trouble and make sound flight decisions *before* it is too late. This is the real purpose of this manual.

AVIATION WEATHER is in two parts. Part I explains weather facts every pilot should know. Part II contains topics of special interest discussing high altitude, Arctic, tropical, and soaring weather. A glossary defines terms for your reference while reading this or other weather writings. To get a complete operational study, you will need in addition to this manual a copy of AVIATION WEATHER SERVICES, AC 00-45, which is explained in the Preface.

We sincerely believe you will enjoy this book and at the same time increase your flying safety and economy and, above all, enhance the pleasure and satisfaction of using today's most modern transportation.

Part ONE

WHAT YOU SHOULD KNOW ABOUT WEATHER

Chapter 1
THE EARTH'S ATMOSPHERE

Planet Earth is unique in that its atmosphere sustains life as we know it. Weather—the state of the atmosphere—at any given time and place strongly influences our daily routine as well as our general life patterns. Virtually all of our activities are affected by weather, but of all man's endeavors, none is influenced more intimately by weather than aviation.

Weather is complex and at times difficult to understand. Our restless atmosphere is almost constantly in motion as it strives to reach equilibrium. These never-ending air movements set up chain reactions which culminate in a continuing variety of weather. Later chapters in this book delve into the atmosphere in motion. This chapter looks briefly at our atmosphere in terms of its composition; vertical structure; the standard atmosphere; and of special concern to you, the pilot, density and hypoxia.

COMPOSITION

Air is a mixture of several gases. When completely dry, it is about 78% nitrogen and 21% oxygen. The remaining 1% is other gases such as Argon, Carbon Dioxide, Neon, Helium, and others. Figure 1 graphs these proportions. However, in nature, air is never completely dry. It always contains some water vapor in amounts varying from *almost* zero to about 5% by volume. As water vapor content increases, the other gases decrease proportionately.

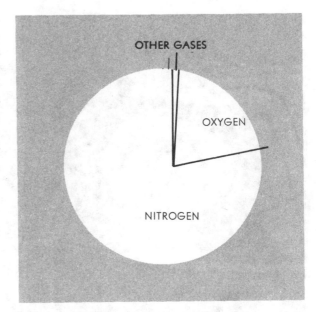

FIGURE 1. Composition of a dry atmosphere. Nitrogen comprises about 78%; oxygen, about 21%; and other gases, about 1%. When water vapor is added, the percentages decrease proportionately. Water vapor varies from almost none to about 5% by volume.

VERTICAL STRUCTURE

We classify the atmosphere into layers, or spheres, by characteristics exhibited in these layers. Figure 2 shows one division which we use in this book. Since most weather occurs in the troposphere and since most flying is in the troposphere and stratosphere, we restrict our discussions mostly to these two layers.

The TROPOSPHERE is the layer from the surface to an average altitude of about 7 miles. It is characterized by an overall decrease of temperature with increasing altitude. The height of the troposphere varies with latitude and seasons. It slopes from about 20,000 feet over the poles to about 65,000 feet over the Equator; and it is higher in summer than in winter.

At the top of the troposphere is the TROPO-PAUSE, a very thin layer marking the boundary between the troposphere and the layer above. The height of the tropopause and certain weather phenomena are related. Chapter 13 discusses in detail the significance of the tropopause to flight.

Above the tropopause is the STRATOSPHERE. This layer is typified by relatively small changes in temperature with height except for a warming trend near the top.

THE STANDARD ATMOSPHERE

Continual fluctuations of temperature and pressure in our restless atmosphere create some problems for engineers and meteorologists who require a fixed standard of reference. To arrive at a standard, they averaged conditions throughout the atmosphere for all latitudes, seasons, and altitudes. The result is a STANDARD ATMOSPHERE with specified sea-level temperature and pressure and specific rates of change of temperature and pressure with height. It is the standard for calibrating the pressure altimeter and developing aircraft performance data. We refer to it often throughout this book.

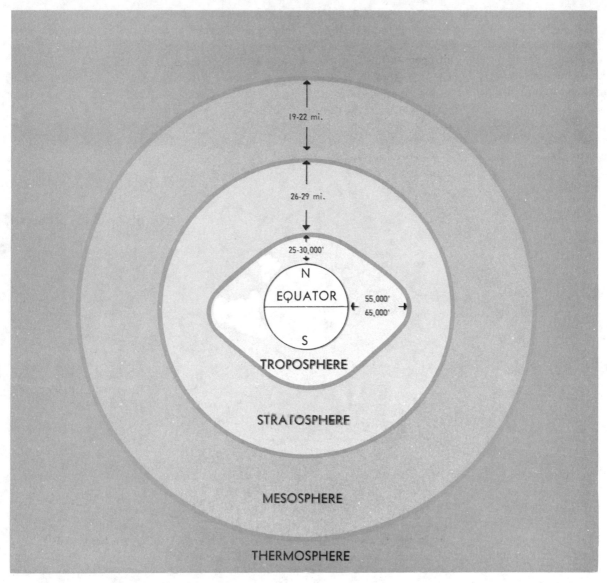

FIGURE 2. The atmosphere divided into layers based on temperature. This book concentrates on the lower two layers, the troposphere and the stratosphere.

DENSITY AND HYPOXIA

Air is matter and has weight. Since it is gaseous, it is compressible. Pressure the atmosphere exerts on the surface is the result of the weight of the air above. Thus, air near the surface is much more dense than air at high altitudes. This decrease of density and pressure with height enters frequently into our discussions in later chapters.

The decrease in air density with increasing height has a physiological effect which we cannot ignore. The rate at which the lungs absorb oxygen depends on the partial pressure exerted by oxygen in the air. The atmosphere is about one-fifth oxygen, so the oxygen pressure is about one-fifth the total pressure at any given altitude. Normally, our lungs are accustomed to an oxygen pressure of about 3 pounds per square inch. But, since air pressure decreases as altitude increases, the oxygen pressure also decreases. A pilot continuously gaining altitude or making a prolonged flight at high altitude without supplemental oxygen will likely suffer from HYPOXIA—a deficiency of oxygen. The effects are a feeling of exhaustion; an impairment of vision and judgment; and finally, unconsciousness. Cases are known where a person lapsed into unconsciousness without realizing he was suffering the effects.

When flying at or above 10,000 feet, force yourself to remain alert. Any feeling of drowsiness or undue fatigue may be from hypoxia. If you do not have oxygen, descend to a lower altitude. If fatigue or drowsiness continues after descent, it is caused by something other than hypoxia.

A safe procedure is to use auxiliary oxygen during prolonged flights above 10,000 feet and for even short flights above 12,000 feet. Above about 40,000 feet, pressurization becomes essential.

Chapter 2
TEMPERATURE

Since early childhood, you have expressed the comfort of weather in degrees of temperature. Why, then, do we stress temperature in aviation weather? Look at your flight computer; temperature enters into the computation of most parameters on the computer. In fact, temperature can be critical to some flight operations. As a foundation for the study of temperature effects on aviation and weather, this chapter describes commonly used temperature scales, relates heat and temperature, and surveys temperature variations both at the surface and aloft.

TEMPERATURE SCALES

Two commonly used temperature scales are Celsius (Centigrade) and Fahrenheit. The Celsius scale is used exclusively for upper air temperatures and is rapidly becoming the world standard for surface temperatures also.

Traditionally, two common temperature references are the melting point of pure ice and the boiling point of pure water at sea level. The melting point of ice is 0° C or 32° F; the boiling point of water is 100° C or 212° F. Thus, the difference between melting and boiling is 100 degrees Celsius or 180 degrees Fahrenheit; the ratio between degrees Celsius and Fahrenheit is 100/180 or 5/9. Since 0° F is 32 Fahrenheit degrees colder than 0° C, you must apply this difference when comparing temperatures on the two scales. You can convert from one scale to the other using one of the following formulae:

$$C = \frac{5}{9}(F - 32)$$

$$F = \frac{9}{5}C + 32$$

where C is degrees Celsius and F is degrees Fahrenheit. Figure 3 compares the two scales. Many flight computers provide for direct conversion of temperature from one scale to the other. Section 16, AVIATION WEATHER SERVICES has a graph for temperature conversion.

Temperature we measure with a thermometer. But what makes a thermometer work? Simply the addition or removal of heat. Heat and temperature are not the same; how are they related?

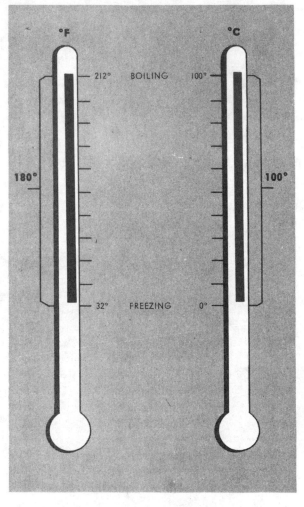

FIGURE 3. The two temperature scales in common use are the Fahrenheit and the Celsius. 9 degrees on the Fahrenheit scale equal 5 degrees on the Celsius.

HEAT AND TEMPERATURE

Heat is a form of energy. When a substance contains heat, it exhibits the property we measure as temperature—the degree of "hotness" or "coldness." A specific amount of heat absorbed by or removed from a substance raises or lowers its temperature a definite amount. However, the amount of temperature change depends on characteristics of the substance. Each substance has its unique temperature change for the specific change in heat. For example, if a land surface and a water surface have the same temperature and an equal amount of heat is added, the land surface becomes hotter than the water surface. Conversely, with equal heat loss, the land becomes colder than the water.

The Earth receives energy from the sun in the form of solar radiation. The Earth and its atmosphere reflect about 55 percent of the radiation and absorb the remaining 45 percent converting it to heat. The Earth, in turn, radiates energy, and this outgoing radiation is "terrestrial radiation." It is evident that the average heat gained from incoming solar radiation must equal heat lost through terrestrial radiation in order to keep the earth from getting progressively hotter or colder. However, this balance is world-wide; we must consider regional and local imbalances which create temperature variations.

TEMPERATURE VARIATIONS

The amount of solar energy received by any region varies with time of day, with seasons, and with latitude. These differences in solar energy create temperature variations. Temperatures also vary with differences in topographical surface and with altitude. These temperature variations create forces that drive the atmosphere in its endless motions.

DIURNAL VARIATION

Diurnal variation is the change in temperature from day to night brought about by the daily rotation of the Earth. The Earth receives heat during the day by solar radiation but continually loses heat by terrestrial radiation. Warming and cooling depend on an imbalance of solar and terrestrial radiation. During the day, solar radiation exceeds terrestrial radiation and the surface becomes warmer. At night, solar radiation ceases, but terrestrial radiation continues and cools the surface. Cooling continues after sunrise until solar radiation again exceeds terrestrial radiation. Minimum temperature usually occurs after sunrise, sometimes as much as one hour after. The continued cooling after sunrise is one reason that fog sometimes forms shortly after the sun is above the horizon. We will have more to say about diurnal variation and topographic surfaces.

SEASONAL VARIATION

In addition to its daily rotation, the Earth revolves in a complete orbit around the sun once each year. Since the axis of the Earth tilts to the plane of orbit, the angle of incident solar radiation varies seasonally between hemispheres. The Northern Hemisphere is warmer in June, July, and August because it receives more solar energy than does the Southern Hemisphere. During December, January, and February, the opposite is true; the Southern Hemisphere receives more solar energy and is warmer. Figures 4 and 5 show these seasonal surface temperature variations.

VARIATION WITH LATITUDE

The shape of the Earth causes a geographical variation in the angle of incident solar radiation. Since the Earth is essentially spherical, the sun is more nearly overhead in equatorial regions than at higher latitudes. Equatorial regions, therefore, receive the most radiant energy and are warmest. Slanting rays of the sun at higher latitudes deliver less energy over a given area with the least being received at the poles. Thus, temperature varies with latitude from the warm Equator to the cold poles. You can see this average temperature gradient in figures 4 and 5.

VARIATIONS WITH TOPOGRAPHY

Not related to movement or shape of the earth are temperature variations induced by water and terrain. As stated earlier, water absorbs and radiates energy with less temperature change than does land. Large, deep water bodies tend to minimize temperature changes, while continents favor large changes. Wet soil such as in swamps and marshes is almost as effective as water in suppressing temperature changes. Thick vegetation tends to control temperature changes since it contains some water and also insulates against heat transfer between the ground and the atmosphere. Arid, barren surfaces permit the greatest temperature changes.

These topographical influences are both diurnal and seasonal. For example, the difference between a daily maximum and minimum may be 10° or less over water, near a shore line, or over a swamp or marsh, while a difference of 50° or more is common over rocky or sandy deserts. Figures 4 and 5 show the seasonal topographical variation. Note that in the Northern Hemisphere in July, temperatures are warmer over continents than over oceans; in January they are colder over continents than over oceans. The opposite is true in the Southern Hemisphere, but not as pronounced because of more water surface in the Southern Hemisphere.

To compare land and water effect on seasonal temperature variation, look at northern Asia and at southern California near San Diego. In the deep continental interior of northern Asia, July average temperature is about 50° F; and January average, about −30° F. Seasonal range is about 80° F. Near San Diego, due to the proximity of the Pacific

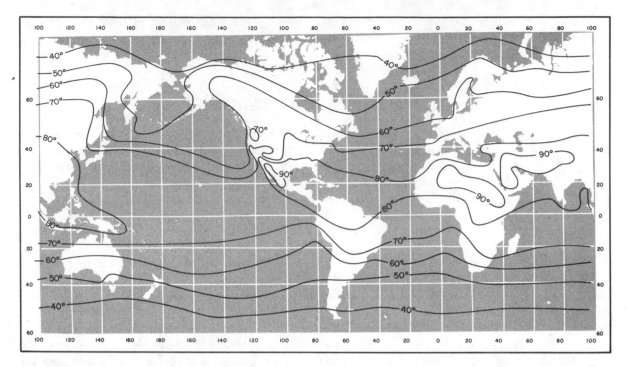

FIGURE 4. World-wide average surface temperatures in July. In the Northern Hemisphere, continents generally are warmer than oceanic areas at corresponding latitudes. The reverse is true in the Southern Hemisphere, but the contrast is not so evident because of the sparcity of land surfaces.

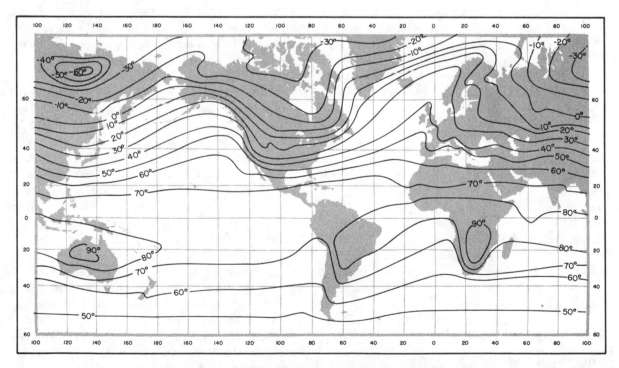

FIGURE 5. World-wide average surface temperatures in January when the Northern Hemisphere is in the cold season and the Southern Hemisphere is warm. Note that in the Northern Hemisphere, continents are colder than oceanic areas at corresponding latitudes, and in the Southern Hemisphere continents are warmer than oceans.

Ocean, July average is about 70° F and January average, 50° F. Seasonal variation is only about 20° F.

Abrupt temperature differences develop along lake and ocean shores. These variations generate pressure differences and local winds which we will study in later chapters. Figure 6 illustrates a possible effect.

Prevailing wind is also a factor in temperature controls. In an area where prevailing winds are from large water bodies, temperature changes are rather small. Most islands enjoy fairly constant temperatures. On the other hand, temperature changes are more pronounced where prevailing wind is from dry, barren regions.

Air transfers heat slowly from the surface upward. Thus, temperature changes aloft are more gradual than at the surface. Let's look at temperature changes with altitude.

VARIATION WITH ALTITUDE

In chapter 1, we learned that temperature normally decreases with increasing altitude throughout the troposphere. This *decrease of temperature with altitude* is defined as *lapse rate*. The average decrease of temperature—average lapse rate—in the troposphere is 2° C per 1,000 feet. But since this is an average, the exact value seldom exists. In fact, temperature sometimes increases with height through a layer. *An increase in temperature with altitude is* defined as *an inversion*, i.e., lapse rate is inverted.

An inversion often develops near the ground on clear, cool nights when wind is light. The ground radiates and cools much faster than the overlying air. Air in contact with the ground becomes cold while the temperature a few hundred feet above changes very little. Thus, temperature increases

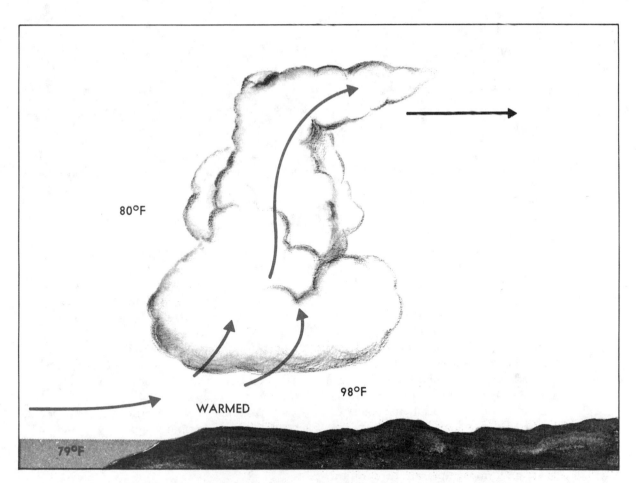

FIGURE 6. Temperature differences create air movement and, at times, cloudiness.

with height. Inversions may also occur at any altitude when conditions are favorable. For example, a current of warm air aloft overrunning cold air near the surface produces an inversion aloft. Figure 7 diagrams temperature inversions both surface and aloft. Inversions are common in the stratosphere.

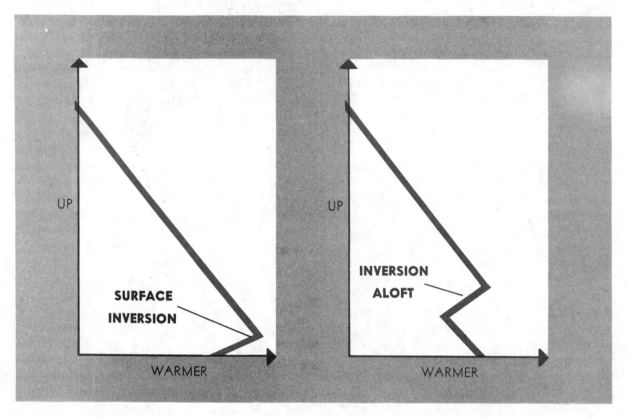

FIGURE 7.   Inverted lapse rates or "inversions." A lapse rate is a decrease of temperature with height. An inversion is an increase of temperature with height, i.e., the lapse rate is inverted. Shown here are a surface inversion and an inversion aloft.

IN CLOSING

Temperature affects aircraft performance and is critical to some operations. Following are some operational pointers to remember, and most of them are developed in later chapters:

1. The aircraft thermometer is subject to inaccuracies no matter how good the instrument and its installation. Position of the aircraft relative to the sun can cause errors due to radiation, particularly on a parked aircraft. At high speeds, aerodynamical effects and friction are basically the causes of inaccuracies.

2. High temperature reduces air density and reduces aircraft performance (chapter 3).

3. Diurnal and topographical temperature variations create local winds (chapter 4).

4. Diurnal cooling is conducive to fog (chapter 5).

5. Lapse rate contributes to stability (chapter 6), cloud formation (chapter 7), turbulence (chapter 9), and thunderstorms (chapter 11).

6. An inversion aloft permits warm rain to fall through cold air below. Temperature in the cold air can be critical to icing (chapter 10).

7. A ground based inversion favors poor visibility by trapping fog, smoke, and other restrictions into low levels of the atmosphere (chapter 12).

Chapter 3
ATMOSPHERIC PRESSURE AND ALTIMETRY

When you understand pressure, its measurement, and effects of temperature and altitude on pressure, you can more readily grasp the significance of pressure and its application to altimetry.

ATMOSPHERIC PRESSURE

Atmospheric pressure is the force per unit area exerted by the weight of the atmosphere. Since air is not solid, we cannot weigh it with conventional scales. Yet, Toricelli proved three centuries ago that he could weigh the atmosphere by balancing it against a column of mercury. He actually measured pressure converting it directly to weight.

MEASURING PRESSURE

The instrument Toricelli designed for measuring pressure is the barometer. Weather services and the aviation community use two types of barometers in measuring pressure—the mercurial and aneroid.

11

The Mercurial Barometer

The mercurial barometer, diagrammed in figure 8, consists of an open dish of mercury into which we place the open end of an evacuated glass tube. Atmospheric pressure forces mercury to rise in the tube. At stations near sea level, the column of mercury rises on the average to a height of 29.92 inches or 760 millimeters. In other words, a column of mercury of that height weighs the same as a column of air having the same cross section as the column of mercury and extending from sea level to the top of the atmosphere.

Why do we use mercury in the barometer? Mercury is the heaviest substance available which remains liquid at ordinary temperatures. It permits the instrument to be of manageable size. We could use water, but at sea level the water column would be about 34 feet high.

The Aneroid Barometer

Essential features of an aneroid barometer illustrated in figure 9 are a flexible metal cell and the registering mechanism. The cell is partially evacuated and contracts or expands as pressure changes. One end of the cell is fixed, while the other end moves the registering mechanism. The coupling mechanism magnifies movement of the cell driving an indicator hand along a scale graduated in pressure units.

Pressure Units

Pressure is expressed in many ways throughout the world. The term used depends somewhat on its application and the system of measurement. Two popular units are "inches of mercury" or "millimeters of mercury." Since pressure is force per unit area, a more explicit expression of pressure is "pounds per square inch" or "grams per square centimeter." The term "millibar" precisely expresses pressure as a force per unit area, one millibar being a force of 1,000 dynes per square centimeter. The millibar is rapidly becoming a universal pressure unit.

Station Pressure

Obviously, we can measure pressure only at the point of measurement. The pressure measured at a station or airport is "station pressure" or the actual pressure at field elevation. We know that pressure at high altitude is less than at sea level or low altitude. For instance, station pressure at Denver is less than at New Orleans. Let's look more closely at some factors influencing pressure.

PRESSURE VARIATION

Pressure varies with altitude and temperature of the air as well as with other minor influences which we neglect here.

Altitude

As we move upward through the atmosphere, weight of the air above becomes less and less. If we carry a barometer with us, we can measure a decrease in pressure as weight of the air above decreases. Within the lower few thousand feet of the troposphere, pressure decreases roughly one inch for each 1,000 feet increase in altitude. The higher we go, the slower is the rate of decrease with height.

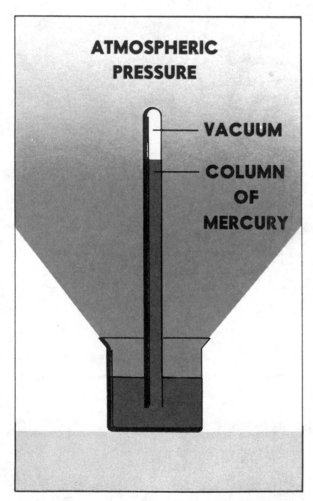

ATMOSPHERIC PRESSURE

VACUUM

COLUMN OF MERCURY

FIGURE 8. The mercurial barometer. Atmospheric pressure forces mercury from the open dish upward into the evacuated glass tube. The height of the mercury column is a measure of atmospheric pressure.

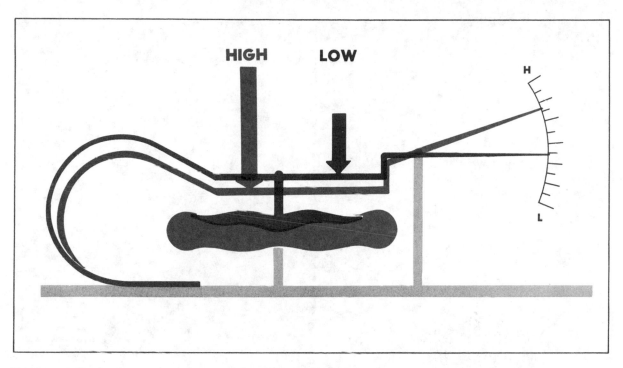

FIGURE 9. The aneroid barometer. The aneroid consists of a partially evacuated metal cell, a coupling mechanism, and an indicator scale. The cell contracts and expands with changing pressure. The coupling mechanism drives the indicator along a scale graduated in pressure units.

Figure 10 shows the pressure decrease with height in the standard atmosphere. These standard altitudes are based on standard temperatures. In the real atmosphere, temperatures are seldom standard, so let's explore temperature effects.

Temperature

Like most substances, air expands as it becomes warmer and shrinks as it cools. Figure 11 shows three columns of air—one colder than standard, one at standard temperature, and one warmer than standard. Pressure is equal at the bottom of each column and equal at the top of each column. Therefore, pressure decrease upward through each column is the same. Vertical expansion of the warm column has made it higher than the column at standard temperature. Shrinkage of the cold column has made it shorter. Since pressure decrease is the same in each column, the *rate of decrease* of pressure with height in warm air is less than standard; the rate of decrease of pressure with height in cold air is greater than standard. You will soon see the importance of temperature in altimetry and weather analysis and on aircraft performance.

Sea Level Pressure

Since pressure varies with altitude, we cannot readily compare station pressures between stations at different altitudes. To make them comparable, we must adjust them to some common level. Mean sea level seems the most feasible common reference. In figure 12, pressure measured at a 5,000-foot station is 25 inches; pressure increases about 1 inch for each 1,000 feet or a total of 5 inches. Sea level pressure is approximately 25 + 5 or 30 inches. The weather observer takes temperature and other effects into account, but this simplified example explains the basic principle of sea level pressure reduction.

We usually express sea level pressure in millibars. Standard sea level pressure is 1013.2 millibars, 29.92 inches of mercury, 760 millimeters of mercury, or about 14.7 pounds per square inch. Figures 23 and 24 in chapter 4 show world-wide averages of sea level pressure for the months of July and January. Pressure changes continually, however, and departs widely from these averages. We use a sequence of weather maps to follow these changing pressures.

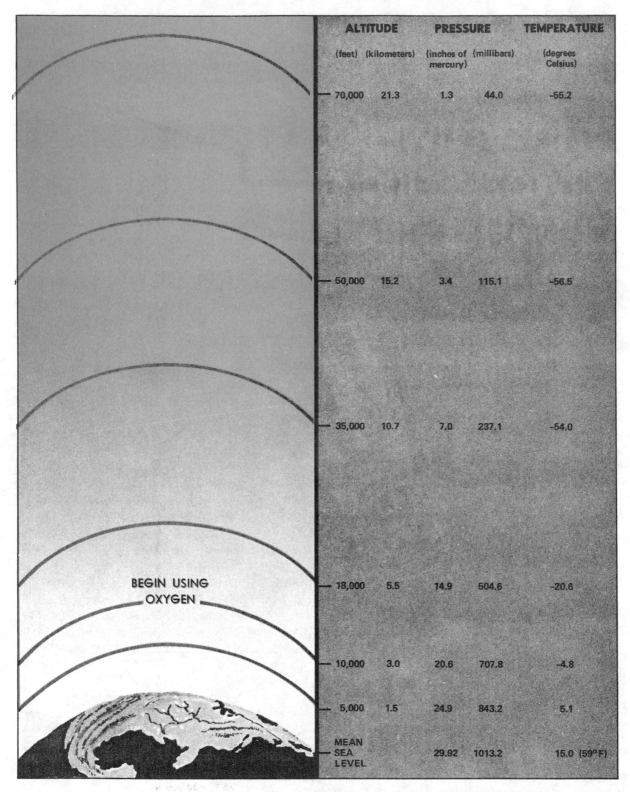

ALTITUDE		PRESSURE		TEMPERATURE
(feet)	(kilometers)	(inches of mercury)	(millibars)	(degrees Celsius)
70,000	21.3	1.3	44.0	-55.2
50,000	15.2	3.4	115.1	-56.5
35,000	10.7	7.0	237.1	-54.0
18,000	5.5	14.9	504.6	-20.6
10,000	3.0	20.6	707.8	-4.8
5,000	1.5	24.9	843.2	5.1
MEAN SEA LEVEL		29.92	1013.2	15.0 (59°F)

BEGIN USING OXYGEN

FIGURE 10.   The standard atmosphere. Note how pressure decreases with increasing height; the rate of decrease with height is greatest in lower levels.

14

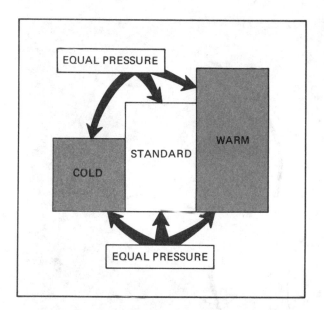

FIGURE 11. Three columns of air showing how decrease of pressure with height varies with temperature. Left column is colder than average and right column, warmer than average. Pressure is equal at the bottom of each column and equal at the top of each column. Pressure decreases most rapidly with height in the cold air and least rapidly in the warm air.

Pressure Analyses

We plot sea level pressures on a map and draw lines connecting points of equal pressure. These lines of equal pressure are *isobars*. Hence, the surface map is an *isobaric analysis* showing identifi-

able, organized pressure patterns. Five pressure systems are shown in figure 13 and are defined as follow:

1. LOW—a center of pressure surrounded on all sides by higher pressure; also called a cyclone. Cyclonic curvature is the curvature of isobars to the left when you stand with lower pressure to your left.
2. HIGH—a center of pressure surrounded on all sides by lower pressure, also called an anticyclone. Anticyclonic curvature is the curvature of isobars to the right when you stand with lower pressure to your left.
3. TROUGH—an elongated area of low pressure with the lowest pressure along a line marking maximum cyclonic curvature.
4. RIDGE—an elongated area of high pressure with the highest pressure along a line marking maximum anticyclonic curvature.
5. COL—the neutral area between two highs and two lows. It also is the intersection of a trough and a ridge. The col on a pressure surface is analogous to a mountain pass on a topographic surface.

Upper air weather maps reveal these same types of pressure patterns aloft for several levels. They also show temperature, moisture, and wind at each level. In fact, a chart is available for a level within a few thousand feet of your planned cruising altitude. AVIATION WEATHER SERVICES lists the approximate heights of upper air maps and shows details of the surface map and each upper air chart.

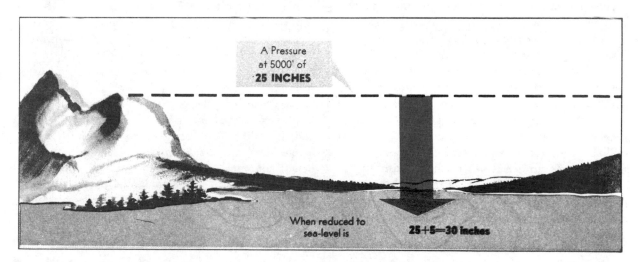

FIGURE 12. Reduction of station pressure to sea level. Pressure increases about 1 inch per 1,000 feet from the station elevation to sea level.

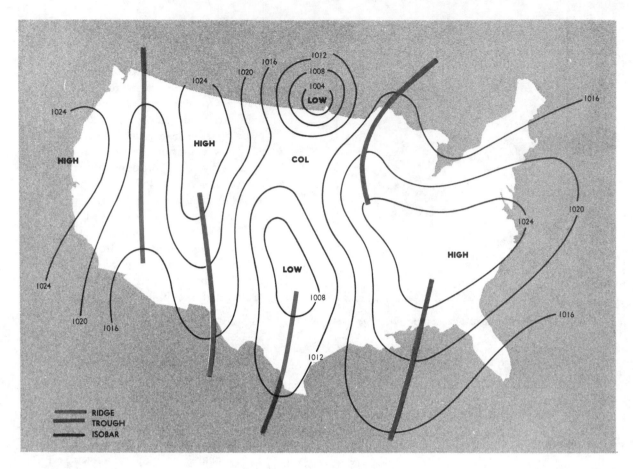

FIGURE 13. Pressure systems.

Chapter 4 of this book ties together the surface chart and upper air charts into a three-dimensional picture.

An upper air map is a *constant pressure analysis*. But, what do we mean by "constant pressure"? Constant pressure simply refers to a specific pressure. Let's arbitrarily choose 700 millibars. Everywhere above the earth's surface, pressure decreases with height; and at some height, it decreases to this constant pressure of 700 millibars. Therefore, there is a "surface" throughout the atmosphere at which pressure is 700 millibars. We call this the 700-millibar constant pressure surface. However, the *height* of this surface is *not* constant. Rising pressure pushes the surface upward into highs and ridges. Falling pressure lowers the height of the surface into lows and troughs. These systems migrate continuously as "waves" on the pressure surface. Remember that we chose this constant pressure surface arbitrarily as a reference. It in no way defines any discrete boundary.

The National Weather Service and military weather services take routine scheduled upper air observations—sometimes called soundings. A balloon carries aloft a radiosonde instrument which consists of miniature radio gear and sensing elements. While in flight, the radiosonde transmits data from which a specialist determines wind, temperature, moisture, and height at selected pressure surfaces.

We routinely collect these observations, plot the heights of a constant pressure surface on a map, and draw lines connecting points of equal height. These lines are *height contours*. But, what is a height contour?

First, consider a topographic map with contours showing variations in elevation. These are height contours of the terrain surface. The Earth surface is a fixed reference and we contour variations in its height.

The same concept applies to height contours on a constant pressure chart, except our reference is a

16

constant pressure surface. We simply contour the heights of the pressure surface. For example, a 700-millibar constant pressure analysis is a contour map of the heights of the 700-millibar pressure surface. While the contour map is based on variations in height, these variations are small when compared to flight levels, and for all practical purposes, you may regard the 700-millibar chart as a weather map at approximately 10,000 feet or 3,048 meters.

A contour analysis shows highs, ridges, lows, and troughs aloft just as the isobaric analysis shows such systems at the surface. What we say concerning pressure patterns and systems applies equally to an isobaric or a contour analysis.

Low pressure systems quite often are regions of poor flying weather, and high pressure areas predominantly are regions of favorable flying weather. A word of caution, however—use care in applying the low pressure-bad weather, high pressure-good weather rule of thumb; it all too frequently fails. When planning a flight, gather *all* information possible on expected weather. Pressure patterns also bear a direct relationship to wind which is the subject of the next chapter. But first, let's look at pressure and altimeters.

ALTIMETRY

The altimeter is essentially an aneroid barometer. The difference is the scale. The altimeter is graduated to read increments of height rather than units of pressure. The standard for graduating the altimeter is the standard atmosphere.

ALTITUDE

Altitude seems like a simple term; it means height. But in aviation, it can have many meanings.

True Altitude

Since existing conditions in a real atmosphere are seldom standard, altitude indications on the altimeter are seldom actual or true altitudes. *True altitude is the actual or exact altitude above mean sea level.* If your altimeter does not indicate true altitude, what does it indicate?

Indicated Altitude

Look again at figure 11 showing the effect of mean temperature on the thickness of the three columns of air. Pressures are equal at the bottoms and equal at the tops of the three layers. Since the altimeter is essentially a barometer, altitude indicated by the altimeter at the top of each column would be the same. To see this effect more clearly, study figure 14. Note that in the warm air, you fly at an altitude higher than indicated. In the cold air, you are at an altitude lower than indicated.

Height indicated on the altimeter also changes with changes in surface pressure. A movable scale on the altimeter permits you to adjust for surface pressure, but you have no means of adjusting the instrument for mean temperature of the column of air below you. *Indicated altitude is the altitude above mean sea level indicated on the altimeter when set at the local altimeter setting.* But what is altimeter setting?

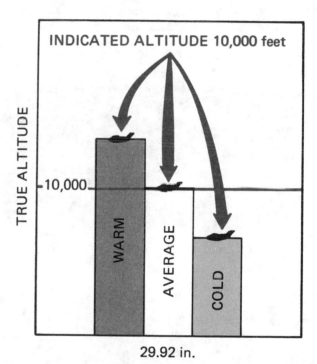

FIGURE 14. Indicated altitude depends on air temperature below the aircraft. Since pressure is equal at the bases and equal at the tops of each column, indicated altitude is the same at the top of each column. When air is colder than average (right), the altimeter reads higher than true altitude. When air is warmer than standard (left), the altimeter reads lower than true altitude.

Altimeter Setting

Since the altitude scale is adjustable, you can set the altimeter to read true altitude at some specified height. Takeoff and landing are the most critical phases of flight; therefore, airport elevation is the most desirable altitude for a true reading of the altimeter. *Altimeter setting is the value to which the scale of the pressure altimeter is set so the altimeter indicates true altitude at field elevation.*

In order to ensure that your altimeter reading is compatible with altimeter readings of other aircraft in your vicinity, keep your altimeter setting current. Adjust it frequently in flight to the altimeter setting reported by the nearest tower or weather reporting station. Figure 15 shows the trouble you can encounter if you are lax in adjusting your altimeter in flight. Note that as you fly from high pressure to low pressure, you are lower than your altimeter indicates.

Figure 16 shows that as you fly from warm to cold air, your altimeter reads too high—you are lower than your altimeter indicates. Over flat terrain this lower than true reading is no great problem; other aircraft in the vicinity also are flying indicated

rather than true altitude, and your altimeter readings are compatible. If flying in cold weather over mountainous areas, however, you must take this difference between indicated and true altitude into account. You must know that your true altitude assures clearance of terrain, so you compute a correction to indicated altitude.

Corrected (Approximately True) Altitude

If it were possible for a pilot always to determine mean temperature of the column of air between the aircraft and the surface, flight computers would be designed to use this mean temperature in computing true altitude. However, the only guide a pilot has to temperature below him is free air temperature at his altitude. Therefore, the flight computer uses outside air temperature to correct indicated altitude to approximate true altitude. *Corrected altitude is indicated altitude corrected for the temperature of the air column below the aircraft, the correction being based on the estimated departure of the existing temperature from standard atmospheric temperature.* It is a close approximation to true altitude and is labeled *true altitude* on flight computers. It is close enough to

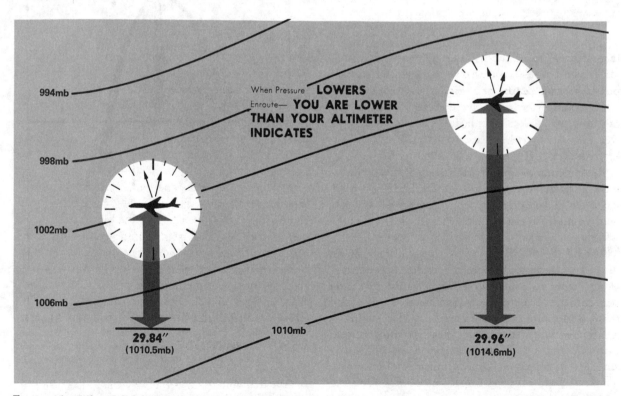

FIGURE 15.   When flying from high pressure to lower pressure without adjusting your altimeter, you are losing true altitude.

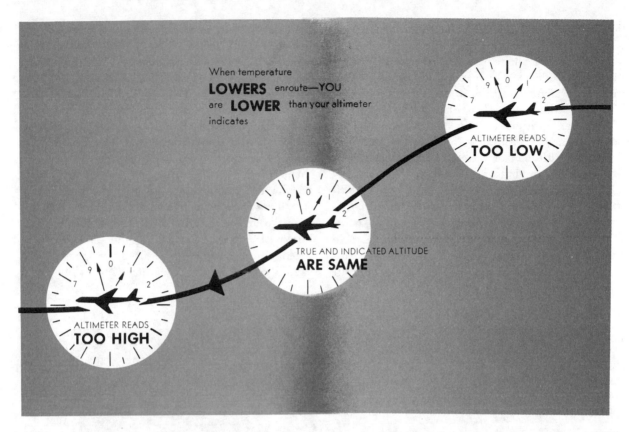

When temperature **LOWERS** enroute—YOU are **LOWER** than your altimeter indicates

ALTIMETER READS
TOO LOW

TRUE AND INDICATED ALTITUDE
ARE SAME

ALTIMETER READS
TOO HIGH

FIGURE 16.   Effect of temperature on altitude. When air is warmer than average, you are higher than your altimeter indicates. When temperature is colder than average, you are lower than indicated. When flying from warm to cold air at a constant indicated altitude, you are losing true altitude.

true altitude to be used for terrain clearance provided you have your altimeter set to the value reported from a nearby reporting station.

Pilots have met with disaster because they failed to allow for the difference between indicated and true altitude. In cold weather when you must clear high terrain, take time to compute true altitude.

FAA regulations require you to fly indicated altitude at low levels and pressure altitude at high levels (at or above 18,000 feet at the time this book was printed). What is pressure altitude?

Pressure Altitude

In the standard atmosphere, sea level pressure is 29.92 inches of mercury or 1013.2 millibars. Pressure falls at a fixed rate upward through this hypothetical atmosphere. Therefore, in the standard atmosphere, a given pressure exists at any specified altitude. *Pressure altitude is the altitude in the standard atmosphere where pressure is the same as where you are.* Since at a specific pressure altitude, pressure is everywhere the same, a constant pres-

sure surface defines a constant pressure altitude. When you fly a constant pressure altitude, you are flying a constant pressure surface.

You can always determine pressure altitude from your altimeter whether in flight or on the ground. Simply set your altimeter at the standard altimeter setting of 29.92 inches, and your altimeter indicates pressure altitude.

A conflict sometimes occurs near the altitude separating flights using indicated altitude from those using pressure altitude. Pressure altitude on one aircraft and indicated altitude on another may indicate altitude separation when, actually, the two are at the same true altitude. All flights using pressure altitude at high altitudes are IFR controlled flights. When this conflict occurs, air traffic controllers prohibit IFR flight at the conflicting altitudes.

DENSITY ALTITUDE

What is density altitude? *Density altitude simply is the altitude in the standard atmosphere where air density is the same as where you are.* Pressure, temperature, and humidity determine air density. On a hot day, the air becomes "thinner" or lighter, and its density where you are is equivalent to a higher altitude in the standard atmosphere—thus the term "high density altitude." On a cold day, the air becomes heavy; its density is the same as that at an altitude in the standard atmosphere lower than your altitude—"low density altitude."

Density altitude is not a height reference; rather, it is an index to aircraft performance. Low density altitude increases performance. *High density altitude* is a real hazard since it *reduces aircraft performance*. It affects performance in three ways. (1) It reduces power because the engine takes in less air to support combustion. (2) It reduces thrust because the propeller gets less grip on the light air

or a jet has less mass of gases to spit out the exhaust. (3) It reduces lift because the light air exerts less force on the airfoils.

You cannot detect the effect of high density altitude on your airspeed indicator. Your aircraft lifts off, climbs, cruises, glides, and lands at the prescribed indicated airspeeds. But at a specified indicated airspeed, your true airspeed and your groundspeed increase proportionally as density altitude becomes higher.

The net results are that high density altitude lengthens your takeoff and landing rolls and reduces your rate of climb. Before lift-off, you must attain a faster groundspeed, and therefore, you need more runway; your reduced power and thrust add a need for still more runway. You land at a

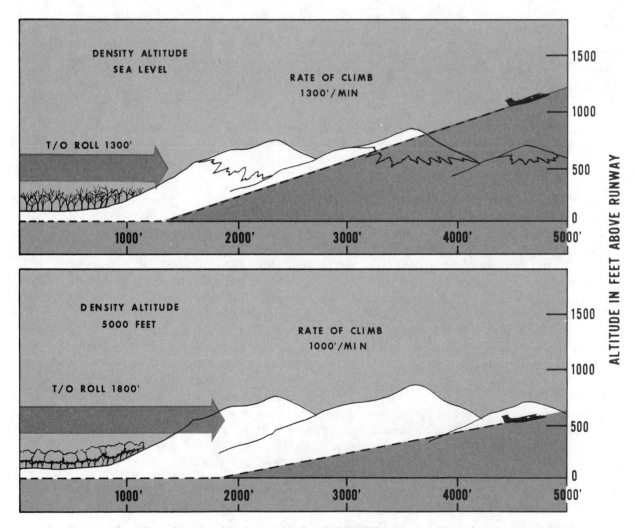

FIGURE 17.   Effect of density altitude on takeoff and climb. High density altitude lengthens takeoff roll and reduces rate of climb.

faster groundspeed and, therefore, need more room to stop. At a prescribed indicated airspeed, you are flying at a faster true airspeed, and therefore, you cover more distance in a given time which means climbing at a more shallow angle. Add to this the problems of reduced power and rate of climb, and you are in double jeopardy in your climb. Figure 17 shows the effect of density altitude on takeoff distance and rate of climb.

High density altitude also can be a problem at cruising altitudes. When air is abnormally warm, the high density altitude lowers your service ceiling. For example, if temperature at 10,000 feet pressure altitude is 20° C, density altitude is 12,700 feet. (Check this on your flight computer.) Your aircraft will perform as though it were at 12,700 indicated with a normal temperature of −8° C.

To compute density altitude, set your altimeter at 29.92 inches or 1013.2 millibars and read pressure altitude from your altimeter. Read outside air temperature and then use your flight computer to get density altitude. On an airport served by a weather observing station, you usually can get density altitude for the airport from the observer. Section 16 of AVIATION WEATHER SERVICES has a graph for computing density altitude if you have no flight computer handy.

IN CLOSING

Pressure patterns can be a clue to weather causes and movement of weather systems, but they give only a part of the total weather picture. Pressure decreases with increasing altitude. The altimeter is an aneroid barometer graduated in increments of altitude in the standard atmosphere instead of units of pressure. Temperature greatly affects the rate of pressure decrease with height; therefore, it influences altimeter readings. Temperature also determines the density of air at a given pressure (density altitude). Density altitude is an index to aircraft performance. Always be alert for departures of pressure and temperature from normals and compensate for these abnormalities.

Following are a few operational reminders:

1. Beware of the low pressure-bad weather, high pressure-good weather rule of thumb. It frequently fails. Always get the *complete* weather picture.
2. When flying from high pressure to low pressure at constant indicated altitude and without adjusting the altimeter, you are losing true altitude.
3. When temperature is colder than standard, you are at an altitude *lower* than your altimeter indicates. When temperature is warmer than standard, you are *higher* than your altimeter indicates.
4. When flying cross country, keep your altimeter setting current. This procedure assures more positive altitude separation from other aircraft.
5. When flying over high terrain in cold weather, compute your true altitude to ensure terrain clearance.
6. When your aircraft is heavily loaded, the temperature is abnormally warm, and/or the pressure is abnormally low, compute density altitude. Then check your aircraft manual to ensure that you can become airborne from the available runway. Check further to determine that your rate of climb permits clearance of obstacles beyond the end of the runway. This procedure is advisable for any airport regardless of altitude.
7. When planning takeoff or landing at a high altitude airport regardless of load, determine density altitude. The procedure is especially critical when temperature is abnormally warm or pressure abnormally low. Make certain you have sufficient runway for takeoff or landing roll. Make sure you can clear obstacles beyond the end of the runway after takeoff or in event of a go-around.
8. Sometimes the altimeter setting is taken from an instrument of questionable reliability. However, if the instrument can cause an error in altitude reading of more than 20 feet, it is removed from service. When altimeter setting is estimated, be prepared for a possible 10- to 20-foot difference between field elevation and your altimeter reading at touchdown.

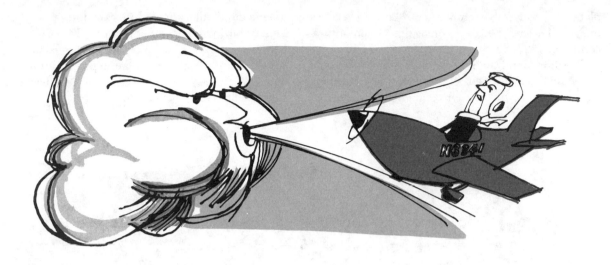

Chapter 4
WIND

Differences in temperature create differences in pressure. These pressure differences drive a complex system of winds in a never ending attempt to reach equilibrium. Wind also transports water vapor and spreads fog, clouds, and precipitation. To help you relate wind to pressure patterns and the movement of weather systems, this chapter ex-plains convection and the pressure gradient force, describes the effects of the Coriolis and frictional forces, relates convection and these forces to the general circulation, discusses local and small-scale wind systems, introduces you to wind shear, and associates wind with weather.

CONVECTION

When two surfaces are heated unequally, they heat the overlying air unevenly. The warmer* air expands and becomes lighter or less dense than the cool* air. The more dense, cool air is drawn to the ground by its greater gravitational force lifting or forcing the warm air upward much as oil is forced to the top of water when the two are mixed. Figure 18 shows the convective process. The rising air spreads and cools, eventually descending to com-

*Frequently throughout this book, we refer to air as *warm, cool,* or *cold.* These terms refer to relative temperatures and not to any fixed temperature reference or to temperatures as they may affect our comfort. For example, compare air at −10° F to air at 0° F; relative to each other, the −10° F air is *cool* and the 0° F, *warm.* 90° F would be *cool* or *cold* relative to 100° F.

plete the convective circulation. As long as the uneven heating persists, convection maintains a continuous "convective current."

The horizontal air flow in a convective current is "wind." Convection of both large and small scales accounts for systems ranging from hemi- spheric circulations down to local eddies. This horizontal flow, wind, is sometimes called "advection." However, the term "advection" more commonly applies to the transport of atmospheric properties by the wind, i.e., warm advection; cold advection; advection of water vapor, etc.

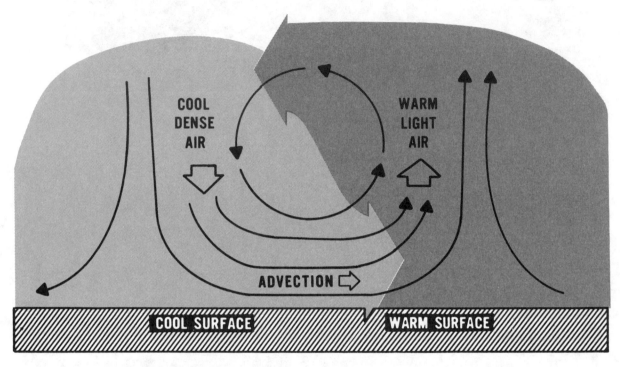

COOL
DENSE
AIR

WARM
LIGHT
AIR

ADVECTION ⇨

COOL SURFACE

WARM SURFACE

FIGURE 18. Convective current resulting from uneven heating of air by contrasting surface temperatures. The cool, heavier air forces the warmer air aloft establishing a convective cell. Convection continues as long as the uneven heating persists.

PRESSURE GRADIENT FORCE

Pressure differences must create a force in order to drive the wind. This force is the *pressure gradient force*. The force is from higher pressure to lower pressure and is perpendicular to isobars or contours. Whenever a pressure difference develops over an area, the pressure gradient force begins moving the air directly across the isobars. The closer the spacing of isobars, the stronger is the pressure gradient force. The stronger the pressure gradient force, the stronger is the wind. Thus, closely spaced isobars mean strong winds; widely spaced isobars mean lighter wind. From a pressure analysis, you can get a general idea of wind speed from contour or isobar spacing.

Because of uneven heating of the Earth, surface pressure is low in warm equatorial regions and high in cold polar regions. A pressure gradient develops from the poles to the Equator. If the Earth did not rotate, this pressure gradient force would be the only force acting on the wind. Circulation would be two giant hemispheric convective currents as shown in figure 19. Cold air would sink at the poles; wind would blow straight from the poles to the Equator; warm air at the Equator would be forced upward; and high level winds would blow directly toward the poles. However, the Earth does rotate; and because of its rotation, this simple circulation is greatly distorted.

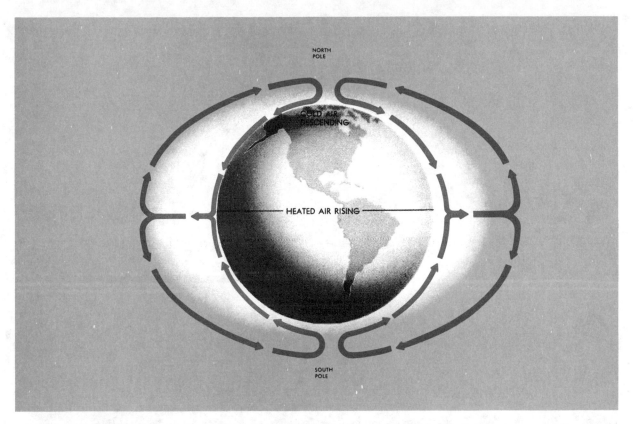

FIGURE 19. Circulation as it would be on a nonrotating globe. Intense heating at the Equator lowers the density. More dense air flows from the poles toward the Equator forcing the less dense air aloft where it flows toward the poles. The circulation would be two giant hemispherical convective currents.

CORIOLIS FORCE

A moving mass travels in a straight line until acted on by some outside force. However, if one views the moving mass from a rotating platform, the path of the moving mass relative to his platform appears to be deflected or curved. To illustrate, start rotating the turntable of a record player. Then using a piece of chalk and a ruler, draw a "straight" line from the center to the outer edge of the turntable. To you, the chalk traveled in a straight line. Now stop the turntable; on it, the line spirals outward from the center as shown in figure 20. To a viewer on the turntable, some "apparent" force deflected the chalk to the right.

A similar apparent force deflects moving particles on the earth. Because the Earth is spherical, the deflective force is much more complex than the simple turntable example. Although the force is termed "apparent," to us on Earth, it is very real. The principle was first explained by a Frenchman, Coriolis, and carries his name—the Coriolis force.

The Coriolis force affects the paths of aircraft; missiles; flying birds; ocean currents; and, most important to the study of weather, air currents. The force deflects air to the right in the Northern Hemisphere and to the left in the Southern Hemisphere. This book concentrates mostly on deflection to the right in the Northern Hemisphere.

Coriolis force is at a right angle to wind direction and directly proportional to wind speed. That is, as wind speed increases, Coriolis force increases. At a given latitude, double the wind speed and you double the Coriolis force. Why at a given latitude?

Coriolis force varies with latitude from zero at the Equator to a maximum at the poles. It influences wind direction everywhere except immediately at the Equator; but the effects are more pronounced in middle and high latitudes.

Remember that the pressure gradient force drives the wind and is perpendicular to isobars. When a pressure gradient force is first established, wind be-

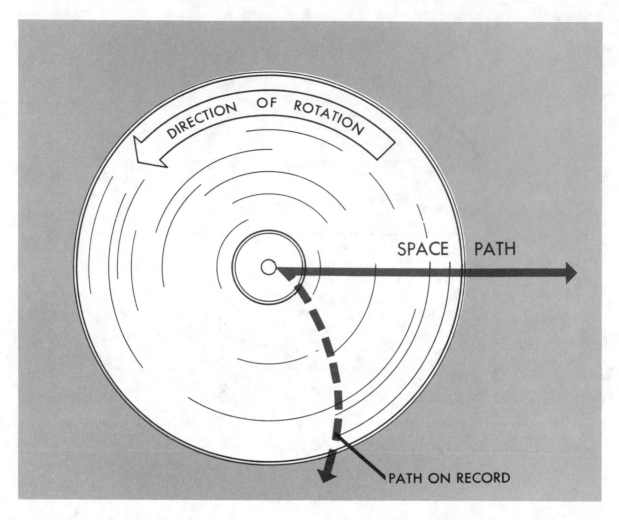

FIGURE 20. Apparent deflective force due to rotation of a horizontal platform. The "space path" is the path taken by a piece of chalk. The "path on the record" is the line traced on the rotating record. Relative to the record, the chalk appeared to curve; in space, it traveled in a straight line.

gins to blow from higher to lower pressure directly across the isobars. However, the instant air begins moving, Coriolis force deflects it to the right. Soon the wind is deflected a full 90° and is parallel to the isobars or contours. At this time, Coriolis force exactly balances pressure gradient force as shown in figure 21. With the forces in balance, wind will remain parallel to isobars or contours. Surface friction disrupts this balance as we discuss later; but first let's see how Coriolis force distorts the fictitious global circulation shown in figure 19.

THE GENERAL CIRCULATION

As air is forced aloft at the Equator and begins its high-level trek northward, the Coriolis force turns it to the right or to the east as shown in figure 22. Wind becomes westerly at about 30° latitude temporarily blocking further northward movement. Similarly, as air over the poles begins its low-level journey southward toward the Equator, it likewise is deflected to the right and becomes an east wind, halting for a while its southerly progress—also shown in figure 22. As a result, air literally "piles up" at about 30° and 60° latitude in both hemispheres. The added weight of the air in-

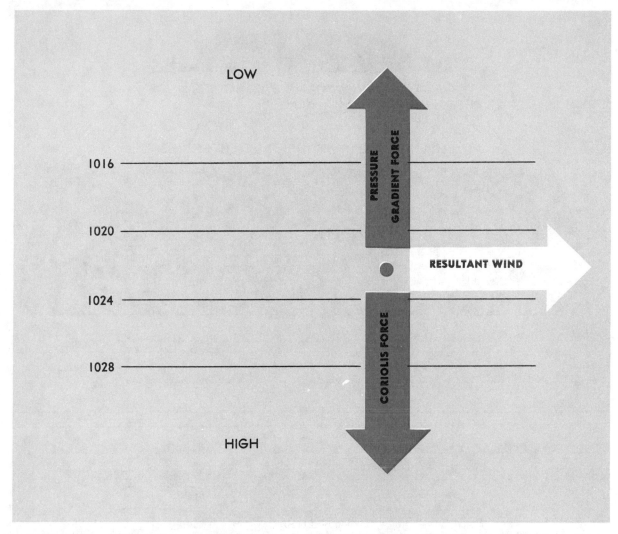

LOW

1016 ————————————————————————————————

1020 ————————————————————————————————

PRESSURE GRADIENT FORCE

RESULTANT WIND

1024 ————————————————————————————————

CORIOLIS FORCE

1028 ————————————————————————————————

HIGH

FIGURE 21.   Effect of Coriolis force on wind relative to isobars. When Coriolis force deflects the wind until it is parallel to the isobars, pressure gradient balances Coriolis force.

creases the pressure into semipermanent high pressure belts. Figures 23 and 24 are maps of mean surface pressure for the months of July and January. The maps show clearly the subtropical high pressure belts near 30° latitude in both the Northern and Southern Hemispheres.

The building of these high pressure belts creates a temporary impasse disrupting the simple convective transfer between the Equator and the poles. The restless atmosphere cannot live with this impasse in its effort to reach equilibrium. Something has to give. Huge masses of air begin overturning in middle latitudes to complete the exchange.

Large masses of cold air break through the northern barrier plunging southward toward the Tropics. Large midlatitude storms develop between cold

outbreaks and carry warm air northward. The result is a midlatitude band of migratory storms with ever changing weather. Figure 25 is an attempt to standardize this chaotic circulation into an average general circulation.

Since pressure differences cause wind, seasonal pressure variations determine to a great extent the areas of these cold air outbreaks and midlatitude storms. But, seasonal pressure variations are largely due to seasonal temperature changes. We have learned that, at the surface, warm temperatures to a great extent determine low pressure and cold temperatures, high pressure. We have also learned that seasonal temperature changes over continents are much greater than over oceans.

During summer, warm continents tend to be

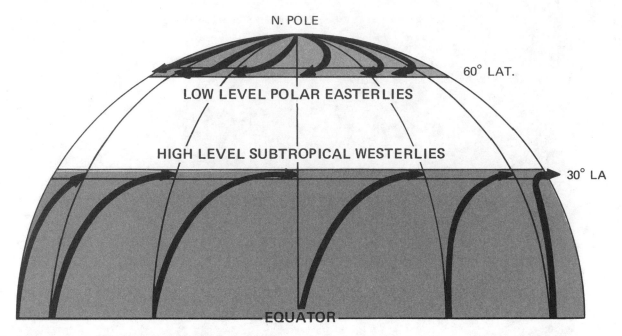

FIGURE 22. In the Northern Hemisphere, Coriolis force turns high level southerly winds to westerlies at about 30° latitude, temporarily halting further northerly progress. Low-level northerly winds from the pole are turned to easterlies, temporarily stopping further southward movement at about 60° latitude. Air tends to "pile up" at these two latitudes creating a void in middle latitudes. The restless atmosphere cannot live with this void; something has to give.

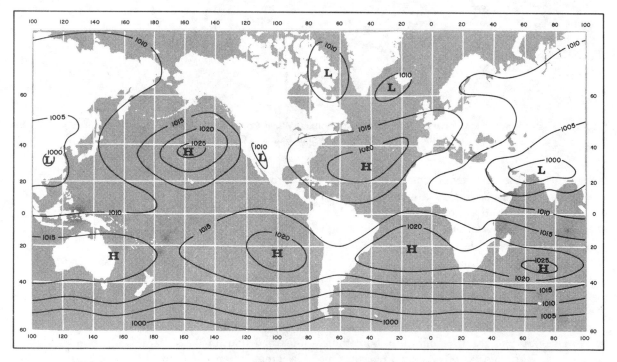

FIGURE 23. Mean world-wide surface pressure distribution in July. In the warm Northern Hemisphere, warm land areas tend to have low pressure, and cool oceanic areas tend to have high pressure. In the cool Southern Hemisphere, the pattern is reversed; cool land areas tend to have high pressure; and water surfaces, low pressure. However, the relationship is not so evident in the Southern Hemisphere because of relatively small amounts of land. The subtropical high pressure belts are clearly evident at about 30° latitude in both hemispheres.

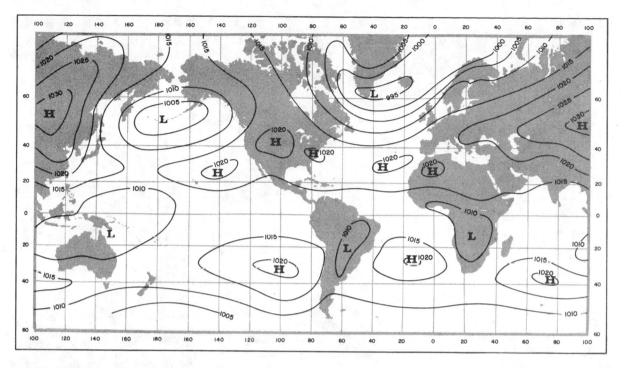

FIGURE 24. Mean world-wide surface pressure distribution in January. In this season, the pattern in figure 23 is reversed. In the cool Northern Hemisphere, cold continental areas are predominantly areas of high pressure while warm oceans tend to be low pressure areas. In the warm Southern Hemisphere, land areas tend to have low pressure; and oceans, high pressure. The subtropical high pressure belts are evident in both hemispheres. Note that the pressure belts shift southward in January and northward in July with the shift in the zone of maximum heating.

areas of low pressure and the relatively cool oceans, high pressure. In winter, the reverse is true—high pressure over the cold continents and low pressure over the relatively warm oceans. Figures 23 and 24 show this seasonal pressure reversal. The same pressure variations occur in the warm and cold seasons of the Southern Hemisphere, although the effect is not as pronounced because of the much larger water areas of the Southern Hemisphere.

Cold outbreaks are strongest in the cold season and are predominantly from cold continental areas. Summer outbreaks are weaker and more likely to originate from cool water surfaces. Since these outbreaks are masses of cool, dense air, they characteristically are high pressure areas.

As the air tries to blow outward from the high pressure, it is deflected to the right by the Coriolis force. Thus, the wind around a high blows clockwise. The high pressure with its associated wind system is an *anticyclone*.

The storms that develop between high pressure systems are characterized by low pressure. As winds try to blow inward toward the center of low pressure, they also are deflected to the right. Thus, the wind around a low is counterclockwise. The low pressure and its wind system is a *cyclone*. Figure 26 shows winds blowing parallel to isobars (contours on upper level charts). The winds are clockwise around highs and counterclockwise around lows.

The high pressure belt at about 30° north latitude forces air outward at the surface to the north and to the south. The northbound air becomes entrained into the midlatitude storms. The southward moving air is again deflected by the Coriolis force becoming the well-known subtropical northeast trade winds. In midlatitudes, high level winds are predominantly from the west and are known as the prevailing westerlies. Polar easterlies dominate low-level circulation north of about 60° latitude.

These three major wind belts are shown in figure 25. Northeasterly trade winds carry tropical storms from east to west. The prevailing westerlies drive midlatitude storms generally from west to east. Few major storm systems develop in the comparatively small Arctic region; the chief influence of the polar easterlies is their contribution to the development of midlatitude storms.

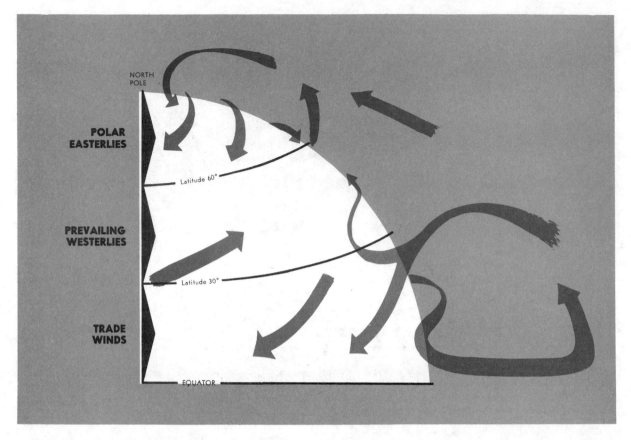

FIGURE 25. General average circulation in the Northern Hemisphere. Note the three belts of prevailing winds, the polar easterlies, the prevailing westerlies in middle latitudes, and the northeasterly "trade" winds. The belt of prevailing westerlies is a mixing zone between the North Pole and the Equator characterized by migrating storms.

Our discussion so far has said nothing about friction. Wind flow patterns aloft follow isobars or contours where friction has little effect. We cannot, however, neglect friction near the surface.

FRICTION

Friction between the wind and the terrain surface slows the wind. The rougher the terrain, the greater is the frictional effect. Also, the stronger the wind speed, the greater is the friction. One may not think of friction as a force, but it is a very real and effective force always acting opposite to wind direction.

As frictional force slows the windspeed, Coriolis force decreases. However, friction does not affect pressure gradient force. Pressure gradient and Coriolis forces are no longer in balance. The stronger pressure gradient force turns the wind at an angle across the isobars toward lower pressure until the three forces balance as shown in figure 27. Frictional and Coriolis forces combine to just balance pressure gradient force. Figure 28 shows how surface wind spirals outward from high pressure into low pressure crossing isobars at an angle.

The angle of surface wind to isobars is about 10° over water increasing with roughness of terrain. In mountainous regions, one often has difficulty relating surface wind to pressure gradient because of immense friction and also because of local terrain effects on pressure.

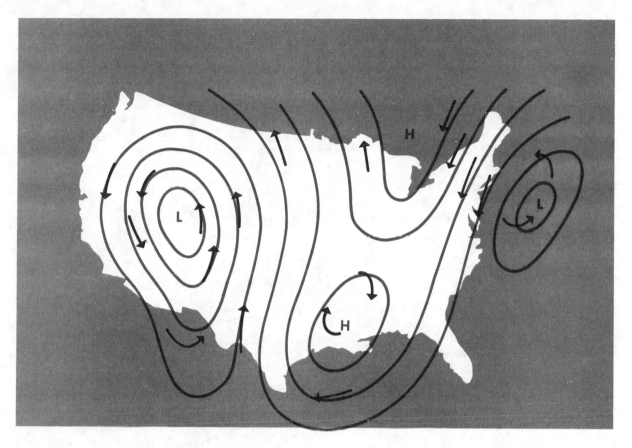

FIGURE 26. Air flow around pressure systems above the friction layer. Wind (black arrows) is parallel to contours and circulates clockwise around high pressure and counterclockwise around low pressure.

THE JET STREAM

A discussion of the general circulation is incomplete when it does not mention the "jet stream." Winds on the average increase with height throughout the troposphere culminating in a maximum near the level of the tropopause. These maximum winds tend to be further concentrated in narrow bands. A jet stream, then, is a narrow band of strong winds meandering through the atmosphere at a level near the tropopause. Since it is of interest primarily to high level flight, further discussion of the jet stream is reserved for chapter 13, "High Altitude Weather."

LOCAL AND SMALL SCALE WINDS

Until now, we have dealt only with the general circulation and major wind systems. Local terrain features such as mountains and shore lines influence local winds and weather.

MOUNTAIN AND VALLEY WINDS

In the daytime, air next to a mountain slope is heated by contact with the ground as it receives radiation from the sun. This air usually becomes warmer than air at the same altitude but farther from the slope.

Colder, denser air in the surroundings settles downward and forces the warmer air near the ground up the mountain slope. This wind is a "valley wind" so called because the air is flowing up out of the valley.

At night, the air in contact with the mountain slope is cooled by terrestrial radiation and becomes heavier than the surrounding air. It sinks along the

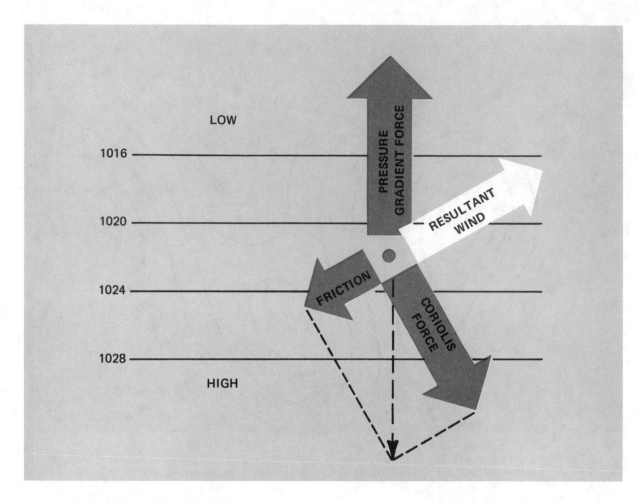

FIGURE 27. Surface friction slows the wind and reduces Coriolis force but does not affect pressure gradient force; winds near the surface are deflected across the isobars toward lower pressure.

slope, producing the "mountain wind" which flows like water down the mountain slope. Mountain winds are usually stronger than valley winds, especially in winter. The mountain wind often continues down the more gentle slopes of canyons and valleys, and in such cases takes the name "drainage wind." It can become quite strong over some terrain conditions and in extreme cases can become hazardous when flowing through canyon restrictions as discussed in chapter 9.

KATABATIC WIND

A katabatic wind is any wind blowing down an incline when the incline is influential in causing the wind. Thus, the mountain wind is a katabatic wind. Any katabatic wind originates because cold, heavy air spills down sloping terrain displacing warmer, less dense air ahead of it. Air is heated and dried as it flows down slope as we will study in

later chapters. Sometimes the descending air becomes warmer than the air it replaces.

Many katabatic winds recurring in local areas have been given colorful names to highlight their dramatic, local effect. Some of these are the Bora, a cold northerly wind blowing from the Alps to the Mediterranean coast; the Chinook, figure 29, a warm wind down the east slope of the Rocky Mountains often reaching hundreds of miles into the high plains; the Taku, a cold wind in Alaska blowing off the Taku glacier; and the Santa Ana, a warm wind descending from the Sierras into the Santa Ana Valley of California.

LAND AND SEA BREEZES

As frequently stated earlier, land surfaces warm and cool more rapidly than do water surfaces; therefore, land is warmer than the sea during the

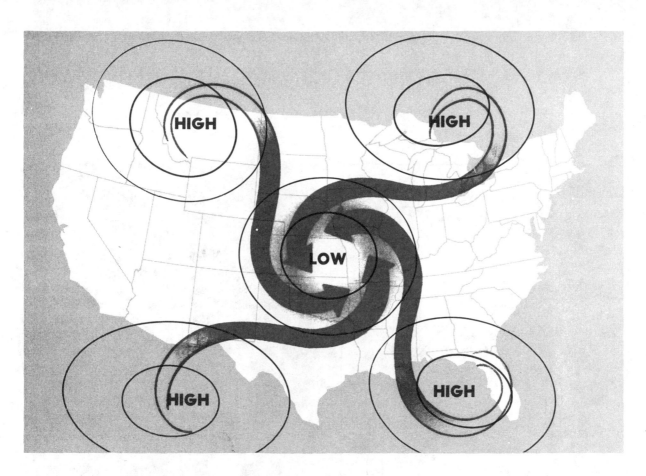

FIGURE 28. Circulation around pressure systems at the surface. Wind spirals outward from high pressure and inward to low pressure, crossing isobars at an angle.

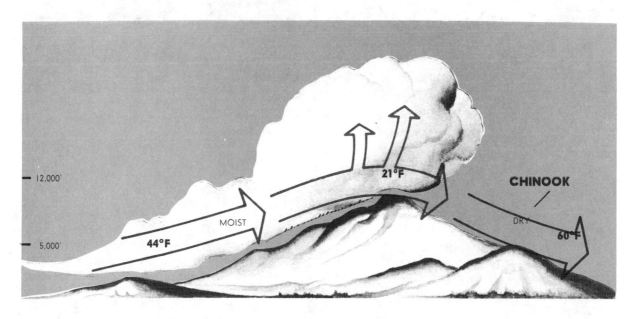

FIGURE 29. The "Chinook" is a katabatic (downslope) wind. Air cools as it moves upslope and warms as it blows downslope. The Chinook occasionally produces dramatic warming over the plains just east of the Rocky Mountains.

day; wind blows from the cool water to warm land—the "sea breeze" so called because it blows from the sea. At night, the wind reverses, blows from cool land to warmer water, and creates a "land breeze." Figure 30 diagrams land and sea breezes.

Land and sea breezes develop only when the overall pressure gradient is weak. Wind with a stronger pressure gradient mixes the air so rapidly that local temperature and pressure gradients do not develop along the shore line.

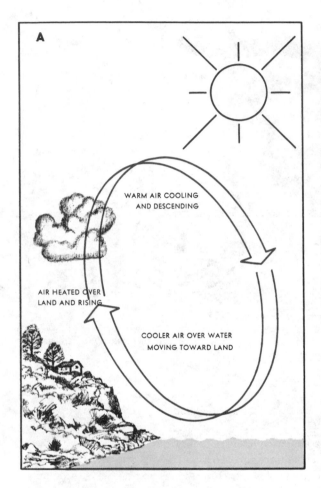
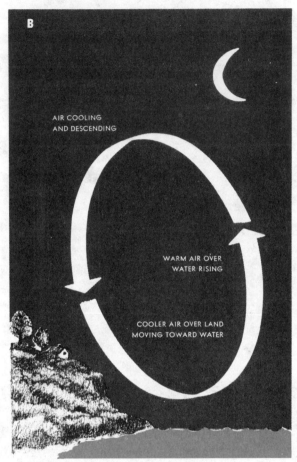

FIGURE 30.   Land and sea breezes. At night, cool air from the land flows toward warmer water—the land breeze. During the day, wind blows from the water to the warmer land—the sea breeze.

WIND SHEAR

Rubbing two objects against each other creates friction. If the objects are solid, no exchange of mass occurs between the two. However, if the objects are fluid currents, friction creates eddies along a common shallow mixing zone, and a mass trans-fer takes place in the shallow mixing layer. This zone of induced eddies and mixing is a shear zone. Figure 31 shows two adjacent currents of air and their accompanying shear zone. Chapter 9 relates wind shear to turbulence.

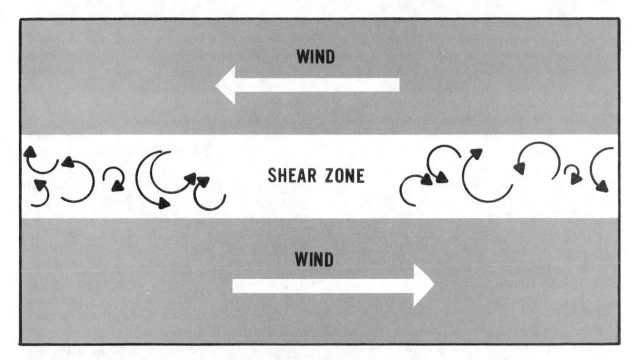

FIGURE 31. Wind shear. Air currents of differing velocities create friction or "shear" between them. Mixing in the shear zone results in a snarl of eddies and whirls.

WIND, PRESSURE SYSTEMS, AND WEATHER

We already have shown that wind speed is proportional to the spacing of isobars or contours on a weather map. However, with the same spacing, wind speed at the surface will be less than aloft because of surface friction.

You also can determine wind direction from a weather map. If you face along an isobar or contour with lower pressure on your left, wind will be blowing in the direction you are facing. On a surface map, wind will cross the isobar at an angle toward lower pressure; on an upper air chart, it will be parallel to the contour.

Wind blows counterclockwise (Northern Hemisphere) around a low and clockwise around a high. At the surface where winds cross the isobars at an angle, you can see a transport of air from high to low pressure. Although winds are virtually parallel to contours on an upper air chart, there still is a slow transport of air from high to low pressure.

At the surface when air converges into a low, it cannot go outward against the pressure gradient, nor can it go downward into the ground; it must go upward.* Therefore, a low or trough is an area of rising air.

Rising air is conducive to cloudiness and precipitation; thus we have the general association of low pressure–bad weather. Reasons for the inclement weather are developed in later chapters.

By similar reasoning, air moving out of a high or ridge depletes the quantity of air. Highs and ridges, therefore, are areas of descending air. Descending air favors dissipation of cloudiness; hence the association, high pressure–good weather.

Many times weather is more closely associated with an upper air pattern than with features shown by the surface map. Although features on the two charts are related, they seldom are identical. A

*You may recall that earlier we said air "piles up" in the vicinity of 30° latitude increasing pressure and forming the subtropical high pressure belt. Why, then, does not air flowing into a low or trough increase pressure and fill the system? Dynamic forces maintain the low or trough; and these forces differ from the forces that maintain the subtropical high.

35

weak surface system often loses its identity in the upper air pattern, while another system may be more evident on the upper air chart than on the surface map.

Widespread cloudiness and precipitation often develop in advance of an upper trough or low. A line of showers and thunderstorms is not uncommon with a trough aloft even though the surface pressure pattern shows little or no cause for the development.

On the other hand, downward motion in a high or ridge places a "cap" on convection, preventing any upward motion. Air may become stagnant in a high, trap moisture and contamination in low levels, and restrict ceiling and visibility. Low stratus, fog, haze, and smoke are not uncommon in high pressure areas. However, a high or ridge aloft with moderate surface winds most often produces good flying weather.

Highs and lows tend to *lean* from the surface into the upper atmosphere. Due to this slope, winds aloft often blow across the associated surface systems. Upper winds tend to steer surface systems in the general direction of the upper wind flow.

An intense, cold, low pressure vortex *leans less* than does a weaker system. The intense low becomes oriented almost vertically and is clearly evident on both surface and upper air charts. Upper winds encircle the surface low and do not blow across it. Thus, the storm moves very slowly and usually causes an extensive and persistent area of clouds, precipitation, strong winds, and generally adverse flying weather. The term *cold low* sometimes used by the weatherman describes such a system.

A contrasting analogy to the cold low is the *thermal low*. A dry, sunny region becomes quite warm from intense surface heating thus generating a surface low pressure area. The warm air is carried to high levels by convection, but cloudiness is scant because of lack of moisture. Since in warm air, pressure decreases slowly with altitude, the warm surface low is not evident at upper levels. Unlike the cold low, the thermal low is relatively shallow with weak pressure gradients and no well defined cyclonic circulation. It generally supports good flying weather. However, during the heat of the day, one must be alert for high density altitude and convective turbulence.

We have cited three exceptions to the low pressure–bad weather, high pressure–good weather rule: (1) cloudiness and precipitation with an upper air trough or low not evident on the surface chart; (2) the contaminated high; and (3) the thermal low. As this book progresses, you can further relate weather systems more specifically to flight operations.

Chapter 5
MOISTURE, CLOUD FORMATION, AND PRECIPITATION

Imagine, if you can, how easy flying would be if skies everywhere were clear! But, flying isn't always that easy; moisture in the atmosphere creates a variety of hazards unmatched by any other weather element. Within Earth's climatic range, water is in the frozen, liquid, and gaseous states.

WATER VAPOR

Water evaporates into the air and becomes an ever-present but variable constituent of the atmosphere. Water vapor is invisible just as oxygen and other gases are invisible. However, we can readily measure water vapor and express it in different ways. Two commonly used terms are (1) relative humidity, and (2) dew point.

RELATIVE HUMIDITY

Relative humidity routinely is expressed in percent. As the term suggests, *relative humidity* is "relative." It relates *the actual water vapor present to that which could be present.*

Temperature largely determines the maximum amount of water vapor air can hold. As figure 32 shows, warm air can hold more water vapor than cool air. Figure 33 relates water vapor, temperature, and relative humidity. Actually, relative humidity expresses the degree of saturation. Air with 100% relative humidity is saturated; less than 100% is unsaturated.

If a given volume of air is cooled to some specific temperature, it can hold no more water vapor than is actually present, relative humidity becomes 100%, and saturation occurs. What is that temperature?

DEW POINT

Dew point is the temperature to which air must be cooled to become saturated by the water vapor already present in the air. Aviation weather reports normally include the air temperature and dew point temperature. Dew point when related to air temperature reveals qualitatively how close the air is to saturation.

TEMPERATURE–DEW POINT SPREAD

The difference between air temperature and dew point temperature is popularly called the "spread." As spread becomes less, relative humidity increases, and it is 100% when temperature and dew point are the same. Surface temperature–dew point spread is important in anticipating fog but has little bearing on precipitation. To support precipitation, air must be saturated through thick layers aloft.

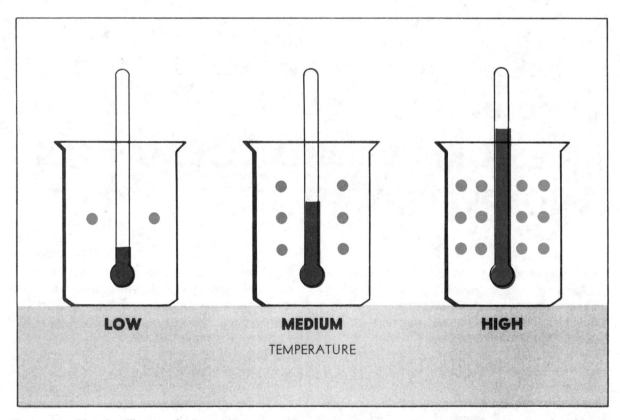

FIGURE 32. Blue dots illustrate the increased water vapor capacity of warmer air. At each temperature, air can hold a specific amount of water vapor—no more.

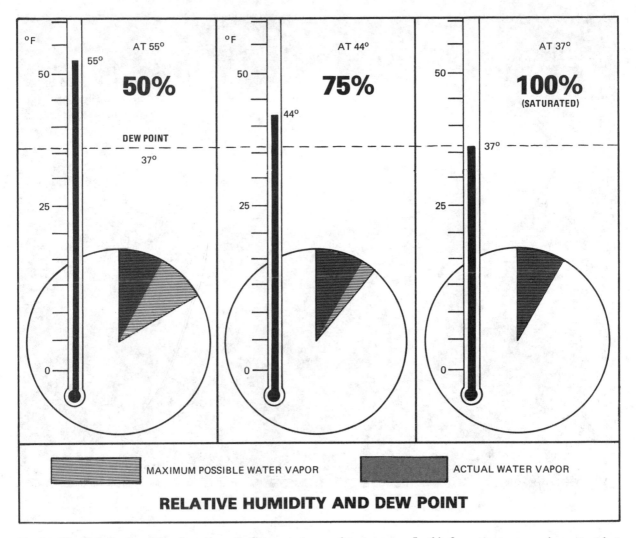

RELATIVE HUMIDITY AND DEW POINT

FIGURE 33.   Relative humidity depends on both temperature and water vapor. In this figure, water vapor is constant but temperature varies. On the left, relative humidity is 50%; the warmer air could hold twice as much water vapor as is actually present. As the air cools, center and right, relative humidity increases. As the air cools to 37° F, its capacity to hold water vapor is reduced to the amount actually present. Relative humidity is 100% and the air is now "saturated." Note that at 100% humidity, temperature and dew point are the same. The air cooled to saturation, i.e., it cooled to the dew point.

Sometimes the spread at ground level may be quite large, yet at higher altitudes the air is saturated and clouds form. Some rain may reach the ground or it may evaporate as it falls into the drier air. Figure 34 is a photograph of "virga"—streamers of precipitation trailing beneath clouds but evaporating before reaching the ground. Our never ending weather cycle involves a continual reversible change of water from one state to another. Let's take a closer look at change of state.

CHANGE OF STATE

Evaporation, condensation, sublimation, freezing, and melting are changes of state. Evaporation is the changing of liquid water to invisible water vapor. Condensation is the reverse process. Sublimation is the changing of ice directly to water vapor, or water vapor to ice, bypassing the liquid

FIGURE 34.   Virga. Precipitation from the cloud evaporates in drier air below and does not reach the ground.

state in each process. Snow or ice crystals result from the sublimation of water vapor directly to the solid state. We are all familiar with freezing and melting processes.

LATENT HEAT

Any change of state involves a heat transaction with no change in temperature. Figure 35 diagrams the heat exchanges between the different states. Evaporation requires heat energy that comes from the nearest available heat source. This heat energy is known as the "latent heat of vaporization," and its removal cools the source it comes from. An example is the cooling of your body by evaporation of perspiration.

What becomes of this heat energy used by evaporation? Energy cannot be created or destroyed, so it is hidden or stored in the invisible water vapor. When the water vapor condenses to liquid water

or sublimates directly to ice, energy originally used in the evaporation reappears as heat and is released to the atmosphere. This energy is "latent heat" and is quite significant as we learn in later chapters. Melting and freezing involve the exchange of "latent heat of fusion" in a similar manner. The latent heat of fusion is much less than that of condensation and evaporation; however, each in its own way plays an important role in aviation weather.

As air becomes saturated, water vapor begins to condense on the nearest available surface. What surfaces are in the atmosphere on which water vapor may condense?

CONDENSATION NUCLEI

The atmosphere is never completely clean; an abundance of microscopic solid particles suspended in the air are condensation surfaces. These particles, such as salt, dust, and combustion byproducts

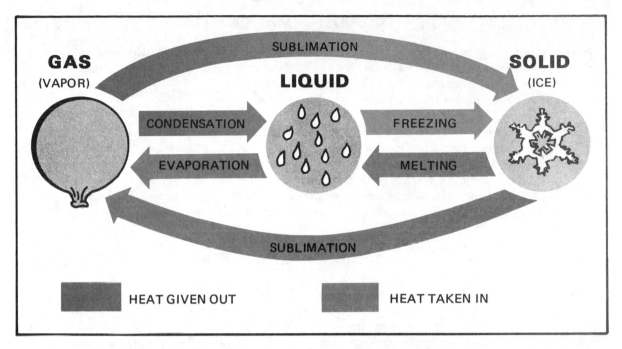

FIGURE 35. Heat transactions when water changes state. Blue arrows indicate changes that absorb heat. The absorbed heat remains hidden, or "latent" until a reverse change occurs. The red arrows show changes that release latent heat back to the surroundings. The heat exchange occurs whenever water changes state even when there is no change in temperature. These heat exchanges play important roles in suppressing temperature changes and in developing instability.

are "condensation nuclei." Some condensation nuclei have an affinity for water and can induce condensation or sublimation even when air is almost but not completely saturated.

As water vapor condenses or sublimates on condensation nuclei, liquid or ice particles begin to grow. Whether the particles are liquid or ice does not depend entirely on temperature. Liquid water may be present at temperatures well below freezing.

SUPERCOOLED WATER

Freezing is complex and liquid water droplets often condense or persist at temperatures colder than 0° C. Water droplets colder than 0° C are supercooled. When they strike an exposed object, the impact induces freezing. Impact freezing of supercooled water can result in aircraft icing.

Supercooled water drops very often are in abundance in clouds at temperatures between 0° C and —15° C with decreasing amounts at colder temperatures. Usually, at temperatures colder than —15° C, sublimation is prevalent; and clouds and fog may be mostly ice crystals with a lesser amount of supercooled water. However, strong vertical currents may carry supercooled water to great heights where temperatures are much colder than

—15° C. Supercooled water has been observed at temperatures colder than —40° C.

DEW AND FROST

During clear nights with little or no wind, vegetation often cools by radiation to a temperature at or below the dew point of the adjacent air. Moisture then collects on the leaves just as it does on a pitcher of ice water in a warm room. Heavy dew often collects on grass and plants when none collects on pavements or large solid objects. These more massive objects absorb abundant heat during the day, lose it slowly during the night, and cool below the dew point only in rather extreme cases.

Frost forms in much the same way as dew. The difference is that the dew point of surrounding air must be colder than freezing. Water vapor then sublimates directly as ice crystals or frost rather than condensing as dew. Sometimes dew forms and later freezes; however, frozen dew is easily distinguished from frost. Frozen dew is hard and transparent while frost is white and opaque.

To now, we have said little about clouds. What brings about the condensation or sublimation that results in cloud formation?

CLOUD FORMATION

Normally, air must become saturated for condensation or sublimation to occur. Saturation may result from cooling temperature, increasing dew point, or both. Cooling is far more predominant.

COOLING PROCESSES

Three basic processes may cool air to saturation. They are (1) air moving over a colder surface, (2) stagnant air overlying a cooling surface, and (3) expansional cooling in upward moving air. Expansional cooling is the major cause of cloud formation. Chapter 6, "Stable and Unstable Air," discusses expansional cooling in detail.

CLOUDS AND FOG

A cloud is a visible aggregate of minute water or ice particles suspended in air. If the cloud is on the ground, it is fog. When entire layers of air cool to saturation, fog or sheet-like clouds result. Saturation of a localized updraft produces a towering cloud. A cloud may be composed entirely of liquid water, of ice crystals, or a mixture of the two.

PRECIPITATION

Precipitation is an all inclusive term denoting drizzle, rain, snow, ice pellets, hail, and ice crystals. Precipitation occurs when these particles grow in size and weight until the atmosphere no longer can suspend them and they fall. These particles grow primarily in two ways.

PARTICLE GROWTH

Once a water droplet or ice crystal forms, it continues to grow by added condensation or sublimation directly onto the particle. This is the slower of the two methods and usually results in drizzle or very light rain or snow.

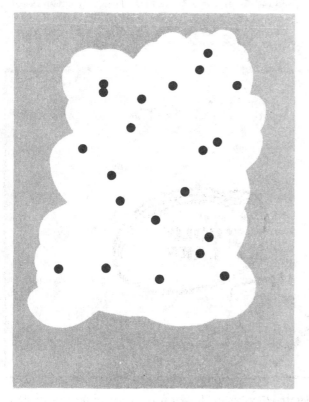

FIGURE 36. Growth of raindrops by collision of cloud droplets.

Cloud particles collide and merge into a larger drop in the more rapid growth process. This process produces larger precipitation particles and does so more rapidly than the simple condensation growth process. Upward currents enhance the growth rate and also support larger drops as shown in figure 36. Precipitation formed by merging drops with mild upward currents can produce light to moderate rain and snow. Strong upward currents support the largest drops and build clouds to great heights. They can produce heavy rain, heavy snow, and hail.

LIQUID, FREEZING, AND FROZEN

Precipitation forming and remaining liquid falls as rain or drizzle. Sublimation forms snowflakes, and they reach the ground as snow if temperatures remain below freezing.

Precipitation can change its state as the temperature of its environment changes. Falling snow may melt in warmer layers of air at lower altitudes to form rain. Rain falling through colder air may become supercooled, freezing on impact as freezing rain; or it may freeze during its descent, falling as ice pellets. Ice pellets always indicate freezing rain at higher altitude.

Sometimes strong upward currents sustain large supercooled water drops until some freeze; subsequently, other drops freeze to them forming hailstones.

PRECIPITATION VERSUS CLOUD THICKNESS

To produce significant precipitation, clouds usually are 4,000 feet thick or more. The heavier the precipitation, the thicker the clouds are likely to be. When arriving at or departing from a terminal reporting precipitation of light or greater intensity, expect clouds to be more than 4,000 feet thick.

LAND AND WATER EFFECTS

Land and water surfaces underlying the atmosphere greatly affect cloud and precipitation development. Large bodies of water such as oceans and large lakes add water vapor to the air. Expect the greatest frequency of low ceilings, fog, and precipitation in areas where prevailing winds have an over-water trajectory. Be especially alert for these hazards when moist winds are blowing upslope.

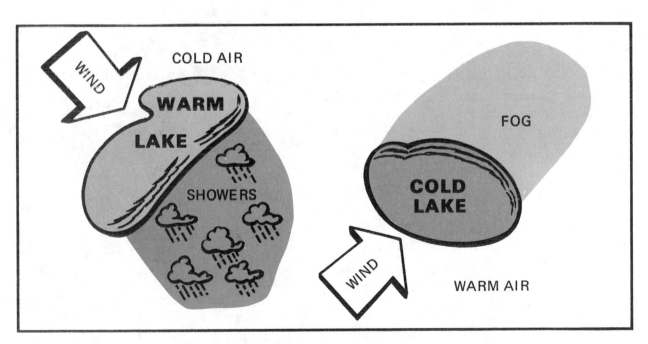

FIGURE 37. Lake effects. Air moving across a sizeable lake absorbs water vapor. Showers may appear on the leeward side if the air is colder than the water. When the air is warmer than the water, fog often develops on the lee side.

In winter, cold air frequently moves over relatively warm lakes. The warm water adds heat and water vapor to the air causing showers to the lee of the lakes. In other seasons, the air may be warmer than the lakes. When this occurs, the air may become saturated by evaporation from the water while also becoming cooler in the low levels by contact with the cool water. Fog often becomes extensive and dense to the lee of a lake. Figure 37 illustrates movement of air over both warm and cold lakes. Strong cold winds across the Great Lakes often carry precipitation to the Appalachians as shown in figure 38.

A lake only a few miles across can influence convection and cause a diurnal fluctuation in cloudiness. During the day, cool air over the lake blows toward the land, and convective clouds form over the land as shown in figure 39, a photograph of Lake Okeechobee in Florida. At night, the pattern reverses; clouds tend to form over the lake as cool air from the land flows over the lake creating convective clouds over the water.

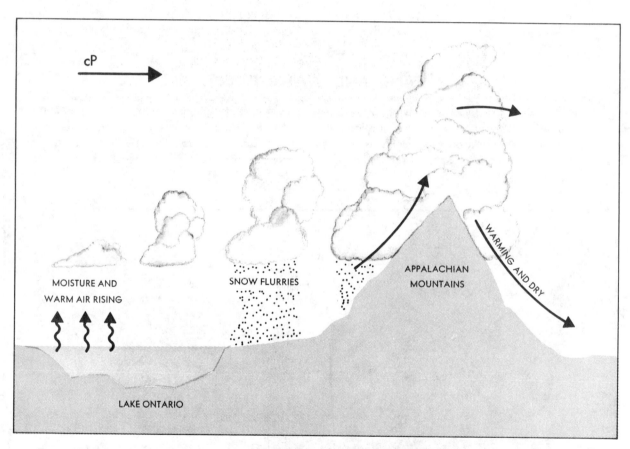

FIGURE 38. Strong cold winds across the Great Lakes absorb water vapor and may carry showers as far eastward as the Appalachians.

FIGURE 39. A view of clouds from 27,000 feet over Lake Okeechobee in southern Florida. Note the lake effect. During daytime, cool air from the lake flows toward the warmer land forming convective clouds over the land.

IN CLOSING

Water exists in three states—solid, liquid, and gaseous. Water vapor is an invisible gas. Condensation or sublimation of water vapor creates many common aviation weather hazards. You may anticipate:

1. Fog when temperature-dew point spread is 5° F or less and decreasing.
2. Lifting or clearing of low clouds and fog when temperature-dew point spread is increasing.
3. Frost on a clear night when temperature-dew point spread is 5° F or less, is decreasing, and dew point is colder than 32° F.
4. More cloudiness, fog, and precipitation when wind blows from water than when it blows from land.
5. Cloudiness, fog, and precipitation over higher terrain when moist winds are blowing uphill.
6. Showers to the lee of a lake when air is cold and the lake is warm. Expect fog to the lee of the lake when the air is warm and the lake is cold.
7. Clouds to be at least 4,000 feet thick when significant precipitation is reported. The heavier the precipitation, the thicker the clouds are likely to be.
8. Icing on your aircraft when flying through liquid clouds or precipitation with temperature freezing or colder.

Chapter 6
STABLE AND UNSTABLE AIR

To a pilot, the stability of his aircraft is a vital concern. A stable aircraft, when disturbed from straight and level flight, returns by itself to a steady balanced flight. An unstable aircraft, when disturbed, continues to move away from a normal flight attitude.

So it is with the atmosphere. A *stable* atmosphere resists any upward or downward displacement. An *unstable* atmosphere allows an upward or downward disturbance to grow into a vertical or convective current.

This chapter first examines fundamental changes in upward and downward moving air and then relates stable and unstable air to clouds, weather, and flying.

CHANGES WITHIN UPWARD AND DOWNWARD MOVING AIR

Anytime air moves upward, it expands because of decreasing atmospheric pressure as shown in figure 40. Conversely, downward moving air is compressed by increasing pressure. But as pressure and volume change, temperature also changes.

When air expands, it cools; and when compressed, it warms. These changes are *adiabatic*, meaning that no heat is removed from or added to the air. We frequently use the terms *expansional* or *adiabatic cooling* and *compressional* or *adiabatic*

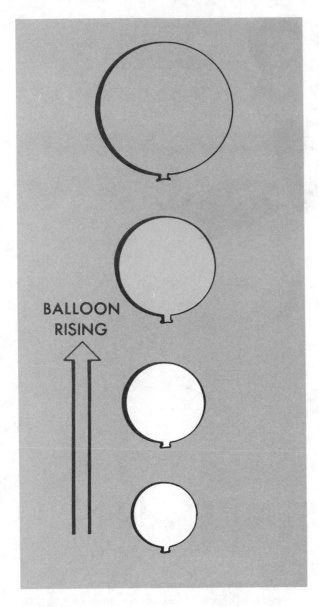

FIGURE 40. Decreasing atmospheric pressure causes the balloon to expand as it rises. Anytime air moves upward, it expands.

heating. The adiabatic rate of change of temperature is virtually fixed in unsaturated air but varies in saturated air.

UNSATURATED AIR

Unsaturated air moving upward and downward cools and warms at about 3.0° C (5.4° F) per 1,000 feet. This rate is *the "dry adiabatic rate of temperature change"* and *is independent of the temperature of the mass of air through which the vertical movements occur*. Figure 41 illustrates a

"Chinook Wind"—an excellent example of dry adiabatic warming.

SATURATED AIR

Condensation occurs when *saturated* air moves upward. Latent heat released through condensation (chapter 5) partially offsets the expansional cooling. Therefore, *the saturated adiabatic rate of cooling is slower than the dry adiabatic rate*. The saturated rate depends on saturation temperature or dew point of the air. Condensation of copious moisture in saturated warm air releases more latent heat to offset expansional cooling than does the scant moisture in saturated cold air. Therefore, *the saturated adiabatic rate of cooling is less in warm air than in cold air*.

When saturated air moves downward, it heats at the same rate as it cools on ascent *provided* liquid water evaporates rapidly enough to maintain saturation. Minute water droplets evaporate at virtually this rate. Larger drops evaporate more slowly and complicate the moist adiabatic process in downward moving air.

ADIABATIC COOLING AND VERTICAL AIR MOVEMENT

If we force a sample of air upward into the atmosphere, we must consider two possibilities:

    (1) The air may become colder than the surrounding air, or

    (2) Even though it cools, the air may remain warmer than the surrounding air.

If the upward moving air becomes colder than surrounding air, it sinks; but if it remains warmer, it is accelerated upward as a convective current. Whether it sinks or rises depends on the ambient or existing temperature lapse rate (chapter 2).

Do not confuse existing lapse rate with adiabatic rates of cooling in vertically moving air.* The difference between the existing lapse rate of a given mass of air and the adiabatic rates of cooling in upward moving air determines if the air is stable or unstable.

---

*Sometimes you will hear the dry and moist adiabatic rates of cooling called the dry adiabatic lapse rate and the moist adiabatic lapse rate. In this book, *lapse rate* refers exclusively to the existing, or actual, decrease of temperature with height in a real atmosphere. The dry or moist adiabatic lapse rate signifies a prescribed rate of expansional cooling or compressional heating. An adiabatic lapse rate becomes real *only* when it becomes a condition brought about by vertically moving air.

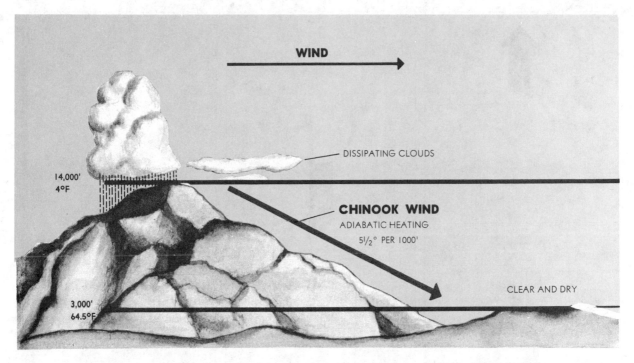

WIND

DISSIPATING CLOUDS

CHINOOK WIND
ADIABATIC HEATING
5½° PER 1000'

CLEAR AND DRY

14,000'
4°F

3,000'
64.5°F

FIGURE 41. Adiabatic warming of downward moving air produces the warm Chinook wind.

STABILITY AND INSTABILITY

Let's use a balloon to demonstrate stability and instability. In figure 42 we have, for three situations, filled a balloon at sea level with air at 31° C —the same as the ambient temperature. We have carried the balloon to 5,000 feet. In each situation, the air in the balloon expanded and cooled at the dry adiabatic rate of 3° C for each 1,000 feet to a temperature of 16° C at 5,000 feet.

In the first situation (left), air inside the balloon, even though cooling adiabatically, remains warmer than surrounding air. Vertical motion is favored. The colder, more dense surrounding air forces the balloon on upward. This air is unstable, and a convective current develops.

In situation two (center) the air aloft is warmer. Air inside the balloon, cooling adiabatically, now becomes colder than the surrounding air. The balloon sinks under its own weight returning to its original position when the lifting force is removed. The air is stable, and spontaneous convection is impossible.

In the last situation, temperature of air inside the balloon is the same as that of surrounding air. The balloon will remain at rest. This condition is

neutrally stable; that is, the air is neither stable nor unstable.

Note that, *in all three situations, temperature of air in the expanding balloon cooled at a fixed rate.* The differences in the three conditions depend, therefore, on the temperature differences between the surface and 5,000 feet, that is, on the ambient lapse rates.

HOW STABLE OR UNSTABLE?

Stability runs the gamut from absolutely stable to absolutely unstable, and the atmosphere usually is in a delicate balance somewhere in between. A change in ambient temperature lapse rate of an air mass can tip this balance. For example, surface heating or cooling aloft can make the air more unstable; on the other hand, surface cooling or warming aloft often tips the balance toward greater stability.

Air may be stable or unstable in layers. A stable layer may overlie and cap unstable air; or, conversely, air near the surface may be stable with unstable layers above.

49

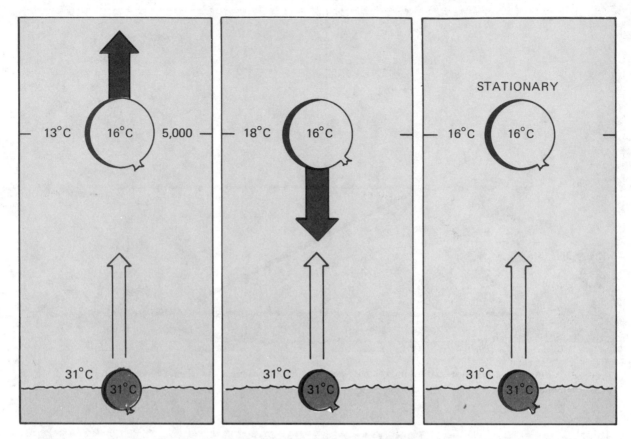

FIGURE 42.   Stability related to temperatures aloft and adiabatic cooling. In each situation, the balloon is filled at sea level
with air at 31° C, carried manually to 5,000 feet, and released. In each case, air in the balloon expands and cools to 16° C
(at the dry adiabatic rate of 3° C per 1,000 feet). But, the temperature of the surrounding air aloft in each situation is
different. The balloon on the left will rise. Even though it cooled adiabatically, the balloon remains warmer and lighter
than the surrounding cold air; when released, it will continue upward spontaneously. The air is unstable; it favors vertical
motion. In the center, the surrounding air is warmer. The cold balloon will sink. It resists our forced lifting and cannot
rise spontaneously. The air is stable—it resists upward motion. On the right, surrounding air and the balloon are at the
same temperature. The balloon remains at rest since no density difference exists to displace it vertically. The air is neutrally stable, i.e., it neither favors nor resists vertical motion. A mass of air in which the temperature decreases rapidly with
height favors instability; but, air tends to be stable if the temperature changes little or not at all with altitude.

CLOUDS—STABLE OR UNSTABLE?

Chapter 5 states that when air is cooling and first
becomes saturated, condensation or sublimation
begins to form clouds. Chapter 7 explains cloud
types and their significance as "signposts in the
sky." Whether the air is stable or unstable within
a layer largely determines cloud structure.

Stratiform Clouds

Since stable air resists convection, clouds in stable
air form in horizontal, sheet-like layers or "strata."
Thus, within a *stable* layer, clouds are *stratiform*.
Adiabatic cooling may be by upslope flow as illustrated in figure 43; by lifting over cold, more dense
air; or by converging winds. Cooling by an underlying cold surface is a stabilizing process and may
produce fog. If clouds are to remain stratiform, the
layer must remain stable after condensation occurs.

Cumuliform Clouds

Unstable air favors convection. A "cumulus"
cloud, meaning "heap," forms in a convective updraft and builds upward, also shown in figure 43.
Thus, within an *unstable* layer, clouds are *cumuliform;* and the vertical extent of the cloud depends
on the depth of the unstable layer.

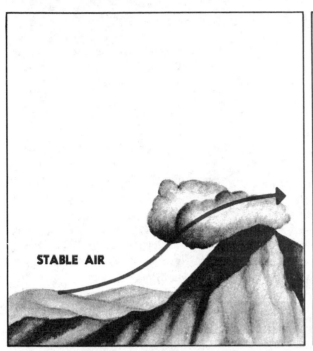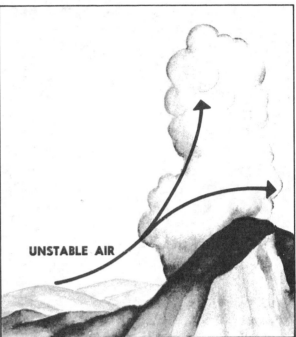

STABLE AIR

UNSTABLE AIR

FIGURE 43. When stable air (left) is forced upward, the air tends to retain horizontal flow, and any cloudiness is flat and stratified. When unstable air is forced upward, the disturbance grows, and any resulting cloudiness shows extensive vertical development.

Initial lifting to trigger a cumuliform cloud may be the same as that for lifting stable air. In addition, convection may be set off by surface heating (chapter 4). Air may be unstable or slightly stable before condensation occurs; but for convective cumuliform clouds to develop, it must be unstable after saturation. Cooling in the updraft is now at the slower moist adiabatic rate because of the release of latent heat of condensation. Temperature in the saturated updraft is warmer than ambient temperature, and convection is spontaneous. Updrafts accelerate until temperature within the cloud cools below the ambient temperature. This condition occurs where the unstable layer is capped by a stable layer often marked by a temperature inversion. Vertical heights range from the shallow fair weather cumulus to the giant thunderstorm cumulonimbus—the ultimate in atmospheric instability capped by the tropopause.

You can estimate height of cumuliform cloud bases using surface temperature-dew point spread. Unsaturated air in a convective current cools at about 5.4° F (3.0° C) per 1,000 feet; dew point decreases at about 1° F (5/9° C). Thus, in a convective current, temperature and dew point con-

verge at about 4.4° F (2.5° C) per 1,000 feet as illustrated in figure 44. We can get a quick *estimate* of a convective cloud base in thousands of feet by rounding these values and dividing into the spread or by multiplying the spread by their reciprocals. When using Fahrenheit, divide by 4 or multiply by .25; when using Celsius, divide by 2.2 or multiply by .45. This method of estimating is reliable only with instability clouds and during the warmer part of the day.

When unstable air lies above stable air, convective currents aloft sometimes form middle and high level cumuliform clouds. In relatively shallow layers they occur as altocumulus and ice crystal cirrocumulus clouds. Altocumulus castellanus clouds develop in deeper midlevel unstable layers.

Merging Stratiform and Cumuliform

A layer of stratiform clouds may sometimes form in a mildly stable layer while a few ambitious convective clouds penetrate the layer thus merging stratiform with cumuliform. Convective clouds may be almost or entirely embedded in a massive stratiform layer and pose an unseen threat to instrument flight.

WHAT DOES IT ALL MEAN?

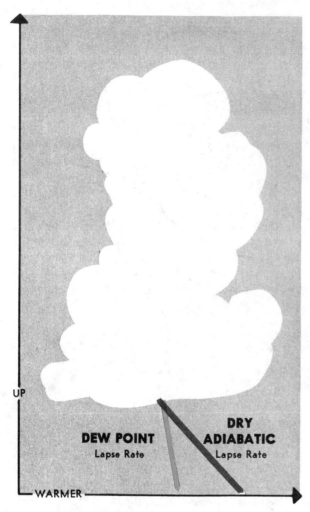

FIGURE 44. Cloud base determination. Temperature and dew point in upward moving air converge at a rate of about 4° F or 2.2° C per 1,000 feet.

Can we fly in unstable air? Stable air? Certainly we can and ordinarily do since air is seldom neutrally stable. The usual convection in unstable air gives a "bumpy" ride; only at times is it violent enough to be hazardous. In stable air, flying is usually smooth but sometimes can be plagued by low ceiling and visibility. It behooves us in preflight planning to take into account stability or instability and any associated hazards. Certain observations you can make on your own:

1. Thunderstorms are sure signs of violently unstable air. Give these storms a wide berth.
2. Showers and clouds towering upward with great ambition indicate strong updrafts and rough (turbulent) air. Stay clear of these clouds.
3. Fair weather cumulus clouds often indicate bumpy turbulence beneath and in the clouds. The cloud tops indicate the approximate upper limit of convection; flight above is usually smooth.
4. Dust devils are a sign of dry, unstable air, usually to considerable height. Your ride may be fairly rough unless you can get above the instability.
5. Stratiform clouds indicate stable air. Flight generally will be smooth, but low ceiling and visibility might require IFR.
6. Restricted visibility at or near the surface over large areas usually indicates stable air. Expect a smooth ride, but poor visibility may require IFR.
7. Thunderstorms may be embedded in stratiform clouds posing an unseen threat to instrument flight.
8. Even in clear weather, you have some clues to stability, viz.:
   a. When temperature decreases uniformly and rapidly as you climb (approaching 3° C per 1,000 feet), you have an indication of unstable air.
   b. If temperature remains unchanged or decreases only slightly with altitude, the air tends to be stable.
   c. If the temperature increases with altitude through a layer—an inversion—the layer is stable and convection is suppressed. Air may be unstable beneath the inversion.
   d. When air near the surface is warm and moist, suspect instability. Surface heating, cooling aloft, converging or upslope winds, or an invading mass of colder air may lead to instability and cumuliform clouds.

Chapter 7
CLOUDS

Clouds, to almost everyone, have some meaning. But to you as a pilot, clouds are your weather "signposts in the sky." They give you an indication of air motion, stability, and moisture. Clouds help you visualize weather conditions and potential weather hazards you might encounter in flight. Let's examine these "signposts" and how to identify them.

IDENTIFICATION

For identification purposes, you need be concerned only with the more basic cloud types, which are divided into four "families." The families are: high clouds, middle clouds, low clouds, and clouds with extensive vertical development. The first three families are further classified according to the way they are formed. Clouds formed by vertical currents in unstable air are *cumulus* meaning *accumulation* or *heap;* they are characterized by their lumpy, billowy appearance. Clouds formed by the cooling of a stable layer are *stratus* meaning *stratified* or *layered;* they are characterized by their uniform, sheet-like appearance.

In addition to the above, the prefix *nimbo* or the suffix *nimbus* means raincloud. Thus, stratified

FIGURE 45. CIRRUS. Cirrus are thin, feather-like ice crystal clouds in patches or narrow bands. Larger ice crystals often trail downward in well-defined wisps called "mares' tails." Wispy, cirrus-like, these contain no significant icing or turbulence. Dense, banded cirrus, which often are turbulent, are discussed in chapter 13.

clouds from which rain is falling are *nimbostratus*. A heavy, swelling cumulus type cloud which produces precipitation is a *cumulonimbus*. Clouds broken into fragments are often identified by adding the suffix *fractus;* for example, fragmentary cumulus is *cumulus fractus*.

HIGH CLOUDS

The high cloud family is cirriform and includes cirrus, cirrocumulus, and cirrostratus. They are composed almost entirely of ice crystals. The height of the bases of these clouds ranges from about 16,500 to 45,000 feet in middle latitudes. Figures 45 through 47 are photographs of high clouds.

MIDDLE CLOUDS

In the middle cloud family are the altostratus, altocumulus, and nimbostratus clouds. These clouds are primarily water, much of which may be supercooled. The height of the bases of these clouds ranges from about 6,500 to 23,000 feet in middle latitudes. Figures 48 through 52 are photographs of middle clouds.

LOW CLOUDS

In the low cloud family are the stratus, stratocumulus, and fair weather cumulus clouds. Low clouds are almost entirely water, but at times the water may be supercooled. Low clouds at subfreezing temperatures can also contain snow and ice particles. The bases of these clouds range from near the surface to about 6,500 feet in middle latitudes. Figures 53 through 55 are photographs of low clouds.

CLOUDS WITH EXTENSIVE VERTICAL DEVELOPMENT

The vertically developed family of clouds includes towering cumulus and cumulonimbus. These clouds usually contain supercooled water above the freezing level. But when a cumulus grows to great heights, water in the upper part of the cloud freezes into ice crystals forming a cumulonimbus. The heights of cumuliform cloud bases range from 1,000 feet or less to above 10,000 feet. Figures 56 and 57 are photographs of clouds with extensive vertical development.

FIGURE 46. CIRROCUMULUS. Cirrocumulus are thin clouds, the individual elements appearing as small white flakes or patches of cotton. May contain highly supercooled water droplets. Some turbulence and icing.

FIGURE 47. CIRROSTRATUS. Cirrostratus is a thin whitish cloud layer appearing like a sheet or veil. Cloud elements are diffuse, sometimes partially striated or fibrous. Due to their ice crystal makeup, these clouds are associated with halos— large luminous circles surrounding the sun or moon. No turbulence and little if any icing. The greatest problem flying in cirriform clouds is restriction to visibility. They can make the strict use of instruments mandatory.

FIGURE 48. ALTOCUMULUS. Altocumulus are composed of white or gray colored layers or patches of solid cloud. The cloud elements may have a waved or roll-like appearance. Some turbulence and small amounts of icing.

FIGURE 49. ALTOSTRATUS. Altostratus is a bluish veil or layer of clouds. It is often associated with altocumulus and sometimes gradually merges into cirrostratus. The sun may be dimly visible through it. Little or no turbulence with moderate amounts of ice.

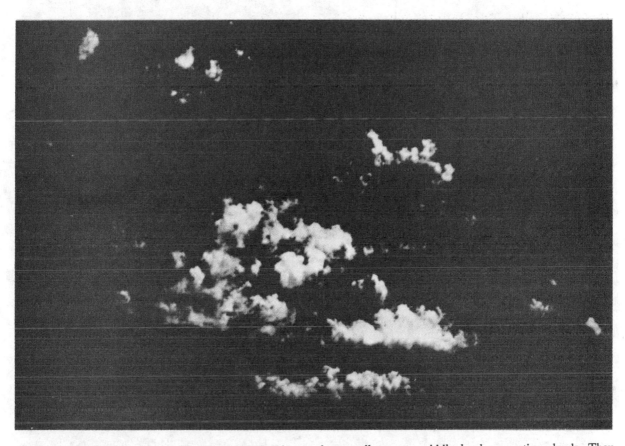

FIGURE 50. ALTOCUMULUS CASTELLANUS. Altocumulus castellanus are middle level convective clouds. They are characterized by their billowing tops and comparatively high bases. They are a good indication of mid-level instability. Rough turbulence with some icing.

FIGURE 51. STANDING LENTICULAR ALTOCUMULUS CLOUDS. Standing lenticular altocumulus clouds are formed on the crests of waves created by barriers in the wind flow. The clouds show little movement, hence the name *standing*. Wind, however, can be quite strong blowing through such clouds. They are characterized by their smooth, polished edges. The presence of these clouds is a good indication of very strong turbulence and should be avoided. Chapter 9, "Turbulence," further explains the significance of this cloud.

FIGURE 52. NIMBOSTRATUS. Nimbostratus is a gray or dark massive cloud layer, diffused by more or less continuous rain, snow, or ice pellets. This type is classified as a middle cloud although it may merge into very low stratus or stratocumulus. Very little turbulence, but can pose a serious icing problem if temperatures are near or below freezing.

FIGURE 53. STRATUS. Stratus is a gray, uniform, sheet-like cloud with relatively low bases. When associated with fog or precipitation, the combination can become troublesome for visual flying. Little or no turbulence, but temperatures near or below freezing can create hazardous icing conditions.

FIGURE 54. STRATOCUMULUS. Stratocumulus bases are globular masses or rolls unlike the flat, sometimes indefinite, bases of stratus. They usually form at the top of a layer mixed by moderate surface winds. Sometimes, they form from the breaking up of stratus or the spreading out of cumulus. Some turbulence, and possible icing at subfreezing temperatures. Ceiling and visibility usually better than with low stratus.

FIGURE 55. CUMULUS. Fair weather cumulus clouds form in convective currents and are characterized by relatively flat bases and dome-shaped tops. Fair weather cumulus do not show extensive vertical development and do not produce precipitation. More often, fair weather cumulus indicates a shallow layer of instability. Some turbulence and no significant icing.

FIGURE 56. TOWERING CUMULUS. Towering cumulus signifies a relatively deep layer of unstable air. It shows considerable vertical development and has billowing *cauliflower* tops. Showers can result from these clouds. Very strong turbulence; some clear icing above the freezing level.

FIGURE 57. CUMULONIMBUS. Cumulonimbus are the ultimate manifestation of instability. They are vertically developed clouds of large dimensions with dense *boiling* tops often crowned with thick veils of dense cirrus (the anvil). Nearly the entire spectrum of flying hazards are contained in these clouds including violent turbulence. They should be avoided at all times! This cloud is the thunderstorm cloud and is discussed in detail in chapter 11, "Thunderstorms."

SIGNPOSTS IN THE SKY

The photographs illustrate some of the basic cloud types. The caption with each photograph describes the type and its significance to flight. In closing, we suggest you take a second look at the cloud photographs. Study the descriptions and potential hazards posed by each type and learn to use the clouds as "signposts in the sky."

Chapter 8
AIR MASSES AND FRONTS

Why is weather today clear and cold over Oklahoma while it is warm and moist over Alabama? What caused the line of thunderstorms that you circumnavigated over eastern Arkansas? Air masses and fronts provide the answer. You can better plan the safety and economy of flight when you can evaluate the expected effects of air masses and fronts. This chapter explains air masses and fronts and relates them to weather and flight planning.

AIR MASSES

When a body of air comes to rest or moves slowly over an extensive area having fairly uniform properties of temperature and moisture, the air takes on those properties. Thus, the air over the area becomes somewhat of an entity as illustrated in figure 58 and has fairly uniform horizontal distribution of its properties. The area over which the air mass acquires its identifying distribution of moisture and temperature is its "source region."

Source regions are many and varied, but the best source regions for air masses are large snow or ice-covered polar regions, cold northern oceans, tropical oceans, and large desert areas. Midlatitudes are poor source regions because transitional disturbances dominate these latitudes giving little opportunity for air masses to stagnate and take on the properties of the underlying region.

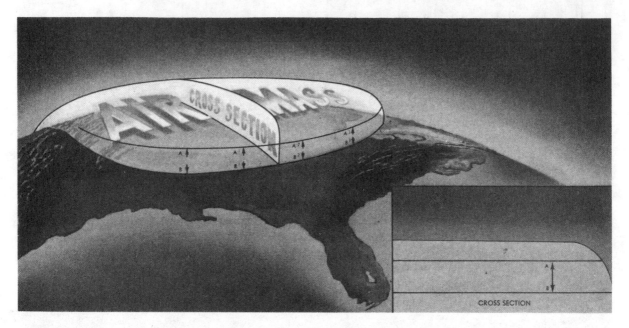

FIGURE 58. Horizontal uniformity of an air mass. (Properties of air at A¹, A², etc., are about the same as those at A; properties at B¹, B², etc., are about the same as those at B.)

AIR MASS MODIFICATION

Just as an air mass took on the properties of its source region, it tends to take on properties of the underlying surface when it moves away from its source region, thus becoming modified.

The degree of modification depends on the speed with which the air mass moves, the nature of the region over which it moves, and the temperature difference between the new surface and the air mass. Some ways air masses are modified are: (1) warming from below, (2) cooling from below, (3) addition of water vapor, and (4) subtraction of water vapor:

1. Cool air moving over a warm surface is heated from below, generating instability and increasing the possibility of showers.
2. Warm air moving over a cool surface is cooled from below, increasing stability. If air is cooled to its dew point, stratus and/or fog forms.
3. Evaporation from water surfaces and falling precipitation adds water vapor to the air. When the water is warmer than the air, evaporation can raise the dew point sufficiently to saturate the air and form stratus or fog.
4. Water vapor is removed by condensation and precipitation.

STABILITY

Stability of an air mass determines its typical weather characteristics. When one type of air mass overlies another, conditions change with height. Characteristics typical of an unstable and a stable air mass are as follows:

Unstable Air	Stable Air
Cumuliform clouds	Stratiform clouds and fog
Showery precipitation	Continuous precipitation
Rough air (turbulence)	Smooth air
Good visibility, except in blowing obstructions	Fair to poor visibility in haze and smoke

FRONTS

As air masses move out of their source regions, they come in contact with other air masses of different properties. The zone between two different air masses is a frontal zone or front. Across this

64

zone, temperature, humidity and wind often change rapidly over short distances.

DISCONTINUITIES

When you pass through a front, the change from the properties of one air mass to those of the other is sometimes quite abrupt. Abrupt changes indicate a narrow frontal zone. At other times, the change of properties is very gradual indicating a broad and diffuse frontal zone.

Temperature

Temperature is one of the most easily recognized discontinuities across a front. At the surface, the passage of a front usually causes noticeable temperature change. When flying through a front, you note a significant change in temperature, especially at low altitudes. Remember that the temperature change, even when gradual, is faster and more pronounced than a change during a flight wholly within one air mass. Thus, for safety, obtain a new altimeter setting after flying through a front. Chapter 3 discussed the effect of a temperature change on the aircraft altimeter.

Dew Point

As you learned in Chapter 5, dew point temperature is a measure of the amount of water vapor in the air. Temperature–dew point spread is a measure of the degree of saturation. Dew point and temperature–dew point spread usually differ across a front. The difference helps identify the front and may give a clue to differences of cloudiness and/or fog.

Wind

Wind always changes across a front. Wind discontinuity may be in direction, in speed, or in both. Be alert for a wind shift when flying in the vicinity of a frontal surface; if the wind shift catches you unaware it can get you off course or even lost in a short time. The relatively sudden change in wind also creates wind shear, and you will study its significance in the next chapter, "Turbulence."

Pressure

A front lies in a pressure trough, and pressure generally is higher in the cold air. Thus, when you cross a front directly into colder air, pressure usually rises abruptly. When you approach a front toward warm air, pressure generally falls until you cross the front and then remains steady or falls slightly in the warm air. However, pressure patterns vary widely across fronts, and your course may not be directly across a front. The important thing to remember is that when crossing a front, you will encounter a difference in the rate of pressure change; be especially alert in keeping your altimeter setting current.

TYPES OF FRONTS

The three principal types of fronts are the cold front, the warm front, and the stationary front.

Cold Front

The leading edge of an advancing cold air mass is a cold front. At the surface, cold air is overtaking and replacing warmer air. Cold fronts move at about the speed of the wind component perpendicular to the front just above the frictional layer. Figure 59 shows the vertical cross section of a cold front and the symbol depicting it on a surface weather chart. A shallow cold air mass or a slow moving cold front may have a frontal slope more like a warm front shown in figure 60.

Warm Front

The edge of an advancing warm air mass is a warm front—warmer air is overtaking and replacing colder air. Since the cold air is denser than the warm air, the cold air hugs the ground. The warm air slides up and over the cold air and lacks direct push on the cold air. Thus, the cold air is slow to retreat in advance of the warm air. This slowness of the cold air to retreat produces a frontal slope that is more gradual than the cold frontal slope as shown in figure 60. Consequently, warm fronts on the surface are seldom as well marked as cold fronts, and they usually move about half as fast when the general wind flow is the same in each case.

Stationary Fronts

When neither air mass is replacing the other, the front is stationary. Figure 61 shows a cross section of a stationary front and its symbol on a surface chart. The opposing forces exerted by adjacent air masses of different densities are such that the frontal surface between them shows little or no movement. In such cases, the surface winds tend to blow parallel to the frontal zone. Slope of a stationary front is normally shallow, although it may be steep depending on wind distribution and density difference.

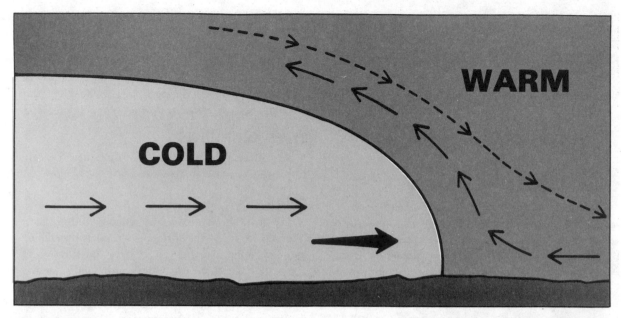

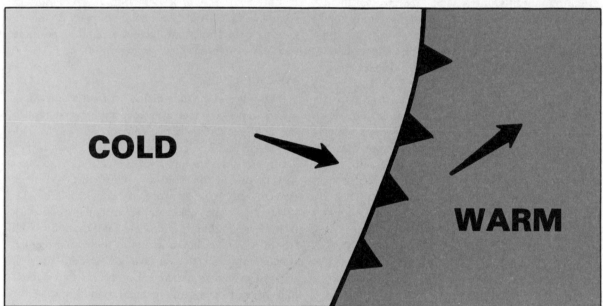

FIGURE 59.   Cross section of a cold front (above) with the weather map symbol (below). The symbol is a line with pointed barbs pointing in the direction of movement. If a map is in color, a blue line represents the cold front. The vertical scale is expanded in the top illustration to show the frontal slope. The frontal slope is steep near the leading edge as cold air replaces warm air. The solid heavy arrow shows movement of the front. Warm air may descend over the front as indicated by the dashed arrows; but more commonly, the cold air forces warm air upward over the frontal surface as shown by the solid arrows.

FRONTAL WAVES AND OCCLUSION

Frontal waves and cyclones (areas of low pressure) usually form on slow-moving cold fronts or on stationary fronts. The life cycle and movement of a cyclone is dictated to a great extent by the upper wind flow.

In the initial condition of frontal wave development in figure 62, the winds on both sides of the front are blowing parallel to the front (A). Small disturbances then may start a wavelike bend in the front (B).

If this tendency persists and the wave increases in size, a cyclonic (counterclockwise) circulation

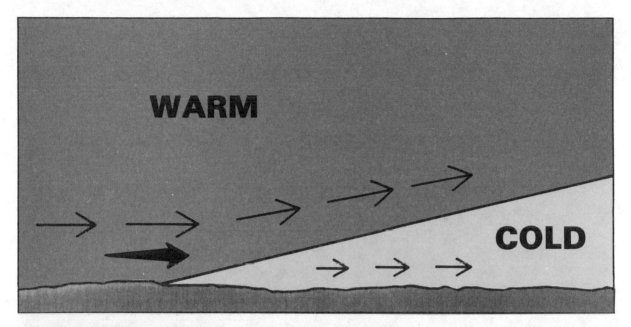

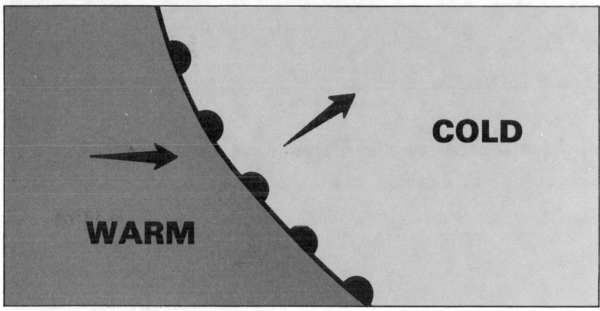

FIGURE 60.   Cross section of a warm front (top) with the weather map symbol (bottom). The symbol is a line with rounded
barbs pointing in the direction of movement. If a map is in color, a red line represents the warm front. Slope of a warm
front generally is more shallow than slope of a cold front. Movement of a warm front shown by the heavy black arrow is
slower than the wind in the warm air represented by the light solid arrows. The warm air gradually erodes the cold air.

develops. One section of the front begins to move as a warm front, while the section next to it begins to move as a cold front (C). This deformation is a frontal wave.

The pressure at the peak of the frontal wave falls, and a low-pressure center forms. The cyclonic circulation becomes stronger, and the surface winds are now strong enough to move the fronts; the cold front moves faster than the warm front (D). When the cold front catches up with the warm front, the two of them *occlude* (close together). The result is an *occluded front* or, for brevity, an *occlusion* (E). This is the time of maximum intensity for the wave cyclone. Note that the symbol depicting the occlusion is a combination of the symbols for the warm and cold fronts.

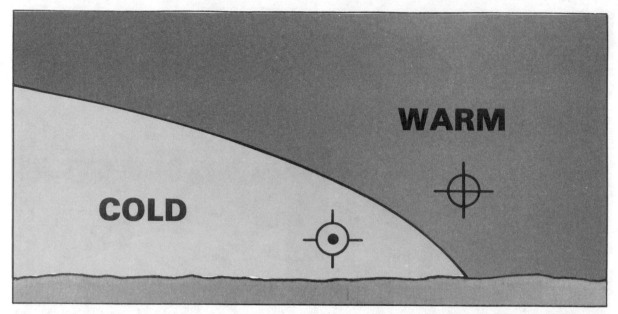

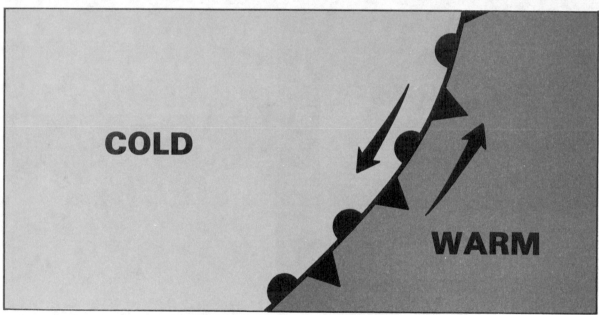

FIGURE 61. Cross section of a stationary front (top) and its weather map symbol (bottom). The symbol is a line with alternating pointed and rounded barbs on opposite sides of the line, the pointed barbs pointing away from the cold air and the rounded barbs away from the warm air. If a map is in color, the symbol is a line of alternating red and blue segments. The front has little or no movement and winds are nearly parallel to the front. The symbol in the warm air is the tail of a wind arrow into the page. The symbol in the cold air is the point of a wind arrow out of the page. Slope of the front may vary considerably depending on wind and density differences across the front.

As the occlusion continues to grow in length, the cyclonic circulation diminishes in intensity and the frontal movement slows down (F). Sometimes a new frontal wave begins to form on the long westward-trailing portion of the cold front (F,G), or a secondary low pressure system forms at the apex where the cold front and warm front come together to form the occlusion. In the final stage, the two fronts may have become a single stationary front again. The low center with its remnant of the occlusion is disappearing (G).

Figure 63 indicates a warm-front occlusion in vertical cross section. This type of occlusion occurs when the air is colder in advance of the warm

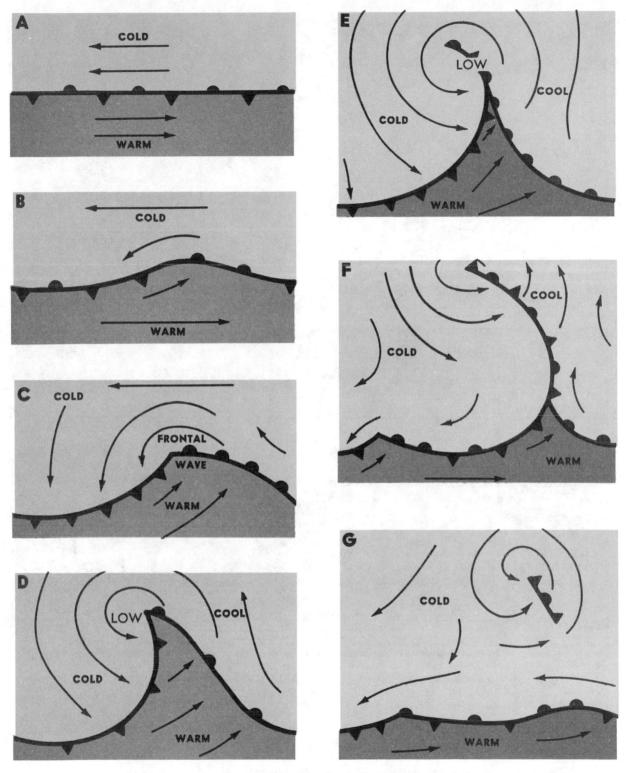

FIGURE 62. The life cycle of a frontal wave.

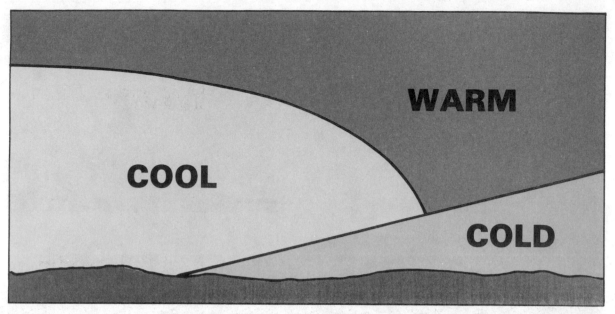

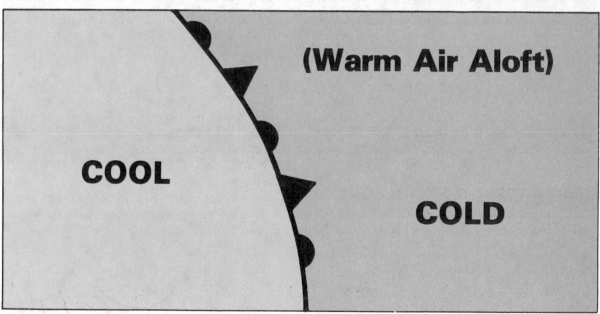

FIGURE 63.   Cross section of a warm-front occlusion (top) and its weather map symbol (bottom). The symbol is a line with alternating pointed and rounded barbs on the same side of the line pointing in the direction of movement. Shown in color on a weather map, the line is purple. In the warm front occlusion, air under the cold front is not as cold as air ahead of the warm front; and when the cold front overtakes the warm front, the less cold air rides over the colder air. In a warm front occlusion, cool air replaces cold air at the surface.

front than behind the cold front, lifting the cold front aloft.

Figure 64 indicates a cold-front occlusion in vertical cross section. This type of occlusion occurs when the air behind the cold front is colder than the air in advance of the warm front, lifting the warm front aloft.

NON-FRONTAL LOWS

Since fronts are boundaries between air masses of different properties, fronts are not associated with lows lying solely in a homogeneous air mass. Nonfrontal lows are infrequent east of the Rocky Mountains in midlatitudes but do occur occasion-

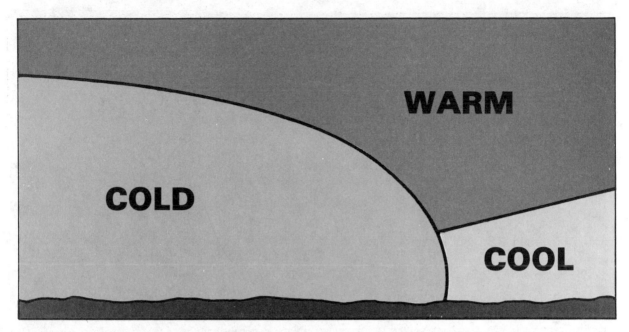

FIGURE 64. Cross section of a cold-front occlusion. Its weather map symbol is the same as for a warm-front occlusion shown in Figure 63. In the cold-front occlusion, the coldest air is under the cold front. When it overtakes the warm front, it lifts the warm front aloft; and cold air replaces cool air at the surface.

ally during the warmer months. Small nonfrontal lows over the western mountains are common as is the semistationary thermal low in extreme Southwestern United States. Tropical lows are also nonfrontal.

FRONTOLYSIS AND FRONTOGENESIS

As adjacent air masses modify and as temperature and pressure differences equalize across a front, the front dissipates. This process, frontolysis, is illustrated in figure 65. Frontogenesis is the generation of a front. It occurs when a relatively sharp zone of transition develops over an area between two air masses which have densities gradually becoming more and more in contrast with each other. The necessary wind flow pattern develops at the same time. Figure 66 shows an example of frontogenesis with the symbol.

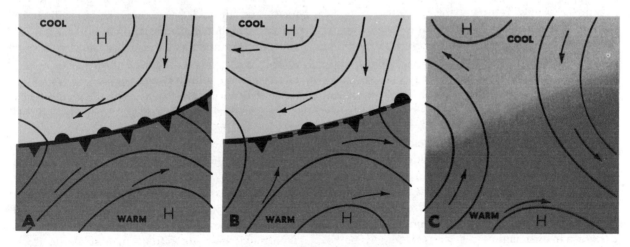

FIGURE 65. Frontolysis of a stationary front.

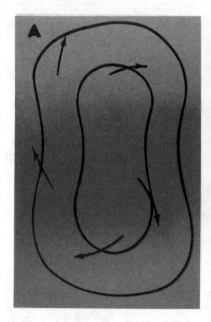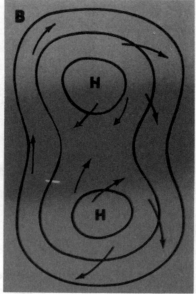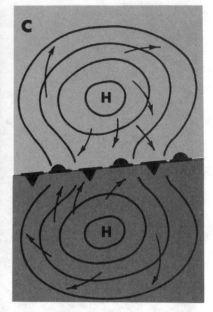

FIGURE 66. Frontogenesis of a stationary front.

FRONTAL WEATHER

In fronts, flying weather varies from virtually clear skies to extreme hazards including hail, turbulence, icing, low clouds, and poor visibility. Weather occurring with a front depends on (1) the amount of moisture available, (2) the degree of stability of the air that is forced upward, (3) the slope of the front, (4) the speed of frontal movement, and (5) the upper wind flow.

Sufficient moisture must be available for clouds to form, or there will be no clouds. As an inactive front comes into an area of moisture, clouds and precipitation may develop rapidly. A good example of this is a cold front moving eastward from the dry slopes of the Rocky Mountains into a tongue of moist air from the Gulf of Mexico over the Plains States. Thunderstorms may build rapidly and catch a pilot unaware.

The degree of stability of the lifted air determines whether cloudiness will be predominately stratiform or cumuliform. If the warm air overriding the front is stable, stratiform clouds develop. If the warm air is unstable, cumuliform clouds develop. Precipitation from stratiform clouds is usually steady as illustrated in figure 67 and there is little or no turbulence. Precipitation from cumuliform clouds is of a shower type as in figure 68, and the clouds are turbulent.

Shallow frontal surfaces tend to give extensive cloudiness with large precipitation areas (figure 69). Widespread precipitation associated with a gradual sloping front often causes low stratus and fog. In this case, the rain raises the humidity of the cold air to saturation. This and related effects may produce low ceiling and poor visibility over thousands of square miles. If temperature of the cold air near the surface is below freezing but the warmer air aloft is above freezing, precipitation falls as freezing rain or ice pellets; however, if temperature of the warmer air aloft is well below freezing, precipitation forms as snow.

When the warm air overriding a shallow front is moist and unstable, the usual widespread cloud mass forms; but embedded in the cloud mass are altocumulus, cumulus, and even thunderstorms as in figures 70 and 71. These embedded storms are more common with warm and stationary fronts but may occur with a slow moving, shallow cold front. A good preflight briefing helps you to foresee the presence of these hidden thunderstorms. Radar also helps in this situation and is discussed in chapter 11.

A fast moving, steep cold front forces upward motion of the warm air along its leading edge. If the warm air is moist, precipitation occurs immediately along the surface position of the front as shown in figure 72.

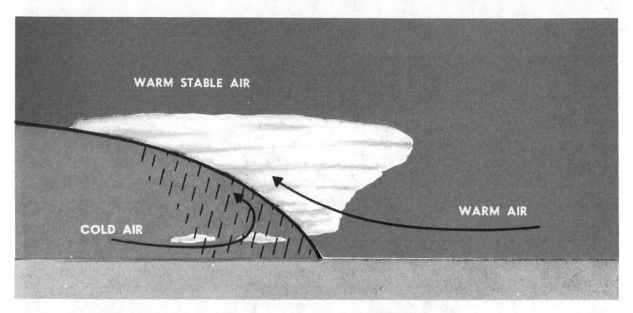

FIGURE 67.   A cold front underrunning warm, moist, stable air. Clouds are stratified and precipitation continuous. Precipitation induces stratus in the cold air.

FIGURE 68.   A cold front underrunning warm, moist, unstable air. Clouds are cumuliform with possible showers or thunderstorms near the surface position of the front. Convective clouds often develop in the warm air ahead of the front. The warm, wet ground behind the front generates low-level convection and fair weather cumulus in the cold air.

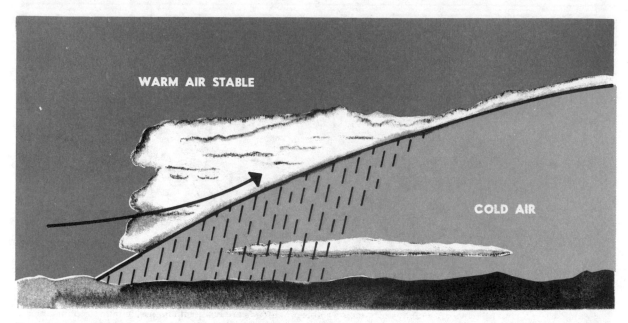

FIGURE 69. A warm front with overrunning moist, stable air. Clouds are stratiform and widespread over the shallow front. Precipitation is continuous and induces widespread stratus in the cold air.

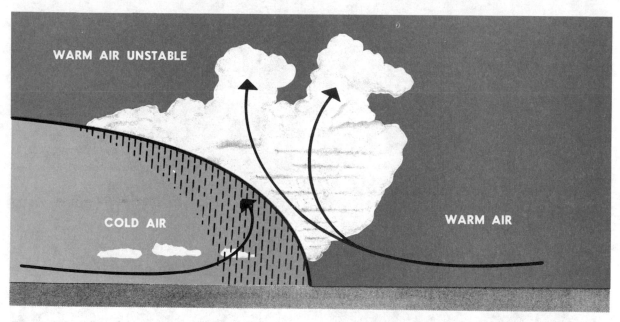

FIGURE 70. A slow-moving cold front underrunning warm, moist, unstable air. Note that the front is more shallow than the fast-moving front shown in figure 68. Clouds are stratified with embedded cumulonimbus and thunderstorms. This type of frontal weather is especially hazardous since the individual thunderstorms are hidden and cannot be avoided unless the aircraft is equipped with airborne radar.

Since an occluded front develops when a cold front overtakes a warm front, weather with an occluded front is a combination of both warm and cold frontal weather. Figures 73 and 74 show warm and cold occlusions and associated weather.

A front may have little or no cloudiness associated with it. Dry fronts occur when the warm air aloft is flowing down the frontal slope or the air is so dry that any cloudiness that occurs is at high levels.

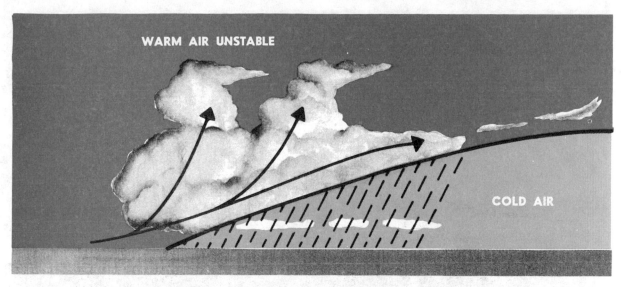

FIGURE 71. A warm front with overrunning warm, moist, unstable air. Weather, clouds, and hazards are similar to those described in figure 70 except that they generally are more widespread.

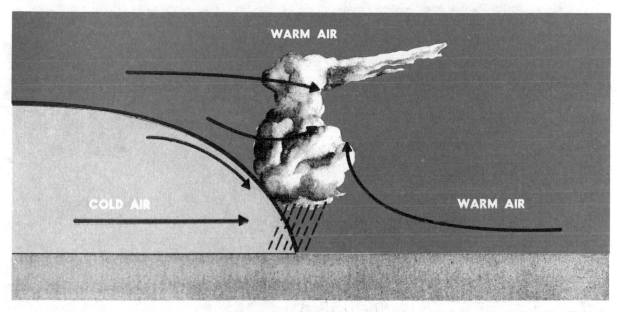

FIGURE 72. A fast moving cold front underrunning warm, moist, unstable air. Showers and thunderstorms develop along the surface position of the front.

The upper wind flow dictates to a great extent the amount of cloudiness and rain accompanying a frontal system as well as movement of the front itself. Remember in chapter 4 we said that systems tend to move with the upper winds. When winds aloft blow across a front, it tends to move with the wind. When winds aloft parallel a front, the front moves slowly if at all. A deep, slow moving trough aloft forms extensive cloudiness and precipitation,

while a rapid moving minor trough more often restricts weather to a rather narrow band. However, the latter often breeds severe, fast moving, turbulent spring weather.

INSTABILITY LINE

An instability line is a narrow, nonfrontal line or band of convective activity. If the activity is fully developed thunderstorms, figure 75, the line is a

FIGURE 73. A warm front occlusion lifting warm, moist, unstable air. Note that the associated weather is complex and encompasses all types of weather associated with both the warm and cold fronts when air is moist and unstable.

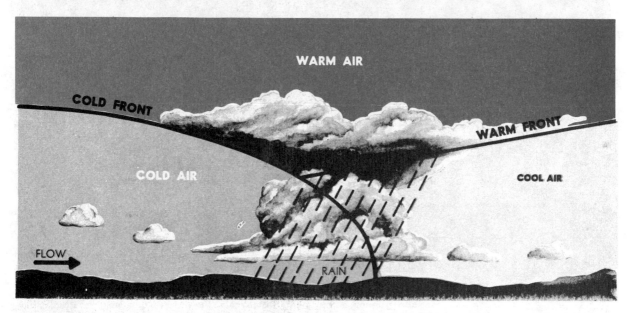

FIGURE 74. A cold front occlusion lifting warm, moist, stable air. Associated weather encompasses types of weather associated with both warm and cold fronts when air is moist and stable.

squall line (chapter 11, "Thunderstorms"). Instability lines form in moist unstable air. An instability line may develop far from any front. More often, it develops ahead of a cold front, and sometimes a series of these lines move out ahead of the front. A favored location for instability lines which frequently erupt into severe thunderstorms is a dew point front or dry line.

DEW POINT FRONT OR DRY LINE

During a considerable part of the year, dew point fronts are common in Western Texas and New Mexico northward over the Plains States. Moist air flowing north from the Gulf of Mexico abuts the dryer and therefore slightly denser air flowing from the southwest. Except for moisture differences, there is seldom any significant air mass contrast across this "Front"; and therefore, it is commonly called a "dry line." Nighttime and early morning fog and low-level clouds often prevail on the moist side of the line while generally clear skies mark the dry side. In spring and early summer over Texas, Oklahoma, and Kansas, and for some distance eastward, the dry line is a favored spawning area for squall lines and tornadoes.

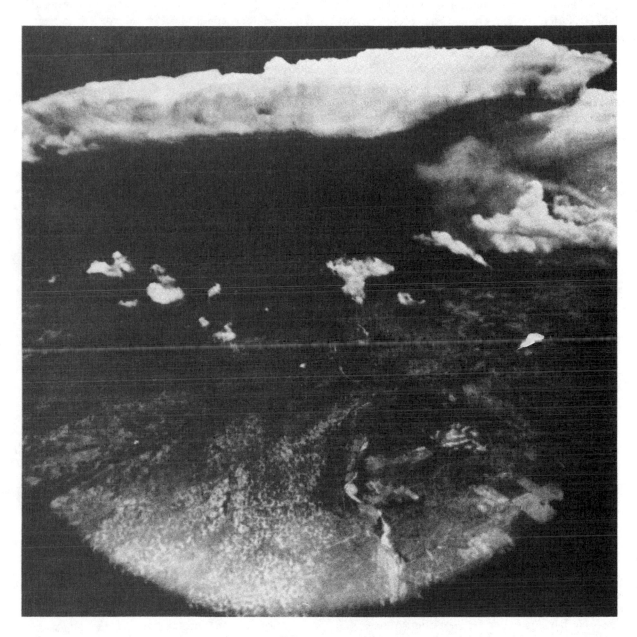

FIGURE 75.   An aerial view of a portion of a squall line.

FRONTS AND FLIGHT PLANNING

Surface weather charts pictorially portray fronts and, in conjunction with other forecast charts and special analyses, aid you in determining expected weather conditions along your proposed route. Knowing the locations of fronts and associated weather helps you determine if you can proceed as planned. Often you can change your route to avoid adverse weather.

Frontal weather may change rapidly. For example, there may be only cloudiness associated with a cold front over northern Illinois during the morning but with a strong squall line forecast by afternoon. Skies may be partly cloudy during the afternoon over Atlanta in advance of a warm front, but by sunset drizzle and dense fog are forecast. A cold front in Kansas is producing turbulent thunderstorms, but by midnight the upper flow is expected to dissipate the thunderstorms and weaken the front. A Pacific front is approaching Seattle and is expected to produce heavy rain by midnight.

A mental picture of what is happening and what is forecast should greatly aid you in avoiding adverse weather conditions. If unexpected adverse weather develops en route, your mental picture aids you in planning the best diversion. *If possible, always obtain a good preflight weather briefing.*

We suggest you again look at figures 67 through 75 and review weather conditions associated with different types of fronts and stability conditions. These are only a few of many possibilities, but they should give some help during preflight planning or inflight diversion.

Chapter 9
TURBULENCE

Everyone who flies encounters turbulence at some time or other. A turbulent atmosphere is one in which air currents vary greatly over short distances. These currents range from rather mild eddies to strong currents of relatively large dimensions. As an aircraft moves through these currents, it undergoes changing accelerations which jostle it from its smooth flight path. This jostling is turbulence. Turbulence ranges from bumpiness which can annoy crew and passengers to severe jolts which can structurally damage the aircraft or injure its passengers.

Aircraft reaction to turbulence varies with the difference in windspeed in adjacent currents, size of the aircraft, wing loading, airspeed, and aircraft attitude. When an aircraft travels rapidly from one current to another, it undergoes abrupt changes in acceleration. Obviously, if the aircraft moved more slowly, the changes in acceleration would be more gradual. The first rule in flying turbulence is to reduce airspeed. Your aircraft manual most likely lists recommended airspeed for penetrating turbulence.

Knowing where to expect turbulence helps a

pilot avoid or minimize turbulence discomfort and hazards. The main causes of turbulence are (1) convective currents, (2) obstructions to wind flow, and (3) wind shear. Turbulence also occurs in the wake of moving aircraft whenever the airfoils exert lift—wake turbulence. Any combination of causes may occur at one time.

CONVECTIVE CURRENTS

Convective currents are a common cause of turbulence, especially at low altitudes. These currents are localized vertical air movements, both *ascending* and *descending*. For every rising current, there

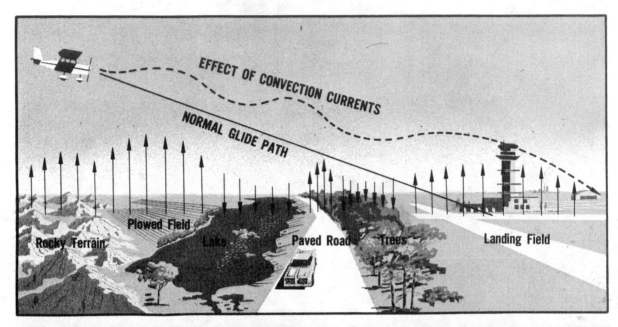

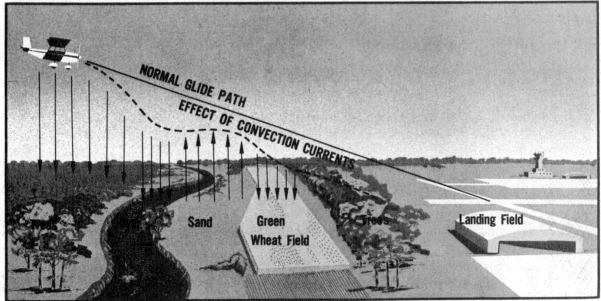

FIGURE 76. Effect of convective currents on final approach. Predominantly upward currents (top) tend to cause the aircraft to overshoot. Predominantly downward currents (bottom) tend to cause the craft to undershoot.

is a compensating downward current. The downward currents frequently occur over broader areas than do the upward currents, and therefore, they have a slower vertical speed than do the rising currents.

Convective currents are most active on warm summer afternoons when winds are light. Heated air at the surface creates a shallow, unstable layer, and the warm air is forced upward. Convection increases in strength and to greater heights as surface heating increases. Barren surfaces such as sandy or rocky wastelands and plowed fields become hotter than open water or ground covered by vegetation. Thus, air at and near the surface heats unevenly. Because of uneven heating, the strength of convective currents can vary considerably within short distances.

When cold air moves over a warm surface, it becomes unstable in lower levels. Convective currents extend several thousand feet above the surface resulting in rough, choppy turbulence when flying in the cold air. This condition often occurs in any season after the passage of a cold front.

Figure 76 illustrates the effect of low-level convective turbulence on aircraft approaching to land. Turbulence on approach can cause abrupt changes in airspeed and may even result in a stall at a dangerously low altitude. To prevent the danger,

increase airspeed slightly over normal approach speed. This procedure may appear to conflict with the rule of reducing airspeed for turbulence penetration; but remember, the approach speed for your aircraft is well below the recommended turbulence penetration speed.

As air moves upward, it cools by expansion. A convective current continues upward until it reaches a level where its temperature cools to the same as that of the surrounding air. If it cools to saturation, a cloud forms. Billowy fair weather cumulus clouds, usually seen on sunny afternoons, are signposts in the sky indicating convective turbulence. The cloud top usually marks the approximate upper limit of the convective current. A pilot can expect to encounter turbulence beneath or in the clouds, while above the clouds, air generally is smooth. You will find most comfortable flight above the cumulus as illustrated in figure 77.

When convection extends to greater heights, it develops larger towering cumulus clouds and cumulonimbus with anvil-like tops. The cumulonimbus gives visual warning of violent convective turbulence discussed in more detail in chapter 11.

The pilot should also know that when air is too dry for cumulus to form, convective currents still can be active. He has little indication of their presence until he encounters turbulence.

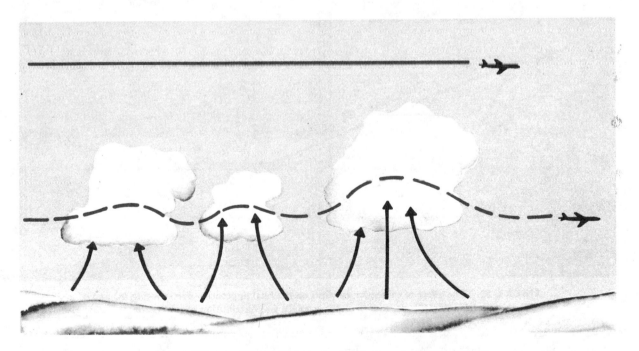

FIGURE 77. Avoiding turbulence by flying above convective clouds.

OBSTRUCTIONS TO WIND FLOW

Obstructions such as buildings, trees, and rough terrain disrupt smooth wind flow into a complex snarl of eddies as diagrammed in figure 78. An aircraft flying through these eddies experiences turbulence. This turbulence we classify as "mechanical" since it results from mechanical disruption of the ambient wind flow.

The degree of mechanical turbulence depends on wind speed and roughness of the obstructions. The higher the speed and/or the rougher the sur-

face, the greater is the turbulence. The wind carries the turbulent eddies downstream—how far depends on wind speed and stability of the air. Unstable air allows larger eddies to form than those that form in stable air; but the instability breaks up the eddies quickly, while in stable air they dissipate slowly.

Mechanical turbulence can also cause cloudiness near the top of the mechanically disturbed layer. However, the type of cloudiness tells you whether

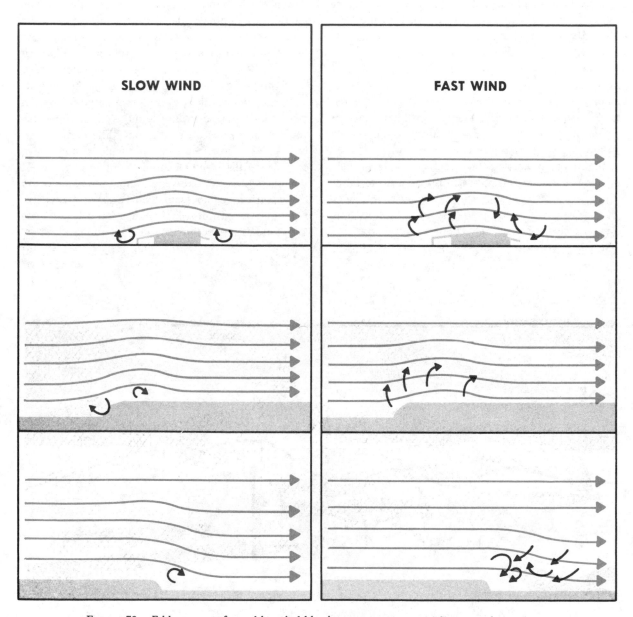

FIGURE 78. Eddy currents formed by wind blowing over uneven ground or over obstructions.

it is from mechanical or convective mixing. Mechanical mixing produces stratocumulus clouds in rows or bands, while convective clouds form a random pattern. The cloud rows developed by mechanical mixing may be parallel to or perpendicular to the wind depending on meteorological factors which we do not discuss here.

The airport area is especially vulnerable to mechanical turbulence which invariably causes gusty surface winds. When an aircraft is in a low-level approach or a climb, airspeed fluctuates in the gusts, and the aircraft may even stall. During extremely gusty conditions, maintain a margin of airspeed above normal approach or climb speed to allow for changes in airspeed. When landing with a gusty crosswind as illustrated in figure 79, be alert for mechanical turbulence and control problems caused by airport structures upwind. Surface gusts also create taxi problems.

Mechanical turbulence can affect low-level cross-country flight about anywhere. Mountains can generate turbulence to altitudes much higher than the mountains themselves.

When flying over rolling hills, you may experience mechanical turbulence. Generally, such turbulence is not hazardous, but it may be annoying or uncomfortable. A climb to higher altitude should reduce the turbulence.

When flying over rugged hills or mountains, however, you may have some real turbulence problems. Again, we cannot discuss mechanical turbulence without considering wind speed and stability. When wind speed across mountains exceeds about 40 knots, you can anticipate turbulence. Where and to what extent depends largely on stability.

If the air crossing the mountains is unstable, turbulence on the windward side is almost certain. If sufficient moisture is present, convective clouds form intensifying the turbulence. Convective clouds over a mountain or along a ridge are a sure sign of unstable air and turbulence on the windward side and over the mountain crest.

As the unstable air crosses the barrier, it spills down the leeward slope often as a violent downdraft. Sometimes the downward speed exceeds the maximum climb rate for your aircraft and may drive the craft into the mountainside as shown in figure 80. In the process of crossing the mountains, mixing reduces the instability to some extent. Therefore, hazardous turbulence in unstable air generally does not extend a great distance downwind from the barrier.

MOUNTAIN WAVE

When stable air crosses a mountain barrier, the turbulent situation is somewhat reversed. Air flowing up the windward side is relatively smooth. Wind flow across the barrier is laminar—that is, it tends to flow in layers. The barrier may set up waves in these layers much as waves develop on

FIGURE 79. Turbulent air in the landing area.

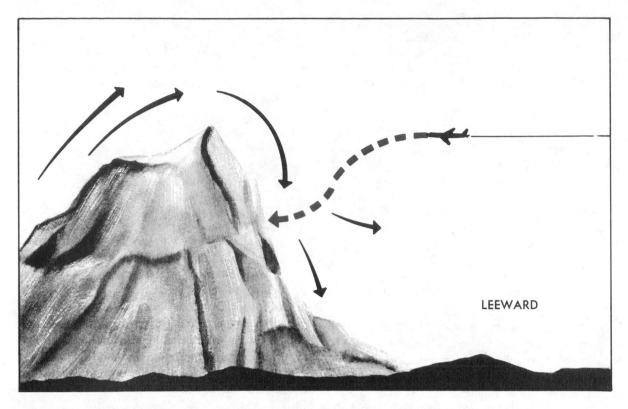

LEEWARD

FIGURE 80. Wind flow in mountain areas. Dangerous downdrafts may be encountered on the lee side.

a disturbed water surface. The waves remain nearly stationary while the wind blows rapidly through them. The wave pattern, diagrammed in figure 81, is a "standing" or "mountain" wave, so named because it remains essentially stationary and is associated with the mountain. The wave pattern may extend 100 miles or more downwind from the barrier.

Wave crests extend well above the highest mountains, sometimes into the lower stratosphere. Under

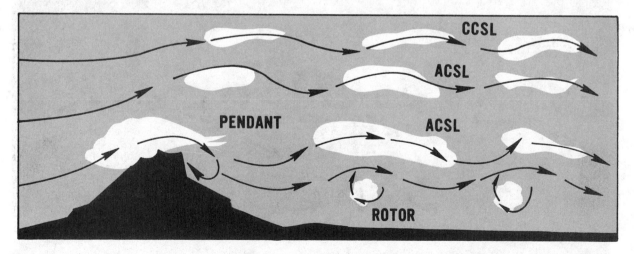

FIGURE 81. Schematic cross section of a mountain wave. Note the standing wave pattern downwind from the mountain. Note also the rotary circulation below the wave crests. When the air contains sufficient moisture, characteristic clouds form.

each wave crest is a rotary circulation also diagrammed in figure 81. The "rotor" forms below the elevation of the mountain peaks. Turbulence can be violent in the overturning rotor. Updrafts and downdrafts in the waves can also create violent turbulence.

Figure 81 further illustrates clouds often associated with a mountain wave. When moisture is sufficient to produce clouds on the windward side, they are stratified. Crests of the standing waves may be marked by stationary, lens-shaped clouds known as "standing lenticular" clouds. Figure 82 is a photograph of standing lenticular clouds. They form in the updraft and dissipate in the downdraft, so they do not move as the wind blows through them. The rotor may also be marked by a "rotor" cloud. Figure 83 is a photograph of a series of rotor clouds, each under the crest of a wave. But remember, clouds are not always present to mark the mountain wave. Sometimes, the air is too dry. Always anticipate possible mountain wave turbulence when strong winds of 40 knots or greater blow across a mountain or ridge and the air is stable.

You should not be surprised at any degree of turbulence in a mountain wave. Reports of turbulence range from none to turbulence violent enough to damage the aircraft, but most reports show something in between.

MOUNTAIN FLYING

When planning a flight over mountainous terrain, gather as much preflight information as possible on cloud reports, wind direction, wind speed, and stability of air. Satellites often help locate mountain waves. Figures 84 and 85 are photographs of mountain wave clouds taken from spacecraft. Adequate information may not always be available, so remain alert for signposts in the sky. What should you look for both during preflight planning and during your inflight observations?

Wind at mountain top level in excess of 25 knots suggests some turbulence. Wind in excess of 40 knots across a mountain barrier dictates caution. Stratified clouds mean stable air. Standing lentic-

FIGURE 82.   Standing lenticular clouds associated with a mountain wave.

FIGURE 83. Standing wave rotor clouds marking the rotary circulation beneath mountain waves.

ular and/or rotor clouds suggest a mountain wave; expect turbulence many miles to the lee of mountains and relative smooth flight on the windward side. Convective clouds on the windward side of mountains mean unstable air; expect turbulence in close proximity to and on either side of the mountain.

When approaching mountains from the leeward side during strong winds, begin your climb well away from the mountains—100 miles in a mountain wave and 30 to 50 miles otherwise. Climb to an altitude 3,000 to 5,000 feet above mountain tops before attempting to cross. The best procedure is to approach a ridge at a 45° angle to enable a rapid retreat to calmer air. If unable to make good on your first attempt and you have higher altitude

capabilities, you may back off and make another attempt at higher altitude. Sometimes you may have to choose between turning back or detouring the area.

Flying mountain passes and valleys is not a safe procedure during high winds. The mountains funnel the wind into passes and valleys thus increasing wind speed and intensifying turbulence. If winds at mountain top level are strong, go high, or go around.

Surface wind may be relatively calm in a valley surrounded by mountains when wind aloft is strong. If taking off in the valley, climb above mountain top level before leaving the valley. Maintain lateral clearance from the mountains sufficient to allow recovery if caught in a downdraft.

WIND SHEAR

As discussed in chapter 4, wind shear generates eddies between two wind currents of differing velocities. The differences may be in wind speed, wind direction, or in both. Wind shear may be

associated with either a wind shift or a wind speed gradient at any level in the atmosphere. Three conditions are of special interest—(1) wind shear with a low-level temperature inversion, (2) wind shear

FIGURE 84. Mountain wave clouds over the Tibetan Plateau photographed from a manned spacecraft.

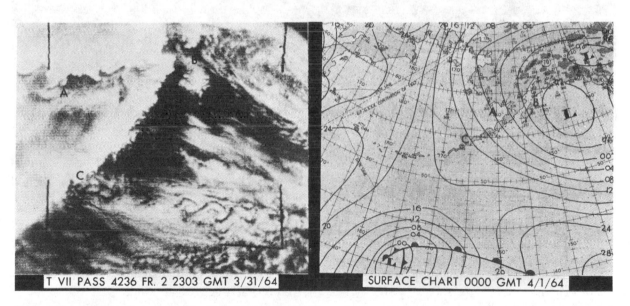

T VII PASS 4236 FR. 2 2303 GMT 3/31/64   SURFACE CHART 0000 GMT 4/1/64

FIGURE 85. Satellite photograph of a mountain wave and the surface weather map for approximately the same time. A single mountain in the Aleutian chain generates the wave. Note how it spirals downwind from the source. Without the satellite, the turbulent wave would have gone undetected unless some aircraft had flown into it.

in a frontal zone, and (3) clear air turbulence (CAT) at high levels associated with a jet stream or strong circulation. High-level clear air turbulence is discussed in detail in chapter 13, "High Altitude Weather."

WIND SHEAR WITH A LOW-LEVEL TEMPERATURE INVERSION

A temperature inversion forms near the surface on a clear night with calm or light surface wind as discussed in chapter 2. Wind just above the inversion may be relatively strong. As illustrated in figure 86, a wind shear zone develops between the calm and the stronger winds above. Eddies in the shear zone cause airspeed fluctuations as an aircraft climbs or descends through the inversion. An aircraft most likely is either climbing from takeoff or approaching to land when passing through the inversion; therefore, airspeed is slow—only a few knots greater than stall speed. The fluctuation in airspeed can induce a stall precariously close to the ground.

Since surface wind is calm or very light, takeoff or landing can be in any direction. Takeoff may be in the direction of the wind above the inversion. If so, the aircraft encounters a sudden tailwind and a corresponding loss of airspeed when climbing through the inversion. Stall is possible. If approach is into the wind above the inversion, the headwind is suddenly lost when descending through the inver-

sion. Again, a sudden loss in airspeed may induce a stall.

When taking off or landing in calm wind under clear skies within a few hours before or after sunrise, be prepared for a temperature inversion near the ground. You can be relatively certain of a shear zone in the inversion if you know the wind at 2,000 to 4,000 feet is 25 knots or more. Allow a margin of airspeed above normal climb or approach speed to alleviate danger of stall in event of turbulence or sudden change in wind velocity.

WIND SHEAR IN A FRONTAL ZONE

As you have learned in chapter 8, a front can contain many hazards. However, a front can be between two dry stable airmasses and can be devoid of clouds. Even so, wind changes abruptly in the frontal zone and can induce wind shear turbulence. The degree of turbulence depends on the magnitude of the wind shear. When turbulence is expected in a frontal zone, follow turbulence penetration procedures recommended in your aircraft manual.

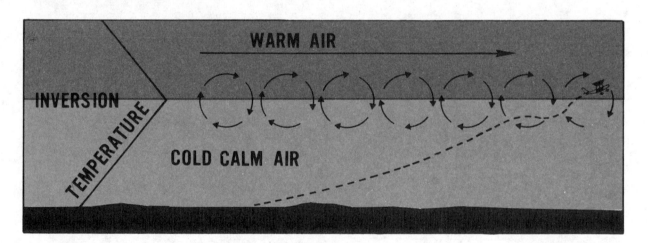

FIGURE 86. Wind shear in a zone between relatively calm wind below an inversion and strong wind above the inversion. This condition is most common at night or in early morning. It can cause an abrupt turbulence encounter at low altitude.

WAKE TURBULENCE

An aircraft receives its lift by accelerating a mass of air downward. Thus, whenever the wings are providing lift, air is forced downward under the wings generating rotary motions or vortices off the wing tips. When the landing gear bears the entire weight of the aircraft, no wing tip vortices

develop. But the instant the pilot "hauls back" on the controls, these vortices begin. Figure 87 illustrates how they might appear if visible behind the plane as it breaks ground. These vortices continue throughout the flight and until the craft again settles firmly on its landing gear.

FIGURE 87. Wake turbulence wing tip vortices developing as aircraft breaks ground. These vortices develop when the aircraft is rotated into a flying attitude and the wings begin developing lift.

These vortices spread downward and outward from the flight path. They also drift with the wind. Strength of the vortices is proportional to the weight of the aircraft as well as other factors. Therefore, wake turbulence is more intense behind large, transport category aircraft than behind small aircraft. Generally, it is a problem only when following the larger aircraft.

The turbulence persists several minutes and may linger after the aircraft is out of sight. At controlled airports, the controller generally warns pilots in the vicinity of possible wake turbulence. When left to your own resources, you could use a few pointers. Most jets when taking off lift the nose wheel about midpoint in the takeoff roll; therefore, vortices begin about the middle of the takeoff roll. Vortices behind propeller aircraft begin only a short distance behind lift-off. Following a landing of either type of aircraft, vortices end at about the point where the nose wheel touches down. Avoid flying through these vortices. More specifically, when using the same runway as a heavier aircraft:

(1) if landing behind another aircraft, keep your approach above his approach and keep your touchdown beyond the point where his nose wheel touched the runway (figure 88 (A));

(2) if landing behind a departing aircraft, land only if you can complete your landing roll before reaching the midpoint of his takeoff roll (figure 88 (B));

(3) if departing behind another departing aircraft, take off only if you can become airborne before reaching the midpoint of his takeoff roll and only if you can climb fast enough to stay above his flight path (figure 88 (C)); and

(4) if departing behind a landing aircraft, don't unless you can taxi onto the runway beyond the point at which his nose wheel touched down and have sufficient runway left for safe takeoff (figure 88 (D)).

If parallel runways are available and the heavier aircraft takes off with a crosswind on the downwind runway, you may safely use the upwind runway. Never land or take off downwind from the heavier aircraft. When using a runway crossing his runway, you may safely use the upwind portion of your runway. You may cross behind a departing aircraft behind the midpoint of his takeoff roll. You may cross ahead of a landing aircraft ahead of the point at which his nose wheel touches down. If none of these procedures is possible, wait 5 minutes or so for the vortices to dissipate or to blow off the runway.

The foregoing procedures are elementary. The problem of wake turbulence is more operational than meteorological. The FAA issues periodic ad-

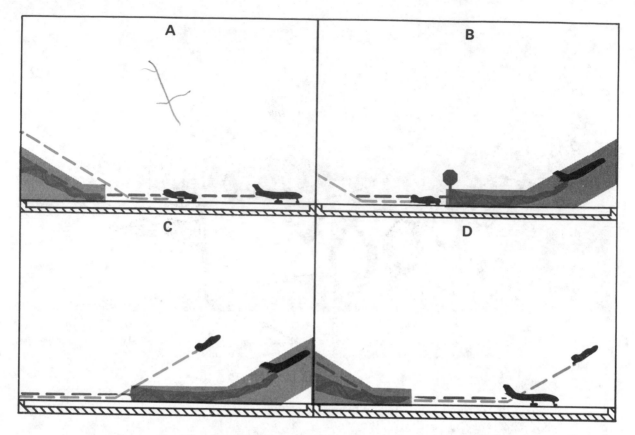

Figure 88.   Planning landing or takeoff to avoid heavy aircraft wake turbulence.

visory circulars of operational problems. If you plan to operate out of airports used routinely by air carriers, we highly recommend you read the latest advisory circulars on wake turbulence. Titles of these circulars are listed in the FAA "Advisory Circular Checklist and Status of Regulations."

IN CLOSING

We have discussed causes of turbulence, classified it into types, and offered some flight procedures to avoid it or minimize its hazards. Occurrences of turbulence, however, are local in extent and transient in character. A forecast of turbulence specifies a volume of airspace that is small when compared to useable airspace but relatively large compared to the localized extent of the hazard. Although general forecasts of turbulence are quite good, forecasting precise locations is at present impossible.

Generally, when a pilot receives a forecast, he plans his flight to avoid areas of *most probable turbulence*. Yet the best laid plans can go astray

and he may encounter turbulence. Since no instruments are currently available for directly observing turbulence, the man on the ground can only confirm its existence or absence via pilot reports. HELP YOUR FELLOW PILOT AND THE WEATHER SERVICE—SEND PILOT REPORTS.

To make reports and forecasts meaningful, turbulence is classified into intensities based on the effects it has on the aircraft and passengers. Section 16 of AVIATION WEATHER SERVICES (AC 00-45) lists and describes these intensities. Use this guide in reporting your turbulence encounters.

Chapter 10
ICING

Aircraft icing is one of the major weather hazards to aviation. Icing is a cumulative hazard. It reduces aircraft efficiency by increasing weight, reducing lift, decreasing thrust, and increasing drag. As shown in figure 89, each effect tends to either slow the aircraft or force it downward. Icing also seriously impairs aircraft engine performance. Other icing effects include false indications on flight instruments, loss of radio communications, and loss of operation of control surfaces, brakes, and landing gear.

In this chapter we discuss the principles of structural, induction system, and instrument icing and relate icing to cloud types and other factors. Although ground icing and frost are structural icing, we discuss them separately because of their different effect on an aircraft. And we wind up the chapter with a few operational pointers.

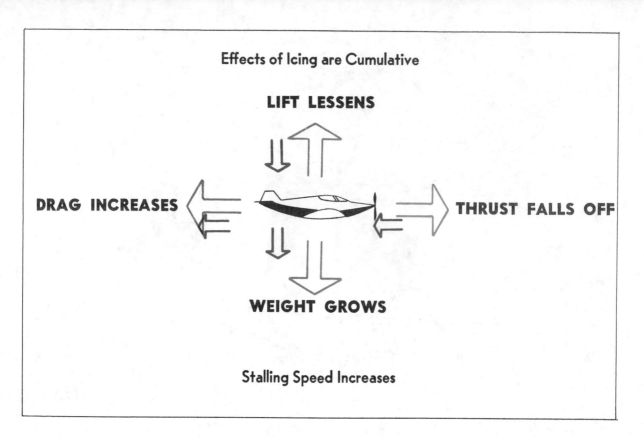

Effects of Icing are Cumulative

LIFT LESSENS

DRAG INCREASES

THRUST FALLS OFF

WEIGHT GROWS

Stalling Speed Increases

FIGURE 89.   Effects of structural icing.

STRUCTURAL ICING

Two conditions are necessary for structural icing in flight: (1) the aircraft must be flying through visible water such as rain or cloud droplets, and (2) the temperature at the point where the moisture strikes the aircraft must be 0° C or colder. Aerodynamic cooling can lower temperature of an airfoil to 0° C even though the ambient temperature is a few degrees warmer.

Supercooled water increases the rate of icing and is essential to rapid accretion. Supercooled water is in an unstable liquid state; when an aircraft strikes a supercooled drop, part of the drop freezes instantaneously. The latent heat of fusion released by the freezing portion raises the temperature of the remaining portion to the melting point. Aerodynamic effects may cause the remaining portion to freeze. The way in which the remaining portion freezes determines the type of icing. The types of structural icing are clear, rime, and a mixture of the two. Each type has its identifying features.

CLEAR ICE

Clear ice forms when, after initial impact, the remaining liquid portion of the drop flows out over the aircraft surface gradually freezing as a smooth sheet of solid ice. This type forms when drops are large as in rain or in cumuliform clouds.

Figure 90 illustrates ice on the cross section of an airfoil, clear ice shown at the top. Figures 91 and 92 are photographs of clear structural icing. Clear ice is hard, heavy, and tenacious. Its removal by deicing equipment is especially difficult.

RIME ICE

Rime ice forms when drops are small, such as those in stratified clouds or light drizzle. The liquid portion remaining after initial impact freezes rapidly before the drop has time to spread over the aircraft surface. The small frozen droplets trap air between them giving the ice a white appearance as

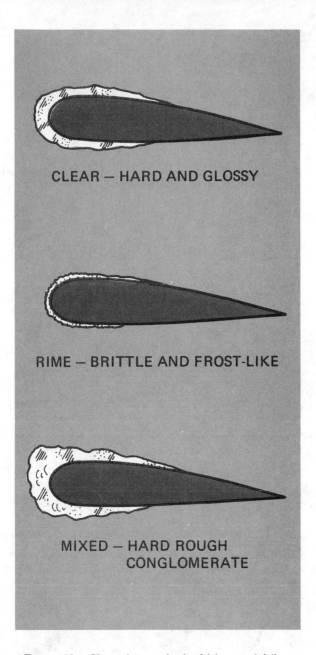

CLEAR — HARD AND GLOSSY

RIME — BRITTLE AND FROST-LIKE

MIXED — HARD ROUGH
CONGLOMERATE

FIGURE 90. Clear, rime, and mixed icing on airfoils.

shown at the center of figure 90. Figure 93 is a photograph of rime.

Rime ice is lighter in weight than clear ice and its weight is of little significance. However, its irregular shape and rough surface make it very effective in decreasing aerodynamic efficiency of airfoils, thus reducing lift and increasing drag. Rime ice is brittle and more easily removed than clear ice.

MIXED CLEAR AND RIME ICING

Mixed ice forms when drops vary in size or when liquid drops are intermingled with snow or ice particles. It can form rapidly. Ice particles become imbedded in clear ice, building a very rough accumulation sometimes in a mushroom shape on leading edges as shown at the bottom of figure 90. Figure 94 is a photo of mixed icing built up on a pitot tube.

ICING INTENSITIES

By mutual agreement and for standardization the FAA, National Weather Service, the military aviation weather services, and aircraft operating organizations have classified aircraft structural icing into intensity categories. Section 16 of AVIATION WEATHER SERVICES (AC 00-45) has a table listing these intensities. The table is your guide in estimating how ice of a specific intensity will affect your aircraft. Use the table also in reporting ice when you encounter it.

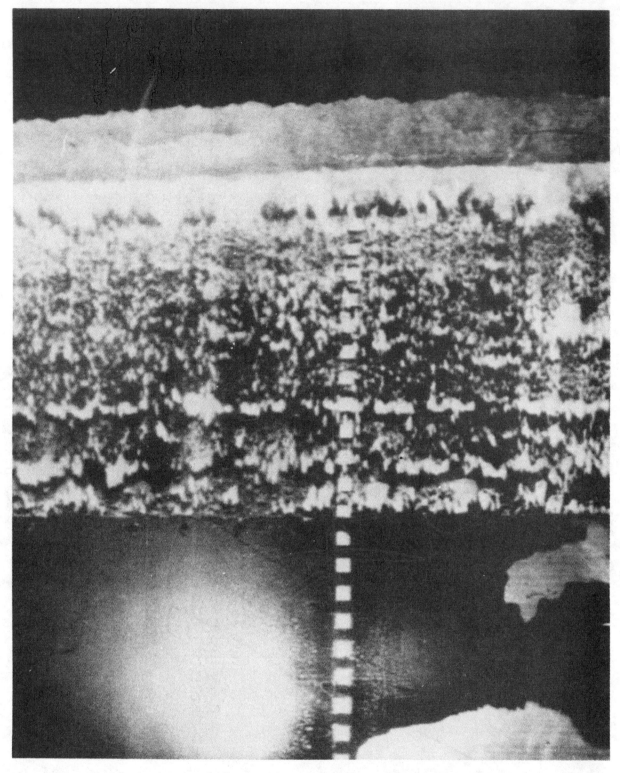

FIGURE 91. Clear wing icing (leading edge and underside). (Courtesy Dean T. Bowden, General Dynamics/Convair.)

FIGURE 92. Propeller icing. Ice may form on propellers just as on any airfoil. It reduces propeller efficiency and may induce severe vibrations.

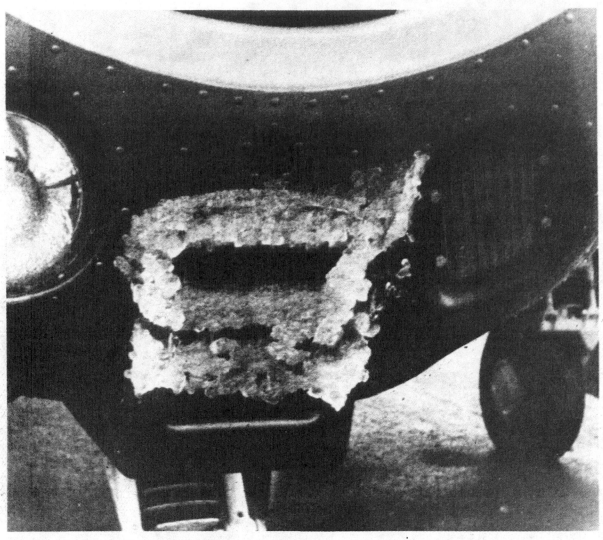

FIGURE 93. Rime icing on the nose of a Mooney "Mark 21" aircraft. (Photo by Norman Hoffman, Mooney Aircraft, Inc., courtesy the A.O.P.A. Pilot Magazine.)

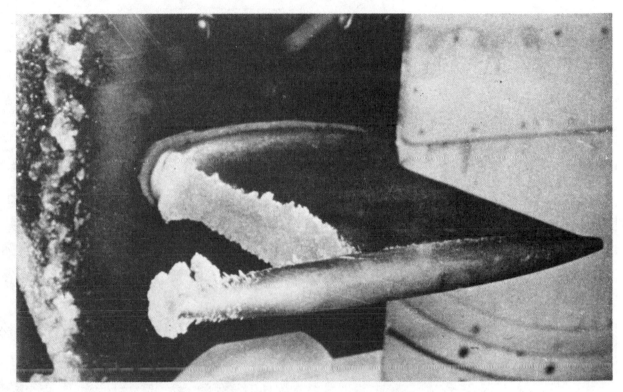

FIGURE 94. External icing on a pitot tube.

INDUCTION SYSTEM ICING

Ice frequently forms in the air intake of an engine robbing the engine of air to support combustion. This type icing occurs with both piston and jet engines, and almost everyone in the aviation community is familiar with carburetor icing. The downward moving piston in a piston engine or the compressor in a jet engine forms a partial vacuum in the intake. Adiabatic expansion in the partial vacuum cools the air. Ice forms when the temperature drops below freezing and sufficient moisture is present for sublimation. In piston engines, fuel evaporation produces additional cooling. Induction icing always lowers engine performance and can even reduce intake flow below that necessary for the engine to operate. Figure 95 illustrates carburetor icing.

Induction icing potential varies greatly among different aircraft and occurs under a wide range of meteorological conditions. It is primarily an engineering and operating problem rather than meteorological.

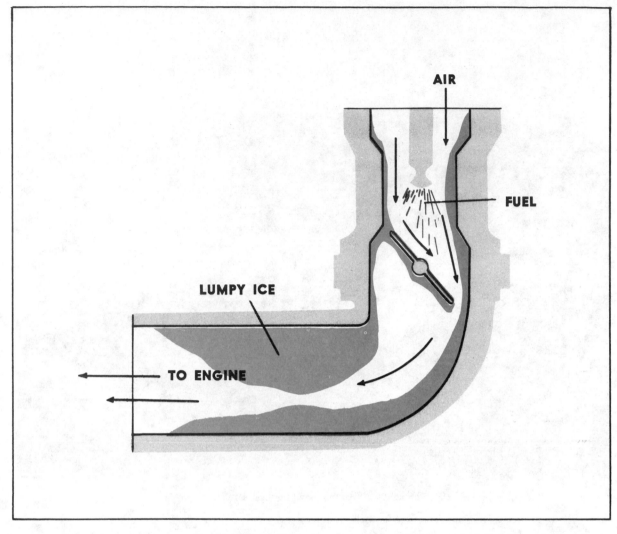

AIR

FUEL

LUMPY ICE

TO ENGINE

FIGURE 95. Carburetor icing. Expansional cooling of air and vaporization of fuel can induce freezing and cause ice to clog the carburetor intake.

INSTRUMENT ICING

Icing of the pitot tube as seen in figure 96 reduces ram air pressure on the airspeed indicator and renders the instrument unreliable. Most modern aircraft also have an outside static pressure port as part of the pitot-static system. Icing of the static pressure port reduces reliability of all instruments on the system—the airspeed, rate-of-climb, and the altimeter.

Ice forming on the radio antenna distorts its shape, increases drag, and imposes vibrations that may result in failure in the communications system of the aircraft. The severity of this icing depends upon the shape, location, and orientation of the antenna. Figure 97 is a photograph of clear ice on an antenna mast.

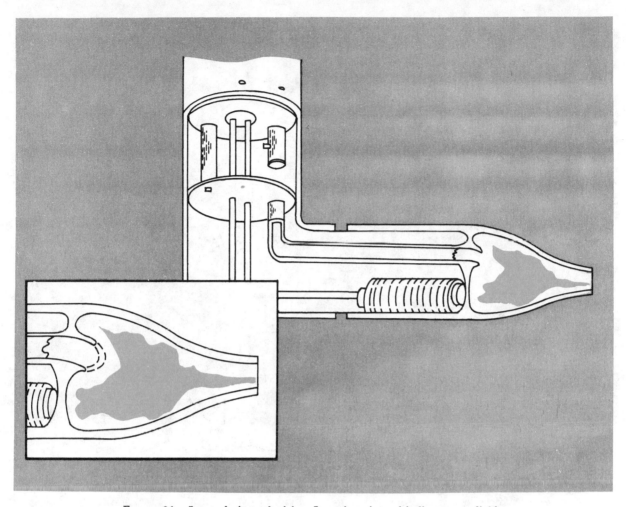

FIGURE 96. Internal pitot tube icing. It renders airspeed indicator unreliable.

ICING AND CLOUD TYPES

Basically, all clouds at subfreezing temperatures have icing potential. However, drop size, drop distribution, and aerodynamic effects of the aircraft influence ice formation. Ice may not form even though the potential exists.

The condition most favorable for very hazardous icing is the presence of many large, supercooled water drops. Conversely, an equal or lesser number of smaller droplets favors a slower rate of icing.

Small water droplets occur most often in fog and low-level clouds. Drizzle or very light rain is evidence of the presence of small drops in such clouds; but in many cases there is no precipitation at all. The most common type of icing found in lower-level stratus clouds is rime.

On the other hand, thick extensive stratified clouds that produce continuous rain such as alto-stratus and nimbostratus usually have an abundance of liquid water because of the relatively larger drop size and number. Such cloud systems in winter may cover thousands of square miles and present very serious icing conditions for protracted flights. Particularly in thick stratified clouds, concentrations of liquid water normally are greater with warmer temperatures. Thus, heaviest icing usually will be found at or slightly above the freezing level where temperature is never more than a few degrees below freezing. In layer type clouds, continuous icing conditions are rarely found to be more than 5,000 feet above the freezing level, and usually are two or three thousand feet thick.

The upward currents in cumuliform clouds are

Figure 97.   Clear ice on an aircraft antenna mast.

favorable for the formation and support of many large water drops. The size of raindrops and rainfall intensity normally experienced from showers and thunderstorms confirm this. When an aircraft enters the heavy water concentrations found in cumuliform clouds, the large drops break and spread rapidly over the leading edge of the airfoil forming a film of water. If temperatures are freezing or colder, the water freezes quickly to form a solid sheet of clear ice. Pilots usually avoid cumuliform clouds when possible. Consequently, icing reports from such clouds are rare and do not indicate the frequency with which it can occur.

The updrafts in cumuliform clouds carry large amounts of liquid water far above the freezing level. On rare occasions icing has been encountered in thunderstorm clouds at altitudes of 30,000 to 40,000 feet where the free air temperature was colder than minus 40° C.

While an upper limit of critical icing potential cannot be specified in cumuliform clouds, the cellular distribution of such clouds usually limits the horizontal extent of icing conditions. An exception, of course, may be found in a protracted flight through a broad zone of thunderstorms or heavy showers.

OTHER FACTORS IN ICING

In addition to the above, other factors also enter into icing. Some of the more important ones are discussed below.

FRONTS

A condition favorable for rapid accumulation of clear icing is freezing rain below a frontal surface.

Rain forms above the frontal surface at temperatures warmer than freezing. Subsequently, it falls through air at temperatures below freezing and becomes supercooled. The supercooled drops freeze on impact with an aircraft surface. Figure 98 diagrams this type of icing. It may occur with either a warm front (top) or a cold front. The icing can be critical because of the large amount of supercooled water. Icing can also become serious in cumulonimbus clouds along a surface cold front, along a squall line, or embedded in the cloud shield of a warm front.

TERRAIN

Air blowing upslope is cooled adiabatically. When the air is cooled below the freezing point, the water becomes supercooled. In stable air blowing up a gradual slope, the cloud drops generally remain comparatively small since larger drops fall out as rain. Ice accumulation is rather slow and you should have ample time to get out of it before the accumulation becomes extremely dangerous. When air is unstable, convective clouds develop a more serious hazard as described in "Icing and Cloud Types."

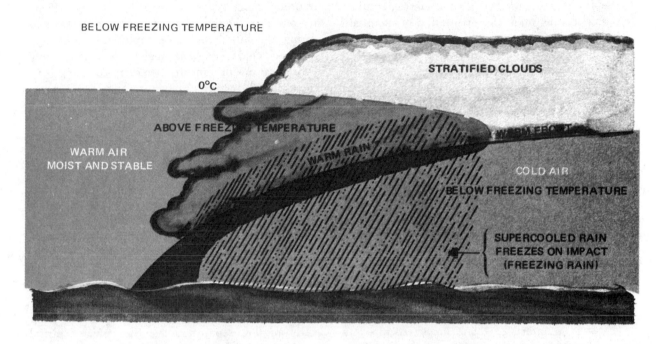

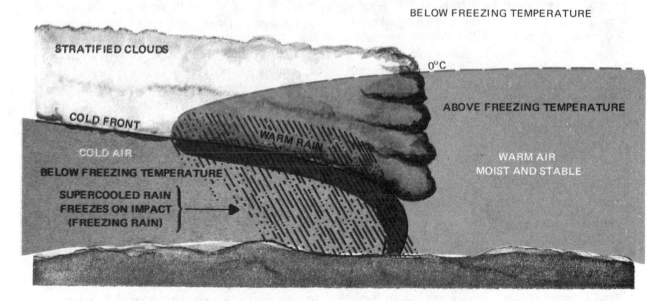

FIGURE 98. Freezing rain with a warm front (top) and a cold front (bottom). Rainfall through warm air aloft into subfreezing cold air near the ground. The rain becomes supercooled and freezes on impact.

Icing is more probable and more hazardous in mountainous regions than over other terrain. Mountain ranges cause rapid upward air motions on the windward side, and these vertical currents support large water drops. The movement of a frontal system across a mountain range often combines the normal frontal lift with the upslope effect of the mountains to create extremely hazardous icing zones.

Each mountainous region has preferred areas of icing depending upon the orientation of mountain ranges to the wind flow. The most dangerous icing takes place above the crests and to the windward side of the ridges. This zone usually extends about 5,000 feet above the tops of the mountains; but when clouds are cumuliform, the zone may extend much higher.

SEASONS

Icing may occur during any season of the year; but in temperate climates such as cover most of the contiguous United States, icing is more frequent in winter. The freezing level is nearer the ground in winter than in summer leaving a smaller low-level layer of airspace free of icing conditions. Cyclonic storms also are more frequent in winter, and the resulting cloud systems are more extensive. Polar regions have the most dangerous icing conditions in spring and fall. During the winter the air is normally too cold in the polar regions to contain heavy concentrations of moisture necessary for icing, and most cloud systems are stratiform and are composed of ice crystals.

GROUND ICING

Frost, ice pellets, frozen rain, or snow may accumulate on parked aircraft. You should remove all ice prior to takeoff, for it reduces flying efficiency of the aircraft. Water blown by propellers or splashed by wheels of an airplane as it taxis or runs through pools of water or mud may result in serious aircraft icing. Ice may form in wheel wells, brake mechanisms, flap hinges, etc., and prevent proper operation of these parts. Ice on runways and taxiways create traction and braking problems.

FROST

Frost is a hazard to flying long recognized in the aviation community. Experienced pilots have learned to remove all frost from airfoils prior to takeoff. Frost forms near the surface primarily in clear, stable air and with light winds—conditions which in all other respects make weather ideal for flying. Because of this, the real hazard is often minimized. Thin metal airfoils are especially vulnerable surfaces on which frost will form. Figure 99 is a photograph of frost on an airfoil.

Frost does not change the basic aerodynamic shape of the wing, but the roughness of its surface spoils the smooth flow of air thus causing a slowing of the airflow. This slowing of the air causes early air flow separation over the affected airfoil resulting in a loss of lift. A heavy coat of hard frost will cause a 5 to 10 percent increase in stall speed. Even a small amount of frost on airfoils may prevent an aircraft from becoming airborne at normal takeoff speed. Also possible is that, once airborne, an aircraft could have insufficient margin of airspeed above stall so that moderate gusts or turning flight could produce incipient or complete stalling.

Frost formation in flight offers a more complicated problem. The extent to which it will form is still a matter of conjecture. At most, it is comparatively rare.

IN CLOSING

Icing is where you find it. As with turbulence, icing may be local in extent and transient in character. Forecasters can identify regions in which icing is possible. However, they cannot define the precise small pockets in which it occurs. You should plan your flight to avoid those areas where icing probably will be heavier than your aircraft can handle. And you must be prepared to avoid or to escape the hazard when encountered en route.

FIGURE 99. Frost on an aircraft. Always remove ice or frost before attempting takeoff.

Here are a few specific points to remember:

1. Before takeoff, check weather for possible icing areas along your planned route. Check for pilot reports, and if possible talk to other pilots who have flown along your proposed route.

2. If your aircraft is not equipped with de-icing or anti-icing equipment, avoid areas of icing. Water (clouds or precipitation) must be visible and outside air temperature must be near 0° C or colder for structural ice to form.

3. Always remove ice or frost from airfoils before attempting takeoff.

4. In cold weather, avoid, when possible, taxiing or taking off through mud, water, or slush. If you have taxied through any of these, make a preflight check to ensure freedom of controls.

5. When climbing out through an icing layer, climb at an airspeed a little faster than normal to avoid a stall.

6. Use deicing or anti-icing equipment when accumulations of ice are not too great. When such equipment becomes less than totally effective, change course or altitude to get out of the icing as rapidly as possible.

7. If your aircraft is not equipped with a pitot-static system deicer, be alert for erroneous readings from your airspeed indicator, rate-of-climb indicator, and altimeter.

8. In stratiform clouds, you can likely alleviate icing by changing to a flight level and above-freezing temperatures or to one colder than —10° C. An altitude change also may take you out of clouds. Rime icing in stratiform clouds can be very extensive horizontally.

9. In frontal freezing rain, you may be able to climb or descend to a layer warmer than freezing. Temperature is always warmer than freezing at some higher altitude. If you are going to climb, move quickly; procrastination may leave you with too much

ice. If you are going to descend, you must know the temperature and terrain below.

10. Avoid cumuliform clouds if at all possible. Clear ice may be encountered anywhere above the freezing level. Most rapid accumulations are usually at temperatures from 0° C to −15° C.

11. Avoid abrupt maneuvers when your aircraft is heavily coated with ice since the aircraft has lost some of its aerodynamic efficiency.

12. When "iced up," fly your landing approach with power.

The man on the ground has no way of observing actual icing conditions. His only confirmation of the existence or absence of icing comes from pilots. Help your fellow pilot and the weather service by sending pilot reports when you encounter icing or when icing is forecast but none encountered. Use the table in Section 16 of AVIATION WEATHER SERVICES as a guide in reporting intensities.

Chapter 11
THUNDERSTORMS

Many times you have to make decisions involving thunderstorms and flying. This chapter looks at where and when thunderstorms occur most frequently, explains what creates a storm, and looks inside the storm at what goes on and what it can do to an aircraft. The chapter also describes how you can use radar and suggests some do's and don'ts of thunderstorm flying.

WHERE AND WHEN?

In some tropical regions, thunderstorms occur year-round. In midlatitudes, they develop most frequently in spring, summer, and fall. Arctic regions occasionally experience thunderstorms during summer.

Figure 100 shows the average number of thunderstorms each year in the adjoining 48 States. Note the frequent occurrences in the south-central and southeastern States. The number of days on which thunderstorms occur varies widely from season to season as shown in figures 101 through 104. In general, thunderstorms are most frequent during July and August and least frequent in December and January.

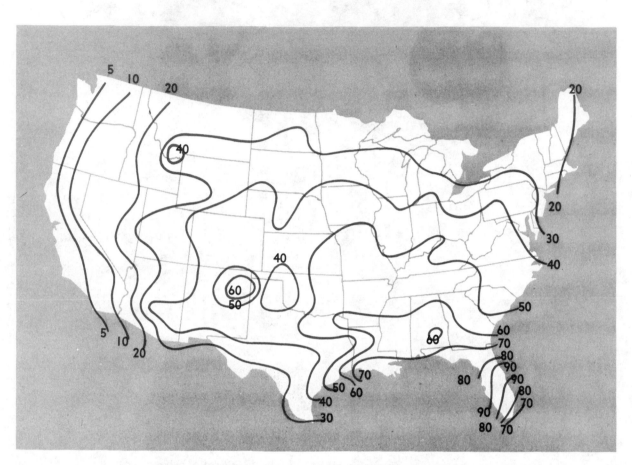

FIGURE 100.   The average number of thunderstorms each year.

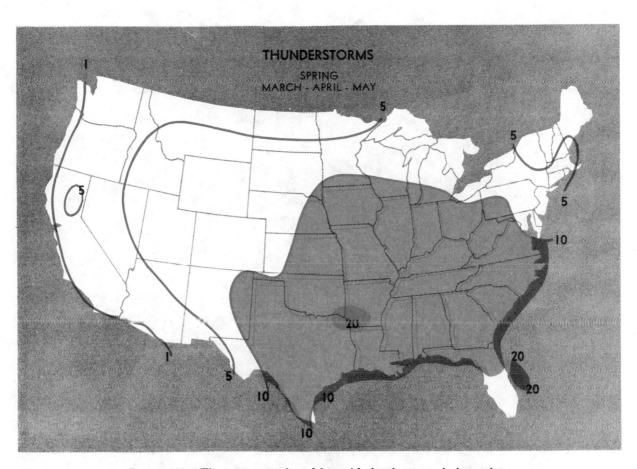

FIGURE 101. The average number of days with thunderstorms during spring.

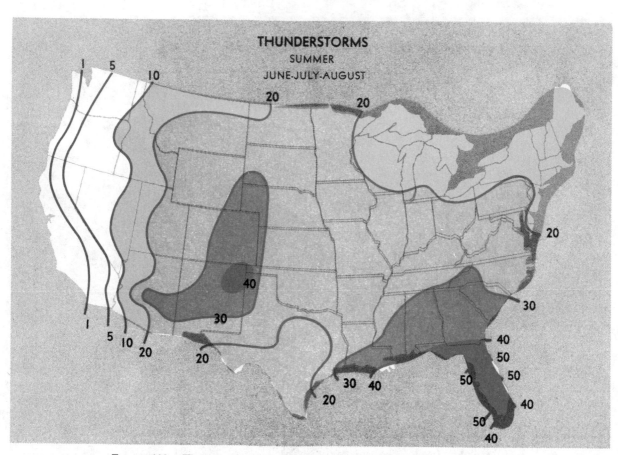

FIGURE 102. The average number of days with thunderstorms during summer.

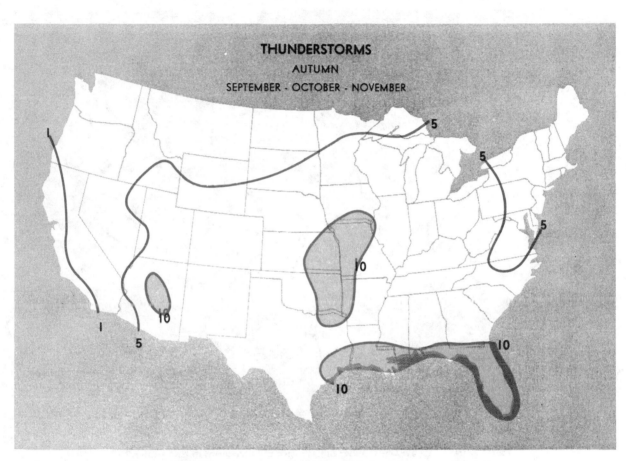

FIGURE 103. The average number of days with thunderstorms during fall.

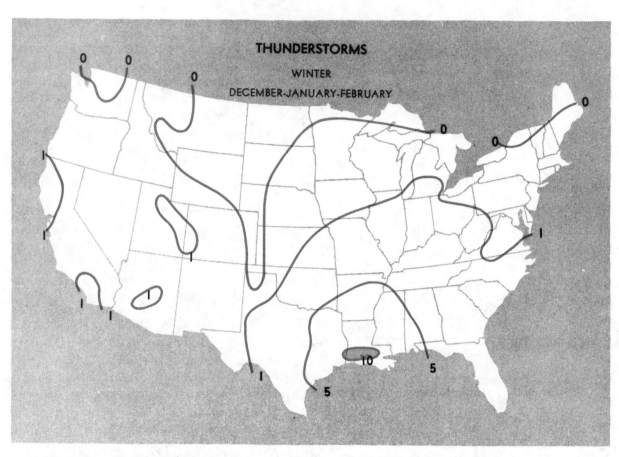

FIGURE 104. The average number of days with thunderstorms during winter.

THEY DON'T JUST HAPPEN

For a thunderstorm to form, the air must have (1) sufficient water vapor, (2) an unstable lapse rate, and (3) an initial upward boost (lifting) to start the storm process in motion. We discussed water vapor in chapter 5 and stability in chapter 6; but, what about lifting? Surface heating, converging winds, sloping terrain, a frontal surface, or any combination of these can provide the lift.

Thunderstorms have been a subject of considerable investigation for many years as they are today. Figuratively speaking, let's look inside a thunderstorm.

THE INSIDE STORY

Forced upward motion creates an initial updraft. Cooling in the updraft results in condensation and the beginning of a cumulus cloud. Condensation releases latent heat which partially offsets cooling in the saturated updraft and increases buoyancy within the cloud. This increased buoyancy drives the updraft still faster drawing more water vapor into the cloud; and, for awhile, the updraft becomes self-sustaining. All thunderstorms progress through a life cycle from their initial development through maturity and into degeneration.

LIFE CYCLE

A thunderstorm cell during its life cycle progresses through three stages—(1) the cumulus, (2) the mature, and (3) the dissipating. It is virtually impossible to visually detect the transition from one stage to another; the transition is subtle and by no means abrupt. Furthermore, a thunderstorm may be a cluster of cells in different stages of the life cycle.

The Cumulus Stage

Although most cumulus clouds do not grow into thunderstorms, every thunderstorm begins as a cumulus. The key feature of the cumulus stage is an updraft as illustrated in figure 105(A). The updraft varies in strength and extends from very near the surface to the cloud top. Growth rate of the cloud may exceed 3,000 feet per minute, so it is inadvisable to attempt to climb over rapidly building cumulus clouds.

Early during the cumulus stage, water droplets are quite small but grow to raindrop size as the cloud grows. The upwelling air carries the liquid water above the freezing level creating an icing hazard. As the raindrops grow still heavier, they fall. The cold rain drags air with it creating a cold downdraft coexisting with the updraft; the cell has reached the mature stage.

The Mature Stage

Precipitation beginning to fall from the cloud base is your signal that a downdraft has developed and a cell has entered the mature stage. Cold rain in the downdraft retards compressional heating, and the downdraft remains cooler than surrounding air. Therefore, its downward speed is accelerated and may exceed 2,500 feet per minute. The downrushing air spreads outward at the surface as shown in figure 105(B) producing strong, gusty surface winds, a sharp temperature drop, and a rapid rise in pressure. The surface wind surge is a "plow wind" and its leading edge is the "first gust."

Meanwhile, updrafts reach a maximum with speeds possibly exceeding 6,000 feet per minute. Updrafts and downdrafts in close proximity create strong vertical shear and a very turbulent environment. All thunderstorm hazards reach their greatest intensity during the mature stage.

The Dissipating Stage

Downdrafts characterize the dissipating stage of the thunderstorm cell as shown in figure 105(C) and the storm dies rapidly. When rain has ended and downdrafts have abated, the dissipating stage is complete. When all cells of the thunderstorm have completed this stage, only harmless cloud remnants remain.

HOW BIG?

Individual thunderstorms measure from less than 5 miles to more than 30 miles in diameter. Cloud bases range from a few hundred feet in very moist climates to 10,000 feet or higher in drier regions. Tops generally range from 25,000 to 45,000 feet but occasionally extend above 65,000 feet.

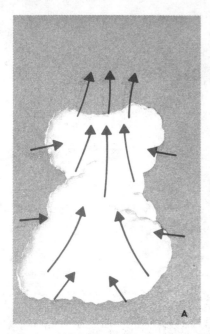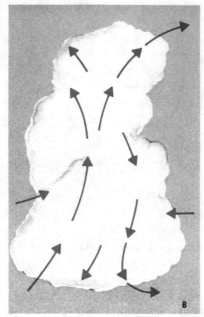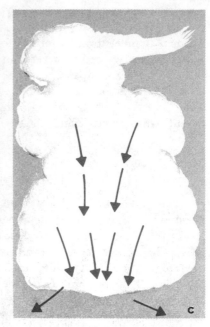

FIGURE 105. The stages of a thunderstorm. (A) is the cumulus stage; (B), the mature stage; and (C), the dissipating stage. Arrows depict air flow.

ROUGH AND ROUGHER

Duration of the mature stage is closely related to severity of the thunderstorm. Some storms occur at random in unstable air, last for only an hour or two, and produce only moderate gusts and rainfall. These are the "air mass" type, but even they are dangerously rough to fly through. Other thunderstorms form in lines, last for several hours, dump heavy rain and possibly hail, and produce strong, gusty winds and possibly tornadoes. These storms are the "steady state" type, usually are rougher than air mass storms, and virtually defy flight through them.

AIR MASS THUNDERSTORMS

Air mass thunderstorms most often result from surface heating. When the storm reaches the mature stage, rain falls through or immediately beside the updraft. Falling precipitation induces frictional drag, retards the updraft and reverses it to a downdraft. The storm is self-destructive. The downdraft and cool precipitation cool the lower portion of the storm and the underlying surface. Thus, it cuts off the inflow of water vapor; the storm runs out of

energy and dies. A self-destructive cell usually has a life cycle of 20 minutes to 1½ hours.

Since air mass thunderstorms generally result from surface heating, they reach maximum intensity and frequency over land during middle and late afternoon. Off shore, they reach a maximum during late hours of darkness when land temperature is coolest and cool air flows off the land over the relatively warm water.

STEADY STATE THUNDERSTORMS

Steady state thunderstorms usually are associated with weather systems. Fronts, converging winds, and troughs aloft force upward motion spawning these storms which often form into squall lines. Afternoon heating intensifies them.

In a steady state storm, precipitation falls outside the updraft as shown in figure 106 allowing the updraft to continue unabated. Thus, the mature stage updrafts become stronger and last much longer than in air mass storms—hence, the name, "steady state." A steady state cell may persist for several hours.

112

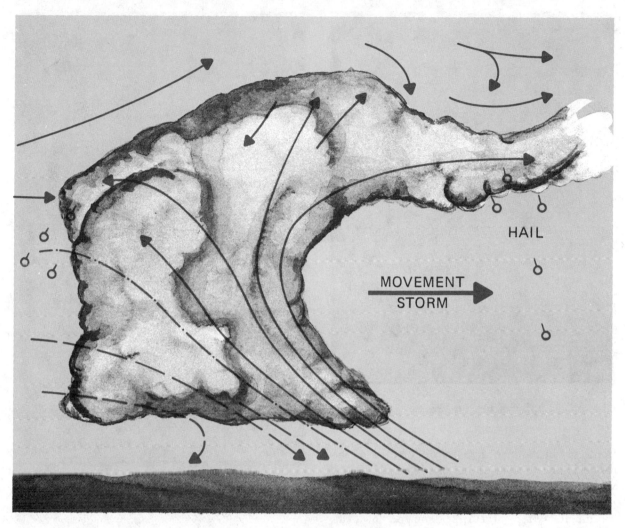

HAIL

MOVEMENT
STORM

FIGURE 106. Schematic of the mature stage of a steady state thunderstorm cell showing a sloping updraft with the down-draft and precipitation outside the updraft not impeding it. The steady state mature cell may continue for many hours and deliver the most violent thunderstorm hazards.

HAZARDS

A thunderstorm packs just about every weather hazard known to aviation into one vicious bundle. Although the hazards occur in numerous combinations, let's separate them and examine each individually.

TORNADOES

The most violent thunderstorms draw air into their cloud bases with great vigor. If the incoming air has any initial rotating motion, it often forms an extremely concentrated vortex from the surface well into the cloud. Meteorologists have estimated

that wind in such a vortex can exceed 200 knots; pressure inside the vortex is quite low. The strong winds gather dust and debris, and the low pressure generates a funnel-shaped cloud extending downward from the cumulonimbus base. If the cloud does not reach the surface, it is a "funnel cloud," figure 109; if it touches a land surface, it is a "tornado," figure 107; if it touches water, it is a "waterspout," figure 108.

Tornadoes occur with isolated thunderstorms at times, but much more frequently, they form with steady state thunderstorms associated with cold

FIGURE 107. A tornado.

FIGURE 108. A waterspout.

fronts or squall lines. Reports or forecasts of tornadoes indicate that atmospheric conditions are favorable for violent turbulence.

An aircraft entering a tornado vortex is almost certain to suffer structural damage. Since the vortex extends well into the cloud, any pilot inadvertently caught on instruments in a severe thunderstorm could encounter a hidden vortex.

Families of tornadoes have been observed as appendages of the main cloud extending several miles outward from the area of lightning and precipitation. Thus, any cloud connected to a severe thunderstorm carries a threat of violence.

Frequently, cumulonimbus mamma clouds occur in connection with violent thunderstorms and tornadoes. The cloud displays rounded, irregular pockets or festoons from its base and is a signpost of violent turbulence. Figure 110 is a photograph of a cumulonimbus mamma cloud. Surface aviation reports specifically mention this and other especially hazardous clouds.

Tornadoes occur most frequently in the Great Plains States east of the Rocky Mountains. Figure 111 shows, however, that they have occurred in every State.

SQUALL LINES

A *squall line* is a non-frontal, narrow band of active thunderstorms. Often it develops ahead of a cold front in moist, unstable air, but it may develop in unstable air far removed from any front. The line may be too long to easily detour and too wide and severe to penetrate. It often contains severe steady-state thunderstorms and presents the single most intense weather hazard to aircraft. It usually forms rapidly, generally reaching maximum intensity during the late afternoon and the first few hours of darkness. Figure 112 is a photograph of an advancing squall line.

TURBULENCE

Hazardous turbulence is present in **all** thunderstorms; and in a severe thunderstorm, it can damage an airframe. Strongest turbulence within the cloud occurs with shear between updrafts and

FIGURE 109. Funnel clouds.
(Photograph by Paul Hexter, NWS.)

downdrafts. Outside the cloud, shear turbulence has been encountered several thousand feet above and 20 miles laterally from a severe storm. A low level turbulent area is the shear zone between the plow wind and surrounding air. Often, a "roll cloud" on the leading edge of a storm marks the eddies in this shear. The roll cloud is most prevalent with cold frontal or squall line thunderstorms and signifies an extremely turbulent zone. The first gust causes a rapid and sometimes drastic change in surface wind ahead of an approaching storm. Figure 113 shows a schematic cross section of a thunderstorm with areas outside the cloud where turbulence may be encountered.

It is almost impossible to hold a constant altitude in a thunderstorm, and maneuvering in an attempt to do so greatly increases stresses on the aircraft. Stresses will be least if the aircraft is held in a constant *attitude* and allowed to "ride the waves." To date, we have no sure way to pick "soft spots" in a thunderstorm.

ICING

Updrafts in a thunderstorm support abundant liquid water; and when carried above the freezing level, the water becomes supercooled. When temperature in the upward current cools to about −15° C, much of the remaining water vapor sublimates as ice crystals; and above this level, the amount of supercooled water decreases.

Supercooled water freezes on impact with an aircraft (see chapter 10). Clear icing can occur at any altitude above the freezing level; but at high levels, icing may be rime or mixed rime and clear. The abundance of supercooled water makes clear icing very rapid between 0° C and −15° C, and encounters can be frequent in a cluster of cells. Thunderstorm icing can be extremely hazardous.

HAIL

Hail competes with turbulence as the greatest thunderstorm hazard to aircraft. Supercooled drops above the freezing level begin to freeze. Once a drop has frozen, other drops latch on and freeze to it, so the hailstone grows—sometimes into a huge iceball. Large hail occurs with severe thunderstorms usually built to great heights. Eventually the hailstones fall, possibly some distance from the storm core. Hail has been observed in clear air several miles from the parent thunderstorm.

As hailstones fall through the melting level, they begin to melt, and precipitation may reach the ground as either hail or rain. Rain at the surface does not mean the absence of hail aloft. You should anticipate possible hail with *any* thunderstorm, especially beneath the anvil of a large cumulonimbus. Hailstones larger than one-half inch in diameter can significantly damage an aircraft in a few seconds. Figure 114 is a photograph of an aircraft flown through a "hail" of a thunderstorm.

LOW CEILING AND VISIBILITY

Visibility generally is near zero within a thunderstorm cloud. Ceiling and visibility also can become restricted in precipitation and dust between the cloud base and the ground. The restrictions create the same problem as all ceiling and visibility restrictions; but the hazards are increased many fold when associated with the other thunderstorm hazards of turbulence, hail, and lightning which make precision instrument flying virtually impossible.

Figure 110. Cumulonimbus Mamma clouds, associated with cumulonimbus clouds, indicate extreme instability.

EFFECT ON ALTIMETERS

Pressure usually falls rapidly with the approach of a thunderstorm, then rises sharply with the onset of the first gust and arrival of the cold downdraft and heavy rain showers, falling back to normal as the storm moves on. This cycle of pressure change may occur in 15 minutes. If the altimeter setting is not corrected, the indicated altitude may be in error by over 100 feet.

THUNDERSTORM ELECTRICITY

Electricity generated by thunderstorms is rarely a great hazard to aircraft, but it may cause damage and is annoying to flight crews. Lightning is the most spectacular of the electrical discharges.

Lightning

A lightning strike can puncture the skin of an aircraft and can damage communication and electronic navigational equipment. Lightning has been suspected of igniting fuel vapors causing explosion; however, serious accidents due to lightning strikes are extremely rare. Nearby lightning can blind the pilot rendering him momentarily unable to navigate either by instrument or by visual reference. Nearby lightning can also induce permanent errors in the magnetic compass. Lightning discharges, even distant ones, can disrupt radio communications on low and medium frequencies.

A few pointers on lightning:
1. The more frequent the lightning, the more severe the thunderstorm.

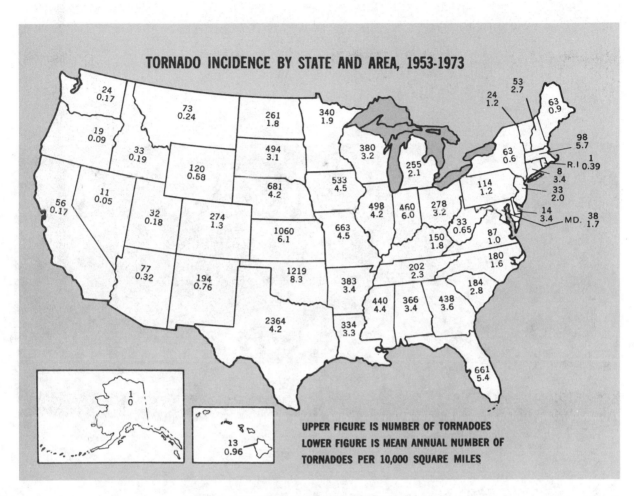

FIGURE 111. Tornado Incidence by State and area.

2. Increasing frequency of lightning indicates a growing thunderstorm.
3. Decreasing lightning indicates a storm nearing the dissipating stage.
4. At night, frequent distant flashes playing along a large sector of the horizon suggest a probable squall line.

Precipitation Static

Precipitation static, a steady, high level of noise in radio receivers is caused by intense corona discharges from sharp metallic points and edges of flying aircraft. It is encountered often in the vicinity of thunderstorms. When an aircraft flies through clouds, precipitation, or a concentration of solid particles (ice, sand, dust, etc.), it accumulates a charge of static electricity. The electricity discharges onto a nearby surface or into the air causing a noisy disturbance at lower frequencies.

The corona discharge is weakly luminous and may be seen at night. Although it has a rather eerie appearance, it is harmless. It was named "St. Elmo's Fire" by Mediterranean sailors, who saw the brushy discharge at the top of ship masts.

FIGURE 112.   Squall line thunderstorms.

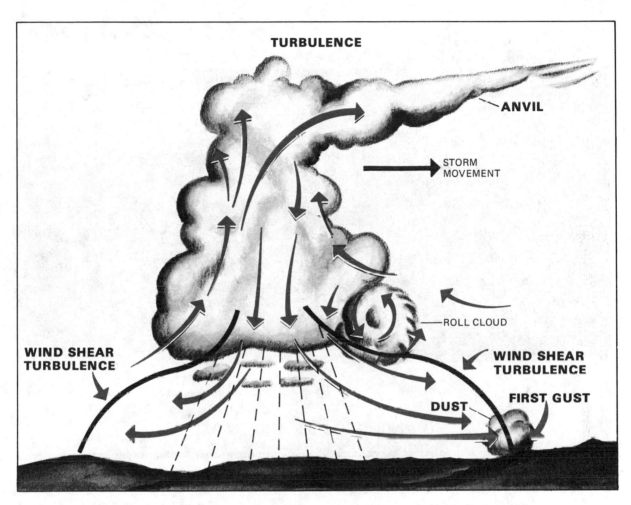

FIGURE 113. Schematic cross section of a thunderstorm. Note areas outside the main cloud where turbulence may be encountered.

FIGURE 114. Hail damage to an aircraft.

THUNDERSTORMS AND RADAR

Weather radar detects droplets of precipitation size. Strength of the radar return (echo) depends on drop size and number. The greater the number of drops, the stronger is the echo; and the larger the drops, the stronger is the echo. Drop size determines echo intensity to a much greater extent than does drop number.

Meteorologists have shown that drop size is almost directly proportional to rainfall rate; and the greatest rainfall rate is in thunderstorms. Therefore, the strongest echoes are thunderstorms. Hailstones usually are covered with a film of water and, therefore, act as huge water droplets giving the strongest of all echoes. Showers show less intense echoes; and gentle rain and snow return the weakest of all echoes. Figure 115 is a photograph of a ground based radar scope.

Since the strongest echoes identify thunderstorms, they also mark the areas of greatest hazards. Radar information can be valuable both from ground based radar for preflight planning and from airborne radar for severe weather avoidance.

Thunderstorms build and dissipate rapidly, and they also may move rapidly. Therefore, **do not attempt to preflight plan a course between echoes.** The best use of ground radar information is to isolate general areas and coverage of echoes. You must evade individual storms from inflight observations either by visual sighting or by airborne radar.

Airborne weather avoidance radar is, as its name implies, for avoiding severe weather—not for penetrating it. Whether to fly into an area of radar echoes depends on echo intensity, spacing between the echoes, and the capabilities of you and your

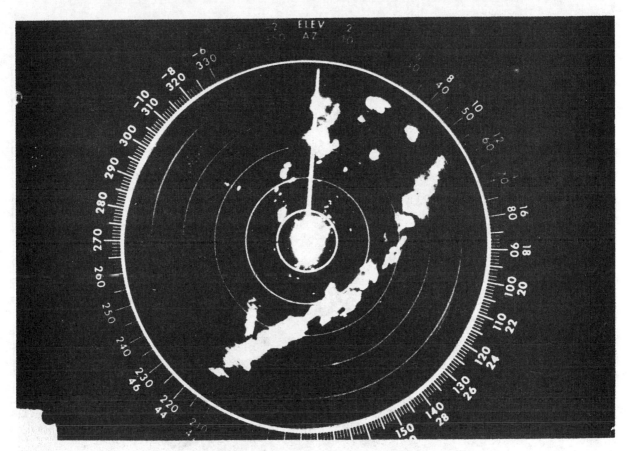

FIGURE 115. Radar photograph of a line of thunderstorms.

aircraft. Remember that weather radar detects only precipitation drops; it does not detect minute cloud droplets. Therefore, *the radar scope provides no assurance of avoiding instrument weather in clouds and fog.* Your scope may be clear between intense echoes; this clear area does not necessarily mean you can fly between the storms and maintain visual sighting of them.

The most intense echoes are severe thunder-storms. Remember that hail may fall several miles from the cloud, and hazardous turbulence may extend as much as 20 miles from the cloud. Avoid the most intense echoes by at least 20 miles; that is, echoes should be separated by at least 40 miles before you fly between them. As echoes diminish in intensity, you can reduce the distance by which you avoid them. Figure 116 illustrates use of airborne radar in avoiding thunderstorms.

DO'S AND DON'TS OF THUNDERSTORM FLYING

Above all, remember this: *never regard any thunderstorm as "light"* even when radar observers report the echoes are of light intensity. *Avoiding thunderstorms is the best policy.* Following are some Do's and Don'ts of thunderstorm *avoidance:*

1. Don't land or take off in the face of an approaching thunderstorm. A sudden wind shift or low level turbulence could cause loss of control.

2. Don't attempt to fly under a thunderstorm even if you can see through to the other side. Turbulence under the storm could be disastrous.

3. Don't try to circumnavigate thunderstorms covering 6/10 of an area or more either visually or by airborne radar.

4. Don't fly without airborne radar into a cloud mass containing scattered embedded

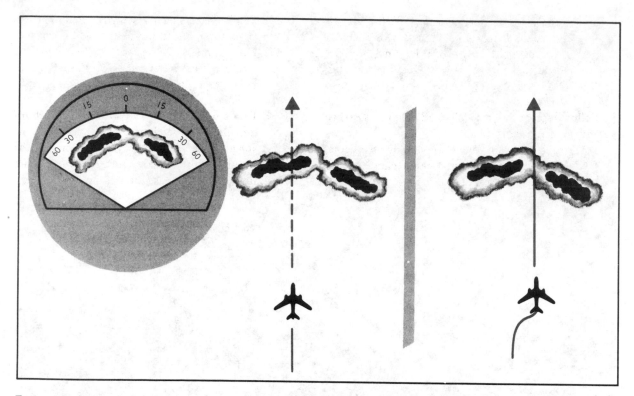

FIGURE 116. Use of airborne radar to avoid heavy precipitation and turbulence. When echoes are extremely intense, avoid the most intense echoes by at least 20 miles. You should avoid flying between these very intense echoes unless they are separated by at least 40 miles. Hazardous turbulence and hail often extend several miles from the storm centers.

thunderstorms. Scattered thunderstorms not embedded usually can be visually circumnavigated.

5. Do avoid by at least 20 miles any thunderstorm identified as severe or giving an intense radar echo. This is especially true under the anvil of a large cumulonimbus.

6. Do clear the top of a known or suspected severe thunderstorm by at least 1,000 feet altitude for each 10 knots of wind speed at the cloud top. This would exceed the altitude capability of most aircraft.

7. Do remember that vivid and frequent lightning indicates a severe thunderstorm.

8. Do regard as severe any thunderstorm with tops 35,000 feet or higher whether the top is visually sighted or determined by radar.

If you *cannot* avoid penetrating a thunderstorm, following are some Do's *Before* entering the storm:

1. Tighten your safety belt, put on your shoulder harness if you have one, and secure all loose objects.

2. Plan your course to take you through the storm in a minimum time and *hold* it.

3. To avoid the most critical icing, establish a penetration altitude below the freezing level or above the level of −15° C.

4. Turn on pitot heat and carburetor or jet inlet heat. Icing can be rapid at any altitude and cause almost instantaneous power failure or loss of airspeed indication.

5. Establish power settings for reduced turbulence penetration airspeed recommended in your aircraft manual. Reduced airspeed lessens the structural stresses on the aircraft.

6. Turn up cockpit lights to highest intensity to lessen danger of temporary blindness from lightning.

7. If using automatic pilot, disengage altitude hold mode and speed hold mode. The automatic altitude and speed controls will increase maneuvers of the aircraft thus increasing structural stresses.

8. If using airborne radar, tilt your antenna

up and down occasionally. Tilting it up may detect a hail shaft that will reach a point on your course by the time you do. Tilting it down may detect a growing thunderstorm cell that may reach your altitude.

Following are some Do's and Don'ts *During* thunderstorm penetration:

1. Do keep your eyes on your instruments. Looking outside the cockpit can increase danger of temporary blindness from lightning.

2. Don't change power settings; maintain settings for reduced airspeed.

3. Do maintain a constant *attitude;* let the aircraft "ride the waves." Maneuvers in trying to maintain constant altitude increase stresses on the aircraft.

4. Don't turn back once you are in the thunderstorm. A straight course through the storm most likely will get you out of the hazards most quickly. In addition, turning maneuvers increase stresses on the aircraft.

Chapter 12
COMMON IFR PRODUCERS

Most aircraft accidents related to low ceilings and visibilities involve pilots who are not instrument qualified. These pilots attempt flight by visual reference into weather that is suitable at best only for instrument flight. When you lose sight of the visual horizon, your senses deceive you; you lose sense of direction—you can't tell up from down. You may doubt that *you* will lose your sense of direction, but one good scare has changed the thinking of many a pilot. ***"Continued VFR into adverse weather" is the cause of about 25 percent of all fatal general aviation accidents.***

Minimum values of ceiling and visibility determine Visual Flight Rules. Lower ceiling and/or visibility require instrument flight. Ceiling is the maximum height from which a pilot can maintain VFR in reference to the ground. Visibility is how far he can see. AVIATION WEATHER SERVICES (AC 00-45) contains details of ceiling and visibility reports.

Don't let yourself be caught in the statistics of "continued VFR into adverse weather." IFR producers are fog, low clouds, haze, smoke, blowing obstructions to vision, and precipitation. Fog and low stratus restrict navigation by visual reference more often than all other weather parameters.

FOG

Fog is a surface based cloud composed of either water droplets or ice crystals. Fog is the most frequent cause of surface visibility below 3 miles, and is one of the most common and persistent weather hazards encountered in aviation. The rapidity with which fog can form makes it especially hazardous. It is not unusual for visibility to drop from VFR to less than a mile in a few minutes. It is primarily a hazard during takeoff and landing, but it is also important to VFR pilots who must maintain visual reference to the ground.

Small temperature-dew point spread is essential for fog to form. Therefore, fog is prevalent in coastal areas where moisture is abundant. However, fog can occur anywhere. Abundant condensation nuclei enhances the formation of fog. Thus, fog is prevalent in industrial areas where byproducts of combustion provide a high concentration of these nuclei. Fog occurs most frequently in the colder months, but the season and frequency of occurrence vary from one area to another.

Fog may form (1) by cooling air to its dew point, or (2) by adding moisture to air near the ground. Fog is classified by the way it forms. Formation may involve more than one process.

RADIATION FOG

Radiation fog is relatively shallow fog. It may be dense enough to hide the entire sky or may conceal only part of the sky. "Ground fog" is a form of radiation fog. As viewed by a pilot in flight, dense radiation fog may obliterate the entire surface below him; a less dense fog may permit his observation of a small portion of the surface directly below him. Tall objects such as buildings, hills, and towers may protrude upward through ground fog giving the pilot fixed references for VFR flight. Figure 117 illustrates ground fog as seen from the air.

Conditions favorable for radiation fog are clear sky, little or no wind, and small temperature-dew point spread (high relative humidity). The fog forms almost exclusively at night or near daybreak. Terrestrial radiation cools the ground; in turn, the cool ground cools the air in contact with it. When the air is cooled to its dew point, fog forms. When rain soaks the ground, followed by clearing skies,

radiation fog is not uncommon the following morning.

Radiation fog is restricted to land because water surfaces cool little from nighttime radiation. It is shallow when wind is calm. Winds up to about 5 knots mix the air slightly and tend to deepen the fog by spreading the cooling through a deeper layer. Stronger winds disperse the fog or mix the air through a still deeper layer with stratus clouds forming at the top of the mixing layer.

Ground fog usually "burns off" rather rapidly after sunrise. Other radiation fog generally clears before noon unless clouds move in over the fog.

ADVECTION FOG

Advection fog forms when moist air moves over colder ground or water. It is most common along coastal areas but often develops deep in continental areas. At sea it is called "sea fog." Advection fog deepens as wind speed increases up to about 15 knots. Wind much stronger than 15 knots lifts the fog into a layer of low stratus or stratocumulus.

The west coast of the United States is quite vulnerable to advection fog. This fog frequently forms offshore as a result of cold water as shown in figure 118 and then is carried inland by the wind. During the winter, advection fog over the central and eastern United States results when moist air from the Gulf of Mexico spreads northward over cold ground as shown in figure 119. The fog may extend as far north as the Great Lakes. Water areas in northern latitudes have frequent dense sea fog in summer as a result of warm, moist, tropical air flowing northward over colder Arctic waters.

A pilot will notice little difference between flying over advection fog and over radiation fog except that skies may be cloudy above the advection fog. Also, advection fog is usually more extensive and much more persistent than radiation fog. Advection fog can move in rapidly regardless of the time of day or night.

UPSLOPE FOG

Upslope fog forms as a result of moist, stable air being cooled adiabatically as it moves up sloping terrain. Once the upslope wind ceases, the fog dissipates. Unlike radiation fog, it can form under cloudy skies. Upslope fog is common along the

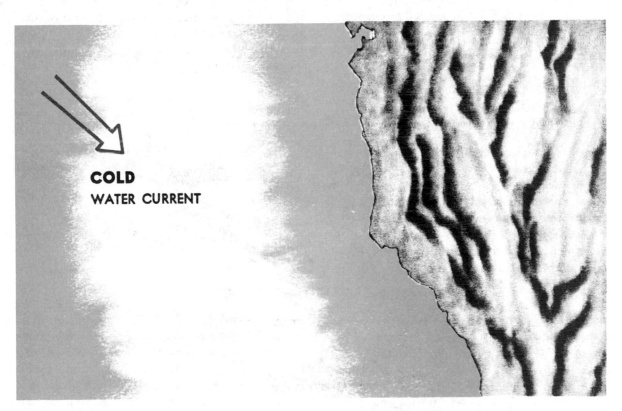

COLD
WATER CURRENT

FIGURE 118.   Advection fog off the coast of California.

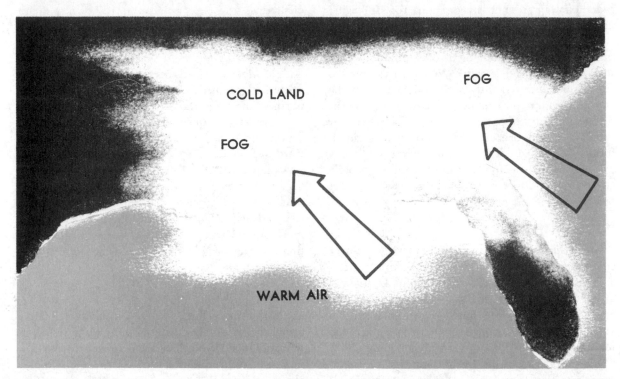

FIGURE 119.   Advection fog over the southeastern United States and Gulf Coast. The fog often may spread to the Great Lakes and northern Appalachians.

eastern slopes of the Rockies and somewhat less frequent east of the Appalachians. Upslope fog often is quite dense and extends to high altitudes.

PRECIPITATION-INDUCED FOG

When relatively warm rain or drizzle falls through cool air, evaporation from the precipitation saturates the cool air and forms fog. Precipitation-induced fog can become quite dense and continue for an extended period of time. This fog may extend over large areas, completely suspending air operations. It is most commonly associated with warm fronts, but can occur with slow moving cold fronts and with stationary fronts.

Fog induced by precipitation is in itself hazard-ous as is any fog. It is especially critical, however, because it occurs in the proximity of precipitation and other possible hazards such as icing, turbulence, and thunderstorms.

ICE FOG

Ice fog occurs in cold weather when the temperature is much below freezing and water vapor sublimates directly as ice crystals. Conditions favorable for its formation are the same as for radiation fog except for cold temperature, usually −25° F or colder. It occurs mostly in the Arctic regions, but is not unknown in middle latitudes during the cold season. Ice fog can be quite blinding to someone flying into the sun.

LOW STRATUS CLOUDS

Stratus clouds, like fog, are composed of extremely small water droplets or ice crystals suspended in air. An observer on a mountain in a stratus layer would call it fog. Stratus and fog frequently exist together. In many cases there is no real line of distinction between the fog and stratus; rather, one gradually merges into the other. Flight visibility may approach zero in stratus clouds. Stratus tends to be lowest during night and early morning, lifting or dissipating due to solar heating during the late morning or afternoon. Low stratus clouds often occur when moist air mixes with a colder air mass or in any situation where temperature-dew point spread is small.

HAZE AND SMOKE

Haze is a concentration of salt particles or other dry particles not readily classified as dust or other phenomenon. It occurs in stable air, is usually only a few thousand feet thick, but sometimes may extend as high as 15,000 feet. Haze layers often have definite tops above which horizontal visibility is good. However, downward visibility from above a haze layer is poor, especially on a slant. Visibility in haze varies greatly depending upon whether the pilot is facing the sun. Landing an aircraft into the sun is often hazardous if haze is present.

Smoke concentrations form primarily in industrial areas when air is stable. It is most prevalent at night or early morning under a temperature inversion but it can persist throughout the day. Figure 120 illustrates smoke trapped under a temperature inversion.

When skies are clear above haze or smoke, visibility generally improves during the day; however, the improvement is slower than the clearing of fog. Fog evaporates, but haze or smoke must be dispersed by movement of air. Haze or smoke may be blown away; or heating during the day may cause convective mixing spreading the smoke or haze to a higher altitude, decreasing the concentration near the surface. At night or early morning, radiation fog or stratus clouds often combine with haze or smoke. The fog and stratus may clear rather rapidly during the day but the haze and smoke will linger. A heavy cloud cover above haze or smoke may block sunlight preventing dissipation; visibility will improve little, if any, during the day.

BLOWING RESTRICTIONS TO VISIBILITY

Strong wind lifts blowing dust in both stable and unstable air. When air is unstable, dust is lifted to great heights (as much as 15,000 feet) and may be spread over wide areas by upper winds. Visibility is restricted both at the surface and aloft. When air is stable, dust does not extend to as great a height as in unstable air and usually is not as widespread.

Dust, once airborne, may remain suspended and restrict visibility for several hours after the wind subsides. Figure 121 is a photograph of a dust storm moving in with an approaching cold front.

Blowing sand is more local than blowing dust; the sand is seldom lifted above 50 feet. However, visibilities within it may be near zero. Blowing sand

FIGURE 120. Smoke trapped in stagnant air under an inversion.

may occur in any dry area where loose sand is exposed to strong wind.

Blowing snow can be troublesome. Visibility at ground level often will be near zero and the sky may become obscured when the particles are raised to great heights.

FIGURE 121. Aerial photograph of blowing dust approaching with a cold front. The dust cloud outlines the leading surface of the advancing cold air.

PRECIPITATION

Rain, drizzle, and snow are the forms of precipitation which most commonly present ceiling and/or visibility problems. Drizzle or snow restricts visibility to a greater degree than rain. Drizzle falls in stable air and, therefore, often accompanies fog, haze, or smoke, frequently resulting in extremely poor visibility. Visibility may be reduced to zero in heavy snow. Rain seldom reduces surface visibility below 1 mile except in brief, heavy showers, but rain does limit cockpit visibility. When rain streams over the aircraft windshield, freezes on it, or fogs over the inside surface, the pilot's visibility to the outside is greatly reduced.

OBSCURED OR PARTIALLY OBSCURED SKY

To be classified as obscuring phenomena, smoke, haze, fog, precipitation, or other visibility restricting phenomena must extend upward from the surface. When the sky is totally hidden by the surface based phenomena, the ceiling is the vertical visibility from the ground upward into the obscuration. If clouds or part of the sky can be seen above the obscuring phenomena, the condition is defined as a partial obscuration; a partial obscuration does not define a ceiling. However, a cloud layer above a partial obscuration may constitute a ceiling.

An obscured ceiling differs from a cloud ceiling. With a cloud ceiling you normally can see the ground and runway once you descend below the cloud base. However, with an obscured ceiling, the obscuring phenomena restricts visibility between your altitude and the ground, and you have restricted slant visibility. Thus, you cannot always clearly see the runway or approach lights even after penetrating the level of the obscuration ceiling as shown in figure 122.

Partial obscurations also present a visibility problem for the pilot approaching to land but usually to a lesser degree than the total obscuration. However, be especially aware of erratic visibility reduction in the partial obscuration. Visibility along the runway or on the approach can instantaneously become zero. This abrupt and unexpected reduction in visibility can be extremely hazardous especially on touchdown.

IN CLOSING

In your preflight preparation, be aware of or alert for phenomena that may produce IFR or marginal VFR flight conditions. Current charts and special analyses along with forecast and prognostic charts are your best sources of information. You may get your preflight weather from a briefer; or, you may rely on recorded briefings; and you always have your own inflight observations. No weather observation is more current or more accurate than the one you make through your cockpit

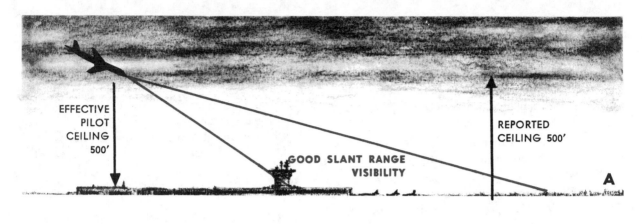

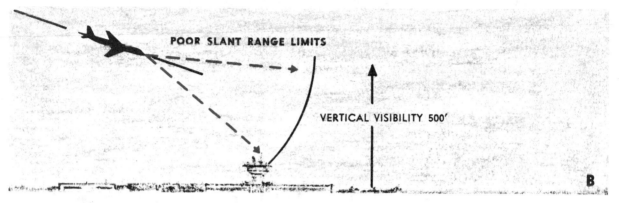

FIGURE 122. Difference between the ceiling caused by a surface-based obscuration (B) and the ceiling caused by a layer aloft (A). When visibility is not restricted, slant range vision is good upon breaking out of the base of a layer aloft.

window. In any event, your understanding of IFR producers will help you make better preflight and inflight decisions.

Do not fly VFR in weather suitable only for IFR. If you do, you endanger not only your own life but the lives of others both in the air and on the ground. Remember, the single cause of the greatest number of general aviation fatal accidents is "continued VFR into adverse weather." The most common cause is vertigo, but you also run the risk of flying into unseen obstructions. Furthermore, pilots who attempt to fly VFR under conditions below VFR minimums are violating Federal Aviation Regulations.

The threat of flying VFR into adverse weather is far greater than many pilots might realize. A pilot may press onward into lowering ceiling and visibility complacent in thinking that better weather still lies behind him. Eventually, conditions are too low to proceed; he no longer can see a horizon ahead. But when he attempts to turn around, he finds so little difference in conditions that he cannot re-establish a visual horizon. He continued too far into adverse weather; he is a prime candidate for vertigo.

Don't let an overwhelming desire to reach your destination entice you into taking the chance of flying too far into adverse weather. The IFR pilot may think it easier to "sneak" through rather than go through the rigors of getting an IFR clearance. The VFR pilot may think, "if I can only make it a little farther." If you can go IFR, get a clearance *before* you lose your horizon. If you must stay VFR, do a 180 while you still have a horizon. The 180 is not the maneuver of cowards. *Any pilot knows how to make a 180; a good pilot knows when.*

Be especially alert for development of:

1. Fog the following morning when at dusk temperature–dew point spread is 15° F or less, skies are clear, and winds are light.
2. Fog when moist air is flowing from a relatively warm surface to a colder surface.

3. Fog when temperature-dew point spread is 5° F or less and decreasing.

4. Fog or low stratus when a moderate or stronger moist wind is blowing over an extended upslope. (Temperature and dew point converge at about 4° F for every 1,000 feet the air is lifted.)

5. Steam fog when air is blowing from a cold surface (either land or water) over warmer water.

6. Fog when rain or drizzle falls through cool air. This is especially prevalent during winter ahead of a warm front and behind a stationary front or stagnating cold front.

7. Low stratus clouds whenever there is an influx of low level moisture overriding a shallow cold air mass.

8. Low visibilities from haze and smoke when a high pressure area stagnates over an industrial area.

9. Low visibilities due to blowing dust or sand over semiarid or arid regions when winds are strong and the atmosphere is unstable. This is especially prevalent in spring. If the dust extends upward to moderate or greater heights, it can be carried many miles beyond its source.

10. Low visibility due to snow or drizzle.

11. An undercast when you must make a VFR descent.

Expect little if any improvement in visibility when:

1. Fog exists below heavily overcast skies.

2. Fog occurs with rain or drizzle and precipitation is forecast to continue.

3. Dust extends to high levels and no frontal passage or precipitation is forecast.

4. Smoke or haze exists under heavily overcast skies.

5. A stationary high persists over industrial areas.

Part TWO

OVER AND BEYOND

Chapter 13
HIGH ALTITUDE WEATHER

Many general aviation as well as air carrier and military aircraft routinely fly the upper troposphere and lower stratosphere. Weather phenomena of these higher altitudes include the tropopause, the jet stream, cirrus clouds, clear air turbulence, condensation trails, high altitude "haze" layers, and canopy static. This chapter explains these phenomena along with the high altitude aspects of the more common icing and thunderstorm hazards.

THE TROPOPAUSE

Why is the high altitude pilot interested in the tropopause? Temperature and wind vary greatly in the vicinity of the tropopause affecting efficiency, comfort, and safety of flight. Maximum winds generally occur at levels near the tropopause. These strong winds create narrow zones of wind shear which often generate hazardous turbulence. Preflight knowledge of temperature, wind, and wind shear is important to flight planning.

In chapter 1, we learned that the tropopause is a thin layer forming the boundary between the troposphere and stratosphere. Height of the tropopause varies from about 65,000 feet over the Equator to 20,000 feet or lower over the poles. The tropopause is not continuous but generally descends step-wise from the Equator to the poles. These steps occur as "breaks." Figure 123 is a cross section of the troposphere and lower stratosphere showing the tropopause and associated features. Note the break between the tropical and the polar tropopauses.

An abrupt change in temperature lapse rate characterizes the tropopause. Note in figure 123 how temperature above the tropical tropopause increases with height and how over the polar tropopause, temperature remains almost constant with height.

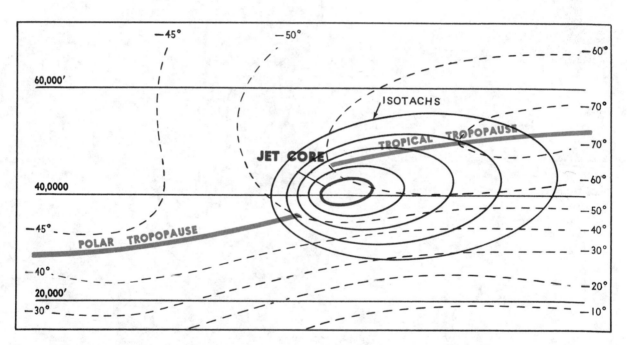

FIGURE 123. A cross section of the upper troposphere and lower stratosphere showing the tropopause and associated features. Note the "break" between the high tropical and the lower polar tropopause. Maximum winds occur in the vicinity of this break.

THE JET STREAM

Diagrammed in figure 124, the jet stream is a narrow, shallow, meandering river of maximum winds extending around the globe in a wavelike pattern. A second jet stream is not uncommon, and three at one time are not unknown. A jet may be as far south as the northern Tropics. A jet in mid-latitudes generally is stronger than one in or near the Tropics. The jet stream typically occurs in a break in the tropopause as shown in figure 123. Therefore, a jet stream occurs in an area of intensified temperature gradients characteristic of the break.

The concentrated winds, by arbitrary definition, must be 50 knots or greater to classify as a jet

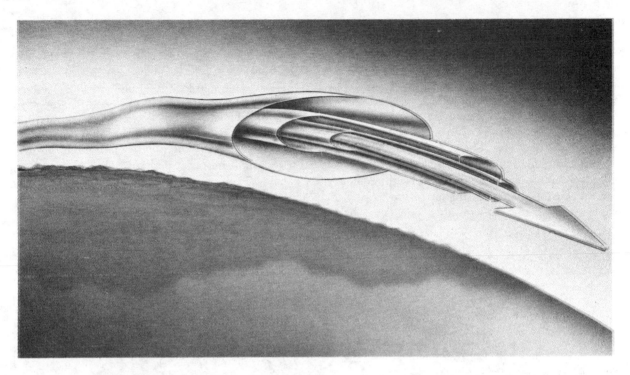

FIGURE 124.   Artist's concept of the jet stream. Broad arrow shows direction of wind.

stream. The jet maximum is not constant; rather, it is broken into segments, shaped something like a boomerang as diagrammed in figure 125.

Jet stream segments move with pressure ridges and troughs in the upper atmosphere. In general they travel faster than pressure systems, and max-imum wind speed varies as the segments progress through the systems. In midlatitude, wind speed in the jet stream averages considerably stronger in winter than in summer. Also the jet shifts farther south in winter than in summer.

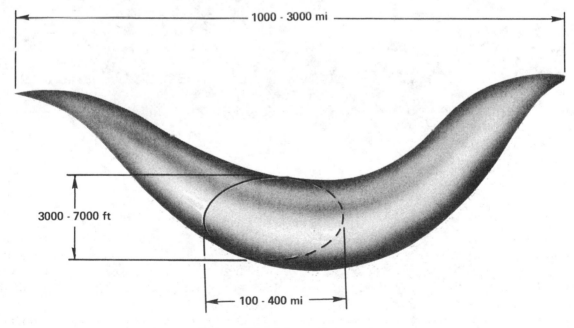

FIGURE 125.   A jet stream segment.

In figure 123 note how wind speed decreases outward from the jet core. Note also that the rate of decrease of wind speed is considerably greater on the polar side than on the equatorial side; hence, the magnitude of wind shear is greater on the polar side than on the equatorial side.

Figure 126 shows a map with two jet streams. The paths of the jets approximately conform to the shape of the contours. The northerly jet has three segments of maximum wind, and the southerly one has two. Note how spacing of the height contours is closer and wind speeds higher in the vicinity of the jets than outward on either side. Thus horizontal wind shear is evident on both sides of the jet and is greatest near the maximum wind segments.

Strong, long-trajectory jet streams usually are associated with well-developed surface lows and frontal systems beneath deep upper troughs or lows. Cyclogenesis is usually south of the jet stream and moves nearer as the low deepens. The occluding low moves north of the jet, and the jet crosses the frontal system near the point of occlusion. Figure 127 diagrams mean jet positions relative to surface systems. These long jets mark high level boundaries between warm and cold air and are favored places for cirriform cloudiness.

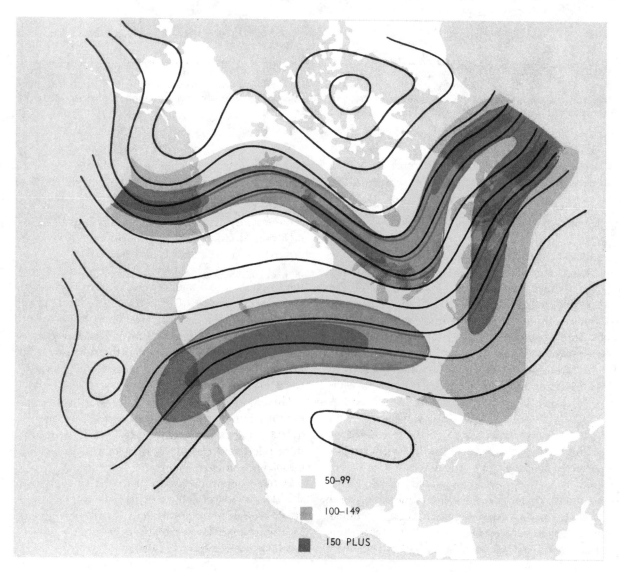

50–99

100–149

150 PLUS

FIGURE 126.   Multiple jet streams. Note the "segments" of maximum winds embedded in the general pattern. Turbulence usually is greatest on the polar sides of these maxima.

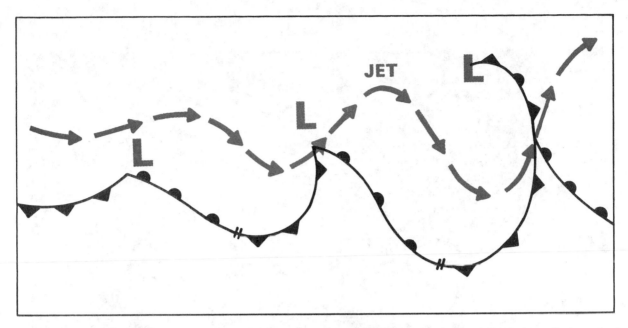

FIGURE 127.   Mean jet positions relative to surface systems. Cyclogenesis (development) of a surface low usually is south of the jet as shown on the left. The deepening low moves nearer the jet, center. As it occludes, the low moves north of the jet, right; the jet crosses the frontal system near the point of occlusion.

CIRRUS CLOUDS

Air travels in a "corkscrew" path around the jet core with upward motion on the equatorial side. Therefore, when high level moisture is available, cirriform clouds form on the equatorial side of the jet. Jet stream cloudiness can form independently of well-defined pressure systems. Such cloudiness ranges primarily from scattered to broken coverage in shallow layers or streaks. Their sometimes fish hook and streamlined, wind-swept appearance always indicates very strong upper wind usually quite far from developing or intense weather systems.

The most dense cirriform clouds occur with well-defined systems. They appear in broad bands. Cloudiness is rather dense in an upper trough, thickens downstream, and becomes most dense at the crest of the downwind ridge. The clouds taper off after passing the ridge crest into the area of descending air. The poleward boundary of the cirrus band often is quite abrupt and frequently casts a shadow on lower clouds, especially in an occluded frontal system. Figure 128a is a satellite photograph showing a cirrus band casting a shadow on lower clouds. Figure 128b is an infrared photo of the same system; the light shade of the cirrus band indicates cold temperatures while warmer low clouds are the darker shades.

The upper limit of dense, banded cirrus is near the tropopause; a band may be either a single layer or multiple layers 10,000 to 12,000 feet thick. Dense, jet stream cirriform cloudiness is most prevalent along midlatitude and polar jets. However, a cirrus band usually forms along the subtropical jet in winter when a deep upper trough plunges southward into the Tropics.

Cirrus clouds, in themselves, have little effect on aircraft. However, dense, continuous coverage requires a pilot's constant reference to instruments; most pilots find this more tiring than flying with a visual horizon even though IFR.

A more important aspect of the jet stream cirrus shield is its association with turbulence. Extensive cirrus cloudiness often occurs with deepening surface and upper lows; and these deepening systems produce the greatest turbulence.

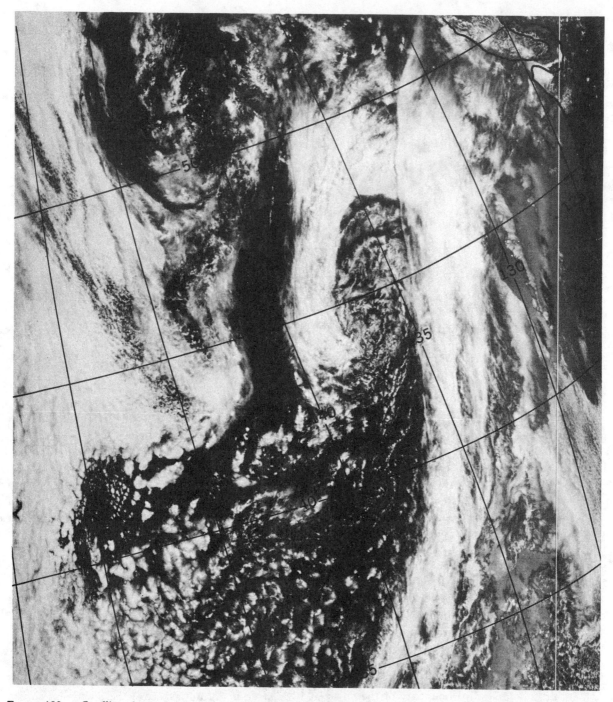

FIGURE 128a. Satellite photograph of an occluded system centered at about 44° N and 137° W. Here, the jet extends south-southwest to north-northeast along the polar (more westerly) boundary of the cirrus band from 35° N, 141° W through 43° N, 135° W to 51° N, 130° W. Shadow of the cirrus band is clearly evident as a narrow dark line from 45° N, 134.5° W to 49° N, 132° W.

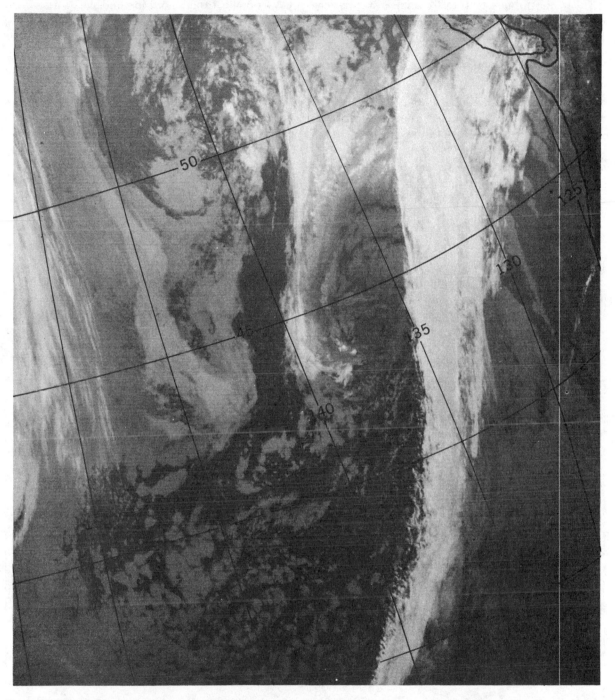

FIGURE 128b. Infrared photograph of the system shown in figure 128a. The warmer the radiating surface, the darker the shade; the cold cirrus appears nearly white. Infrared clearly distinguishes the banded jet stream cirrus from other cirrus and lower clouds.

CLEAR AIR TURBULENCE

Clear air turbulence (CAT) implies turbulence devoid of clouds. However, we commonly reserve the term for high level wind shear turbulence, even when in cirrus clouds.

Cold outbreaks colliding with warm air from the south intensify weather systems in the vicinity of the jet stream along the boundary between the cold and warm air. CAT develops in the turbulent energy exchange between the contrasting air masses. Cold and warm advection along with strong wind shears develop near the jet stream, especially where curvature of the jet stream sharply increases in deepening upper troughs. CAT is most pronounced in winter when temperature contrast is greatest between cold and warm air.

A preferred location of CAT is in an upper trough on the cold (polar) side of the jet stream. Another frequent CAT location, shown in figure 129, is along the jet stream north and northeast of a rapidly deepening surface low.

Even in the absence of a well-defined jet stream,

CAT often is experienced in wind shears associated with sharply curved contours of strong lows, troughs, and ridges aloft, and in areas of strong, cold or warm air advection. Also mountain waves can create CAT. Mountain wave CAT may extend from the mountain crests to as high as 5,000 feet above the tropopause, and can range 100 miles or more downstream from the mountains.

CAT can be encountered where there seems to be no reason for its occurrence. Strong winds may carry a turbulent volume of air away from its source region. Turbulence intensity diminishes downstream, but some turbulence still may be encountered where it normally would not be expected. CAT forecast areas are sometimes elongated to indicate probable turbulence drifting downwind from the main source region.

A forecast of turbulence specifies a volume of airspace which is quite small when compared to the total volume of airspace used by aviation, but is relatively large compared to the localized extent of

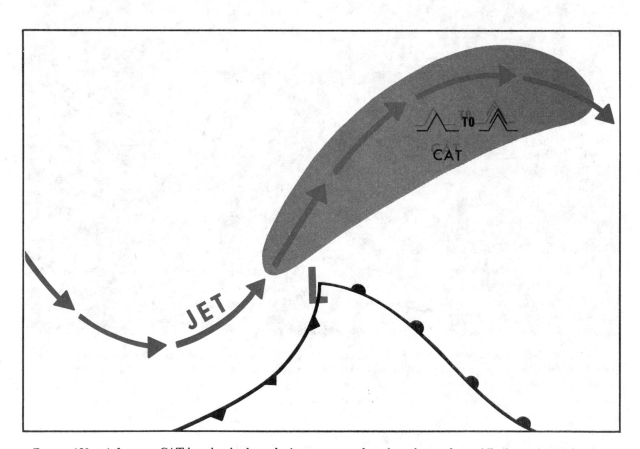

FIGURE 129. A frequent CAT location is along the jet stream north and northeast of a rapidly deepening surface low.

the hazard. Since turbulence in the forecast volume is patchy, you can expect to encounter it only intermittently and possibly not at all. A flight through forecast turbulence, on the average, encounters only light and annoying turbulence 10 to 15 percent of the time; about 2 to 3 percent of the time there is a need to have all objects secured; the pilot experiences control problems only about two-tenths of 1 percent of the time—odds of this genuinely hazardous turbulence are about 1 in 500.

Look again at figure 126. Where are the most probable areas of CAT? Turbulence would be greatest near the windspeed maxima, usually on the polar sides where there is a combination of strong wind shear, curvature in the flow, and cold air advection. These areas would be to the northwest of Vancouver Island, from north of the Great Lakes to east of James Bay and over the Atlantic east of Newfoundland. Also, turbulence in the form of mountain waves is probable in the vicinity of the jet stream from southern California across the Rockies into the Central Plains.

In flight planning, use upper air charts and forecasts to locate the jet stream, wind shears, and areas of most probable turbulence. AVIATION WEATHER SERVICES (AC 00-45) explains in detail how to obtain these parameters. If impractical to avoid completely an area of forecast turbulence, proceed with caution. You will do well to avoid areas where vertical shear exceeds 6 knots per 1,000 feet or horizontal shear exceeds 40 knots per 150 miles.

What can you do if you get into CAT rougher than you care to fly? If near the jet core, you could climb or descend a few thousand feet or you could move farther from the jet core. If caught in CAT not associated with the jet stream, your best bet is to change altitude since you have no positive way of knowing in which direction the strongest shear lies. Pilot reports from other flights, when available, are helpful.

Flight maneuvers increase stresses on the aircraft as does turbulence. The increased stresses are cumulative when the aircraft maneuvers in turbulence. Maneuver gently when in turbulence to minimize stress. The patchy nature of CAT makes current pilot reports extremely helpful to observers, briefers, forecasters, air traffic controllers, and, most important, to your fellow pilots. Always, if at all possible, make inflight weather reports of CAT or other turbulence encounters; negative reports also help when no CAT is experienced where it normally might be expected.

CONDENSATION TRAILS

A condensation trail, popularly contracted to "contrail," is generally defined as a cloud-like streamer which frequently is generated in the wake of aircraft flying in clear, cold, humid air, figure 130. Two distinct types are observed—exhaust trails and aerodynamic trails. "Distrails," contracted from dissipation trails, are produced differently from exhaust and aerodynamic trails.

EXHAUST CONTRAILS

The exhaust contrail is formed by the addition to the atmosphere of sufficient water vapor from aircraft exhaust gases to cause saturation or supersaturation of the air. Since heat is also added to the atmosphere in the wake of an aircraft, the addition of water vapor must be of such magnitude that it saturates or supersaturates the atmosphere in spite of the added heat. There is evidence to support the idea that the nuclei which are necessary for condensation or sublimation may also be donated to the atmosphere in the exhaust gases of aircraft engines, further aiding contrail formation. These nuclei are relatively large. Recent experiments, however, have revealed that visible exhaust contrails may be prevented by adding very minute nuclei material (dust, for example) to the exhaust. Condensation and sublimation on these smaller nuclei result in contrail particles too small to be visible.

AERODYNAMIC CONTRAILS

In air that is almost saturated, aerodynamic pressure reduction around airfoils, engine nacelles, and propellers cools the air to saturation leaving condensation trails from these components. This type of trail usually is neither as dense nor as persistent as exhaust trails. However, under critical atmospheric conditions, an aerodynamic contrail may trigger the formation and spreading of a deck of cirrus clouds.

Contrails create one problem unique to military operations in that they reveal the location of an aircraft attempting to fly undetected. A more general operational problem is a cirrus layer sometimes induced by the contrail. The induced layer

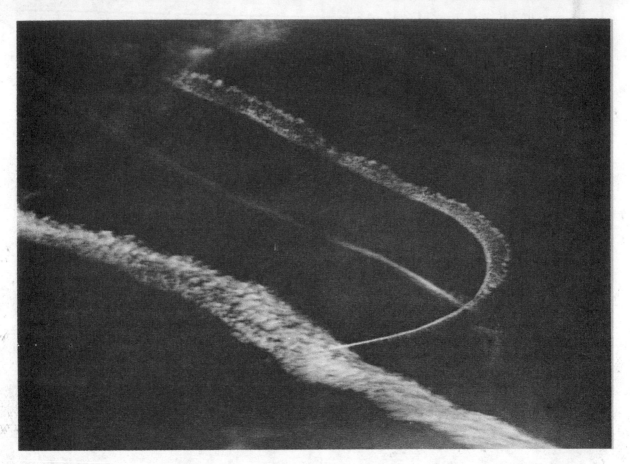

FIGURE 130.   Contrails. The thin contrail is freshly formed by an aircraft (not visible) in the lower right center of the photograph.

may make necessary the strict use of instruments by a subsequent flight at that altitude.

DISSIPATION TRAILS (DISTRAILS)

The term dissipation trail applies to a rift in clouds caused by the heat of exhaust gases from an aircraft flying in a thin cloud layer. The exhaust gases sometimes warm the air to the extent that it is no longer saturated, and the affected part of the cloud evaporates. The cloud must be both thin and relatively warm for a distrail to exist; therefore, they are not common.

HAZE LAYERS

Haze layers not visible from the ground are, at times, of concern at high altitude. These layers are really cirrus clouds with a very low density of ice crystals. Tops of these layers generally are very definite and are at the tropopause. High level haze occurs in stagnant air; it is rare in fresh outbreaks of cold polar air. Cirrus haze is common in Arctic winter. Sometimes ice crystals restrict visibility from the surface to the tropopause.

Visibility in the haze sometimes may be near zero, especially when one is facing the sun. To avoid the poor visibility, climb into the lower stratosphere or descend below the haze. This change may be several thousand feet.

CANOPY STATIC

Canopy static, similar to the precipitation static sometimes encountered at lower levels, is produced by particles brushing against plastic-covered aircraft surfaces. The discharge of static electricity results in a noisy disturbance that interferes with radio reception. Discharges can occur in such rapid succession that interference seems to be continuous. Since dust and ice crystals in cirrus clouds are the primary producers of canopy static, usually you may eliminate it by changing altitude.

ICING

Although icing at high altitude is not as common or extreme as at low altitudes, it can occur. It can form quickly on airfoils and exposed parts of jet engines. Structural icing at high altitudes usually is rime, although clear ice is possible.

High altitude icing generally forms in tops of tall cumulus buildups, anvils, and even in detached cirrus. Clouds over mountains are more likely to contain liquid water than those over more gently sloping terrain because of the added lift of the mountains. Therefore, icing is more likely to occur and to be more hazardous over mountainous areas.

Because ice generally accumulates slowly at high altitudes, anti-icing equipment usually eliminates any serious problems. However, anti-icing systems currently in use are not always adequate. If such is the case, avoid the icing problem by changing altitude or by varying course to remain clear of the clouds. Chapter 10 discusses aircraft icing in more detail.

THUNDERSTORMS

A well-developed thunderstorm may extend upward through the troposphere and penetrate the lower stratosphere. Sometimes the main updraft in a thunderstorm may toss hail out the top or the upper portions of the storm. An aircraft may encounter hail in clear air at a considerable distance from the thunderstorm, especially under the anvil cloud. Turbulence may be encountered in clear air for a considerable distance both above and around a growing thunderstorm.

Thunderstorm avoidance rules given in chapter 11 apply equally at high altitude. When flying in the clear, visually avoid all thunderstorm tops. In a severe thunderstorm situation, avoid tops by at least 20 miles. When you are on instruments, weather avoidance radar assures you of avoiding thunderstorm hazards. If in an area of severe thunderstorms, avoid the most intense echoes by at least 20 miles. Most air carriers now use this distance as the minimum for thunderstorm avoidance.

Chapter 14
ARCTIC WEATHER

The Arctic, strictly speaking, is the region shown in figure 131 which lies north of the Arctic Circle (66½° latitude). However, this chapter includes Alaskan weather even though much of Alaska lies south of the Arctic Circle.

Because of the lack of roads over most Arctic areas, aviation is the backbone of transportation between communities. As the economy expands, so will air transportation.

Your most valuable source of information concerning flying the Arctic is the experienced Arctic flyer. To introduce you to Arctic flying weather, this chapter surveys climate, air masses, and fronts of the Arctic; introduces you to some Arctic weather peculiarities; discusses weather hazards in the Arctic; and comments on Arctic flying.

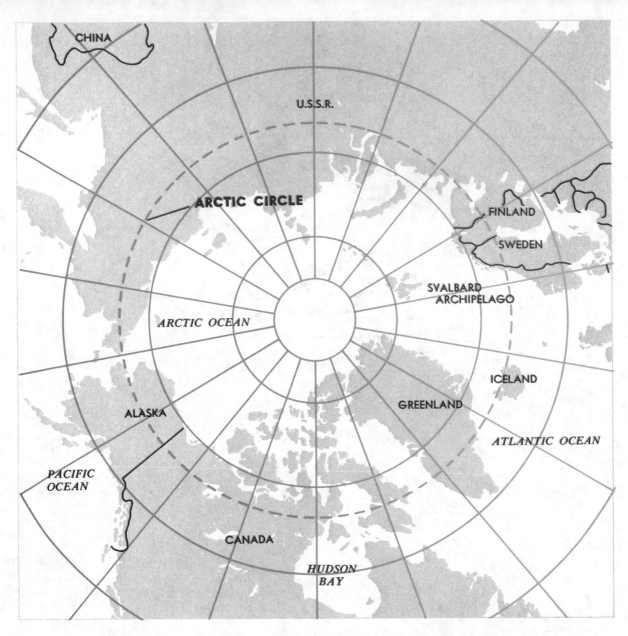

FIGURE 131. The Arctic. The Arctic Circle is at 66½° N latitude.

CLIMATE, AIR MASSES, AND FRONTS

Climate of any region is largely determined by the amount of energy received from the sun; but local characteristics of the area also influence climate.

LONG DAYS AND NIGHTS

A profound seasonal change in length of day and night occurs in the Arctic because of the Earth's tilt and its revolution around the sun. Figure 132 shows that any point north of the Arctic Circle has

autumn and winter days when the sun stays all day below the horizon and days in spring and summer with 24 hours of sunshine. The number of these days increases toward the North Pole; there the sun stays below the horizon for 6 months and shines continuously during the other 6 months.

Twilight in the Arctic is prolonged because of the shallow angle of the sun below the horizon. In more northern latitudes, it persists for days when the sun remains just below the horizon. This

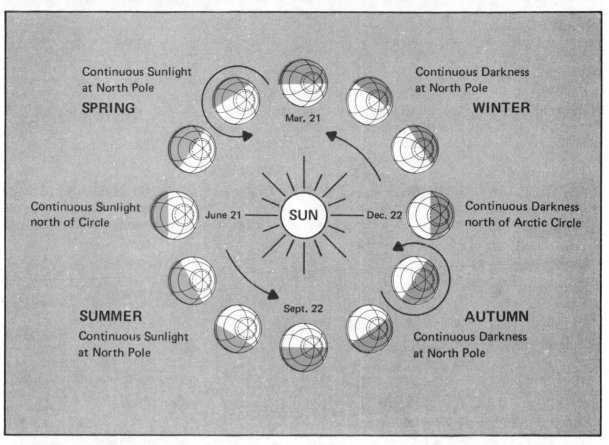

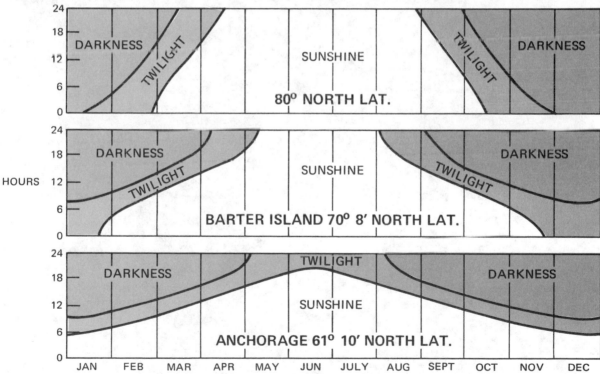

FIGURE 132.   Sunshine in the Northern Hemisphere. The sun shines a full 24 hours on the entire area north of the Arctic Circle (top) on June 21; the amount of sunshine decreases until none falls anywhere in the area on December 22. Graphs (below) show duration of sunshine and nautical twilight per day at two points north of the Arctic Circle and for Anchorage, Alaska, at a latitude about 5½° south of the circle.

abundance of twilight often makes visual reference possible at night.

LAND AND WATER

Figure 131 shows the water and land distribution in the Arctic. Arctic mountain ranges are effective barriers to air movement. Large masses of air stagnate over the inland continental areas. Thus, the Arctic continental areas are air mass source regions.

A large portion of the Arctic Ocean is covered throughout the year by a deep layer of ice—the permanent ice pack as shown in figure 133. Even though the ocean is ice-covered through much of the year, the ice and the water below contain more heat than the surrounding cold land, thus moderating the climate to some extent. Oceanic and coastal areas have a milder climate during winter than would be expected and a cool climate in summer. As opposed to large water bodies, large land areas show a more significant seasonal temperature variation.

TEMPERATURE

As one would expect, the Arctic is very cold in winter; but due to local terrain and the movement of pressure systems, occasionally some areas are sur-

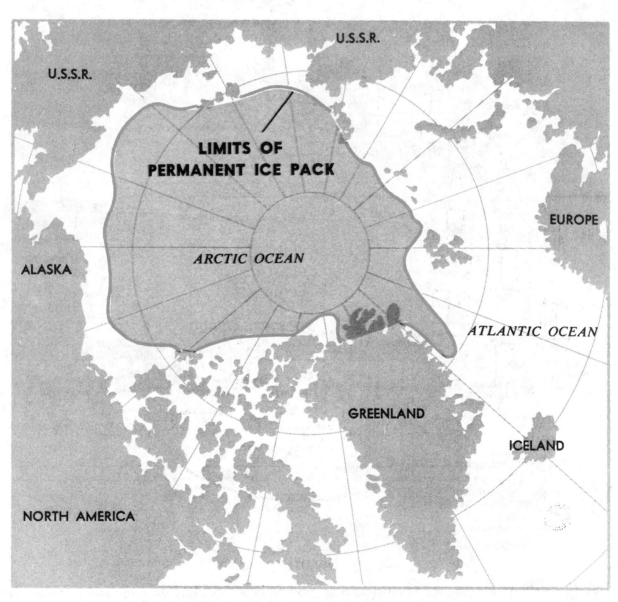

FIGURE 133.   The permanent Arctic ice pack.

prisingly warm. During winter, coastal areas average about 20 degrees warmer than the interior. During summer, interior areas are pleasantly warm with many hours of sunshine. Coastal areas have relatively cool short summers due to their proximity to water.

CLOUDS AND PRECIPITATION

Cloudiness over the Arctic is at a minimum during winter reaching a maximum in summer and fall, figure 134. Spring also brings many cloudy days. During summer afternoons, scattered cumulus clouds forming over the interior occasionally grow into thundershowers. These thundershowers, usually circumnavigable, move generally from northeast to southwest in the polar easterlies which is opposite the general movement in midlatitudes.

Precipitation in the Arctic is generally light. Annual amounts over the ice pack and along the coastal areas are only 3 to 7 inches. The interior is somewhat wetter, with annual amounts of 5 to 15 inches. Precipitation falls mostly in the form of

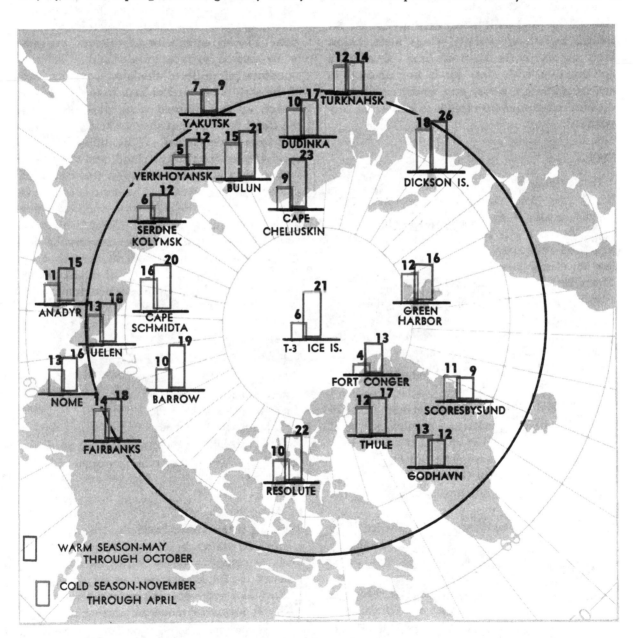

FIGURE 134. Average number of cloudy days per month. Note that most stations show the greatest number of cloudy days in the warmer season.

snow over ice caps and oceanic areas and mostly as summer rain over interior areas.

WIND

Strong winds occur more often along the coasts than elsewhere. The frequency of high winds in coastal areas is greatest in fall and winter. Wind speeds are generally light in the continental interior during the entire year, but are normally at their strongest during summer and fall.

AIR MASSES—WINTER

In winter, air masses form over the expanded ice pack and adjoining snow-covered land areas. These air masses are characterized by very cold surface air, very low humidity, and strong low-level temperature inversions. Occasionally, air from unfrozen ocean areas flows northward over the Arctic. These intrusions of moist, cold air account for most of the infrequent wintertime cloudiness and precipitation in the Arctic.

AIR MASSES—SUMMER

During the summer, the top layer of the Arctic permafrost layer melts leaving very moist ground, and the open water areas of the Polar Basin increase markedly. Thus, the entire area becomes more humid, relatively mild, and semimaritime in character. The largest amount of cloudiness and precipitation occurs inland during the summer months.

FRONTS

Occluded fronts are the rule. Weather conditions with occluded fronts are much the same in the Arctic as elsewhere—low clouds, precipitation, poor visibility, and sudden fog formation. Fronts are much more frequent over coastal areas than over the interior.

ARCTIC PECULIARITIES

Several Arctic phenomena are peculiar to that region. At times, they have a direct bearing on Arctic flying.

EFFECTS OF TEMPERATURE INVERSION

The intense low-level inversion over the Arctic during much of the winter causes sound—including people's voices—to carry over extremely long distances. Light rays are bent as they pass at low angles through the inversion. This bending creates an effect known as looming—a form of mirage that causes objects beyond the horizon to appear above the horizon. Mirages distorting the shape of the sun, moon, and other objects are common with these low level inversions.

AURORA BOREALIS

In theory, certain energy particles from the sun strike the Earth's magnetic field and are carried along the lines of force where they tend to lower and converge near the geomagnetic poles. The energy particles then pass through rarefied gases of the outer atmosphere, illuminating them in much the same way as an electrical charge illuminates neon gas in neon signs.

The Aurora Borealis takes place at high altitudes above the Earth's surface and thus has been observed as far south as Florida. However, the highest frequency of observations is over the northern United States and northward. Displays of aurora vary from a faint glow to an illumination of the Earth's surface equal to a full moon. They frequently change shape and form and are also called dancing lights or northern lights.

LIGHT REFLECTION BY SNOW-COVERED SURFACES

Much more light is reflected by snow-covered surfaces than by darker surfaces. Snow often reflects Arctic sunlight sufficiently to blot out shadows, thus markedly decreasing the contrast between objects. Dark distant mountains may be easily recognized, but a crevasse normally directly in view may be undetected due to lack of contrasts.

LIGHT FROM CELESTIAL BODIES

Illumination from the moon and stars is much more intense in the Arctic than in lower latitudes. Pilots have found that light from a half-moon over a snow-covered field may be sufficient for landing. Even illumination from the stars creates visibility far beyond that found elsewhere. Only under heavy overcast skies does the night darkness in the Arctic begin to approach the degree of darkness in lower latitudes.

WEATHER HAZARDS

Weather hazards include visibility restricting phenomena, blowing snow, icing, frost, and lack of contrast—whiteout.

FOG

Fog limits landing and takeoff in the Arctic more than any other visibility restriction. Water-droplet fog is the main hazard to aircraft operations in coastal areas during the summer. Ice fog is the major restriction in winter.

Ice Fog

Ice fog is common in the Arctic. It forms in moist air during extremely cold, calm conditions in winter, occurring often and tending to persist. Effective visibility is reduced much more in ice fog when one is looking toward the sun. Ice fog may be produced both naturally and artificially. Ice fog affecting aviation operations most frequently is produced by the combustion of aircraft fuel in cold air. When the wind is very light and the temperature is about −30° F or colder, ice fog often forms instantaneously in the exhaust gases of automobiles and aircraft. It lasts from as little as a few minutes to days.

Steam Fog

Steam fog, often called "sea smoke," forms in winter when cold, dry air passes from land areas over comparatively warm ocean waters. Moisture evaporates rapidly from the water surface; but since the cold air can hold only a small amount of water vapor, condensation takes place just above the surface of the water and appears as "steam" rising from the ocean. This fog is composed entirely of water droplets that often freeze quickly and fall back into the water as ice particles. Low level turbulence can occur and icing can become hazardous.

Advection Fog

Advection fog, which may be composed either of water droplets or of ice crystals, is most common in winter and is often persistent. Advection fog forms along coastal areas when comparatively warm, moist, oceanic air moves over cold land. If the land areas are hilly or mountainous, lifting of the air results in a combination of low stratus and fog. The stratus and fog quickly diminish inland. Lee sides of islands and mountains usually are free of advection fog because of drying due to compressional heating as the air descends downslope. Icing in advection fog is in the form of rime and may become quite severe.

BLOWING SNOW

Over the frozen Arctic Ocean and along the coastal areas, blowing snow and strong winds are common hazards during autumn and winter. Blowing snow is a greater hazard to flying operations in the Arctic than in midlatitudes because the snow is "dry" and fine and can be picked up easily by light winds. Winds in excess of 8 knots may raise the snow several feet off the ground obliterating objects such as runway markers as illustrated in figure 135. A sudden increase in surface wind may cause an unlimited visibility to drop to near zero in a few minutes. This sudden loss of visibility occurs frequently without warning in the Arctic. Stronger winds sometimes lift blowing snow to heights above 1,000 feet and produce drifts over 30 feet deep.

ICING

Icing is most likely in spring and fall, but is also encountered in winter. During spring and fall, icing may extend to upper levels along frontal zones. While icing is mostly a problem over water and coastal areas, it does exist inland. It occurs typically as rime, but a combination of clear and rime is not unusual in coastal mountains.

FROST

In coastal areas during spring, fall, and winter, heavy frost and rime may form on aircraft parked outside, especially when fog or ice fog is present. This frost should be removed; it reduces lift and is especially hazardous if surrounding terrain requires a rapid rate of climb.

WHITEOUT

"Whiteout" is a visibility restricting phenomenon that occurs in the Arctic when a layer of cloudiness of uniform thickness overlies a snow or ice-covered surface. Parallel rays of the sun are broken up and diffused when passing through the cloud layer so that they strike the snow surface from many angles. The diffused light then reflects back and forth countless times between the snow and the cloud eliminating all shadows. The result is a loss of depth perception. Buildings, people, and dark-colored objects appear to float in the air, and the

FIGURE 135.   Visibility reduced by blowing snow. Common in Arctic regions since wind easily picks up the dry, powder-like snow.

horizon disappears. Low level flight over icecap terrain or landing on snow surfaces becomes dangerous. Disastrous accidents have occurred as a result of whiteouts.

ARCTIC FLYING WEATHER

A great number of pilots who fly Alaska and the Arctic are well seasoned. They are eager to be of help and are your best sources of information. Alaska and the Arctic are sparsely settled with mostly natural landmarks to guide you as illustrated in figure 136. Before flying in the Arctic, be sure to learn all you can about your proposed route.

Generally, flying conditions in the Arctic are

FIGURE 136.   A typical frozen landscape of the Arctic.

good when averaged over the entire year; however, areas of Greenland compete with the Aleutians for the world's worst weather. These areas are exceptions.

Whiteouts, in conjunction with overcast skies, often present a serious hazard especially for visual flight. Many mountain peaks are treeless and rounded rather than ragged, making them unusually difficult to distinguish under poor visibility conditions.

OCEANIC AND COASTAL AREAS

In oceanic and coastal areas, predominant hazards change with the seasons. In summer, the main hazard is fog in coastal areas.

In winter, ice fog is the major restriction to aircraft operation. Blowing and drifting snow often restrict visibility also. Storms and well-defined frontal passages frequent the coastal areas accompanied by turbulence, especially in the coastal mountains.

Icing is most frequent in spring and fall and may extend to high levels in active, turbulent frontal zones. Fog is also a source of icing when temperature is colder than freezing.

CONTINENTAL AREAS

Over the continental interior, good flying weather prevails much of the year; although during winter, ice fog often restricts aircraft operations. In terms of ceiling and visibility, the summer months provide the best flying weather. However, the number of cloudy days during the summer exceeds those in winter. Thunderstorms develop on occasion during the summer, but they usually can be circumnavigated without much interference with flight plans.

IN CLOSING

If one were to summarize general weather conditions and flight precautions over Alaska, northern Canada, and the Arctic, he would say:

1. Interior areas generally have good flying weather, but coastal areas and Arctic slopes often are plagued by low ceiling, poor visibility, and icing.
2. "Whiteout" conditions over ice and snow covered areas often cause pilot disorientation.
3. Flying conditions are usually worse in mountain passes than at reporting stations along the route.
4. Routes through the mountains are subject to strong turbulence, especially in and near passes.
5. Beware of a false mountain pass that may lead to a dead-end.
6. Thundershowers sometimes occur in the interior during May through August. They are usually circumnavigable and generally move from northeast to southwest.
7. Always file a flight plan. Stay on regularly traversed routes, and if downed, stay with your plane.
8. If lost during summer, fly down-drainage, that is, downstream. Most airports are located near rivers, and chances are you can reach a landing strip by flying downstream. If forced down, you will be close to water on which a rescue plane can land. In summer, the tundra is usually too soggy for landing.
9. Weather stations are few and far between. Adverse weather between stations may go undetected unless reported by a pilot in flight. A report confirming good weather between stations is also just as important. *Help yourself and your fellow pilot by reporting weather en route.*

Chapter 15
TROPICAL WEATHER

Technically, the Tropics lie between latitudes 23½° N and 23½° S. However, weather typical of this region sometimes extends as much as 45° from the Equator. One may think of the Tropics as uniformly rainy, warm, and humid. The facts are, however, that the Tropics contain both the wettest and driest regions of the world. This chapter describes the circulation basic to the Tropics, terrain influences that determine arid and wet regions, and transitory systems that invade or disturb the basic tropical circulation.

CIRCULATION

In chapter 4, we learned that wind blowing out of the subtropical high pressure belts toward the Equator form the northeast and southeast trade winds of the two hemispheres. These trade winds converge in the vicinity of the Equator where air rises. This convergence zone is the "intertropical convergence zone" (ITCZ). In some areas of the world, seasonal temperature differences between land and water areas generate rather large circulation patterns that overpower the trade wind circulation; these areas are "monsoon" regions. Tropical weather discussed here includes the subtropical high pressure belts, the trade wind belts, the intertropical convergence zone, and monsoon regions.

SUBTROPICAL HIGH PRESSURE BELTS

If the surface under the subtropical high pressure belts were all water of uniform temperature, the high pressure belts would be continuous highs around the globe. The belts would be areas of descending or subsiding air and would be characterized by strong temperature inversions and very little precipitation. However, land surfaces at the latitudes of the high pressure belts are generally warmer throughout the year than are water surfaces. Thus, the high pressure belts are broken into semipermanent high pressure anticyclones over oceans with troughs or lows over continents as shown in figures 23 and 24, chapter 4. The subtropical highs shift southward during the Northern Hemisphere winter and northward during summer. The seasonal shift, the height and strength of the inversion, and terrain features determine weather in the subtropical high pressure belts.

Continental Weather

Along the west coasts of continents under a subtropical high, the air is stable. The inversion is strongest and lowest where the east side of an anticyclone overlies the west side of a continent. Moisture is trapped under the inversion; fog and low stratus occur frequently. However, precipitation is rare since the moist layer is shallow and the air is stable. Heavily populated areas also add contaminants to the air which, when trapped under the inversion, create an air pollution problem.

The extreme southwestern United States, for example, is dominated in summer by a subtropical high. We are all familiar with the semi-arid summer climate of southern California. Rainfall is infrequent but fog is common along the coast. Contaminants trapped along with fog under the strong inversion may persist for days creating "smog."

In winter, the subtropical high pressure belts shift southward. Again, let's consider southern California as an example. In winter, the area comes under the influence of midlatitude circulation which increases frequency of rain. Also, an occasional wintertime outbreak of polar air brings clear skies with excellent visibility.

The situation on eastern continental coasts is just the opposite. The inversion is weakest and highest where the west side of an anticyclone overlies the eastern coast of a continent. Convection can penetrate the inversion, and showers and thunderstorms often develop. Precipitation is generally sufficient to support considerable vegetation. For example, in the United States, Atlantic coastal areas at the same latitude as southern California are far from arid in summer.

Low ceiling and fog often prevent landing at a west coast destination, but a suitable alternate generally is available a few miles inland. Alternate selection may be more critical for an eastern coast destination because of widespread instability and associated hazards.

Weather over Open Sea

Under a subtropical high over the open sea, cloudiness is scant. The few clouds that do develop have tops from 3,000 to 6,000 feet depending on height of the inversion. Ceiling and visibility are generally quite ample for VFR flight.

Island Weather

An island under a subtropical high receives very little rainfall because of the persistent temperature inversion. Surface heating over some larger islands causes light convective showers. Cloud tops are only slightly higher than over open water. Temperatures are mild, showing small seasonal and diurnal changes. A good example is the pleasant, balmy climate of Bermuda.

TRADE WIND BELTS

Figures 138 and 139 show prevailing winds throughout the Tropics for July and January. Note that trade winds blowing out of the subtropical highs over ocean areas are predominantly northeasterly in the Northern Hemisphere and southeasterly in the Southern Hemisphere. The inversion from the subtropical highs is carried into the trade winds and is known as the "trade wind inversion." As in a subtropical high, the inversion is strongest where the trades blow away from the west coast of a continent and weakest where they blow onto an eastern continental shore. Daily variations from these prevailing directions are small except during tropical storms. As a result, weather at any specific location in a trade wind belt varies little from day to day.

Weather over Open Sea

In the trade wind belt, skies over open water are about one-half covered by clouds on the average. Tops range from 3,000 to 8,000 feet depending on height of the inversion. Showers, although more common than under a subtropical high, are still light with comparatively little rainfall. Flying weather generally is quite good.

Continental Weather

Where trade winds blow offshore along the west coasts of continents, skies are generally clear and the area is quite arid. The Baja Peninsula of Lower California is a well-known example. Where trade winds blow onshore on the east sides of continents, rainfall is generally abundant in showers and occasional thunderstorms. The east coast of Mexico is a good example. Rainfall may be carried a considerable distance inland where the winds are not blocked by a mountain barrier. Inland areas blocked by a mountain barrier are deserts; examples are the Sahara Desert and the arid regions of southwestern United States. Afternoon convective currents are common over arid regions due to strong surface heating. Cumulus and cumulonimbus clouds can develop, but cloud bases are high and rainfall is scant because of the low moisture content.

Flying weather along eastern coasts and mountains is subject to the usual hazards of showers and thunderstorms. Flying over arid regions is good most of the time but can be turbulent in afternoon convective currents; be especially aware of dust devils. Blowing sand or dust sometimes restricts visibility.

Island Weather

Mountainous islands have the most dramatic effect on trade wind weather. Since trade winds are consistently from approximately the same direction, they always strike the same side of the island; this side is the windward side. The opposite side is the leeward side. Winds blowing up the windward side produce copious and frequent rainfall, although cloud tops rarely exceed 10,000 feet. Thunderstorms are rare. Downslope winds on the leeward slopes dry the air leaving relatively clear skies and much less rainfall. Many islands in the trade wind belt have lush vegetation and even rain forests on the windward side while the leeward is semiarid. For example, the island of Oahu, Hawaii, is about 24 miles wide in the direction of the trade winds. Annual rainfall averages from about 60 inches on the windward coast to 200 inches at the mountain tops, decreasing to 10 inches on the leeward shore.

The greatest flying hazard near these islands is obscured mountain tops. Ceiling and visibility occasionally restrict VFR flight on the windward side in showers. IFR weather is virtually nonexistent on leeward slopes.

Islands without mountains have little effect on cloudiness and rainfall. Afternoon surface heating increases convective cloudiness slightly, but shower activity is light. However, any island in either the subtropical high pressure belt or trade wind belt enhances cumulus development even though tops do not reach great heights. Therefore, a cumulus top higher than the average tops of surrounding cumulus usually marks the approximate location of an island. If it becomes necessary to "ditch" in the ocean, look for a tall cumulus. If you see one, head for it. It probably marks a land surface, increasing your chances of survival.

THE INTERTROPICAL CONVERGENCE ZONE (ITCZ)

Converging winds in the intertropical convergence zone (ITCZ) force air upward. The inversion typical of the subtropical high and trade wind belts disappears. Figures 138 and 139 show the ITCZ and its seasonal shift. The ITCZ is well marked over tropical oceans but is weak and ill-defined over large continental areas.

Weather over Islands and Open Water

Convection in the ITCZ carries huge quantities of moisture to great heights. Showers and thunderstorms frequent the ITCZ and tops to 40,000 feet or higher are common as shown in figure 137. Precipitation is copious. Since convection dominates the ITCZ, there is little difference in weather over islands and open sea under the ITCZ.

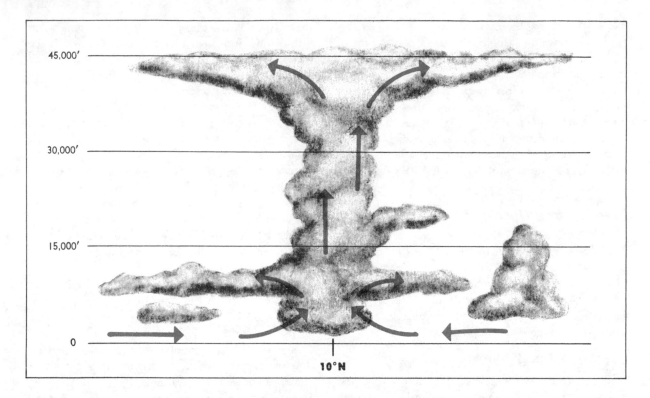

FIGURE 137. Vertical cross section illustrating convection in the Intertropical Convergence Zone.

Flying through the ITCZ usually presents no great problem if one follows the usual practice of avoiding thunderstorms. He usually can find a safe corridor between storms.

Since the ITCZ is ill-defined over continents, we will not attempt to describe ITCZ continental weather as such. Continental weather ranges from arid to rain forests and is more closely related to the monsoon than to the ITCZ.

MONSOON

If you refer again to figures 23 and 24 in chapter 4, you can see that over the large land mass of Asia, the subtropical high pressure breaks down completely. Asia is covered by an intense high during the winter and a well-developed low during the summer. You can also see the same over Australia and central Africa, although the seasons are reversed in the Southern Hemisphere.

The cold, high pressures in winter cause wind to blow from the deep interior outward and offshore. In summer, wind direction reverses and warm moist air is carried far inland into the low pressure area. This large scale seasonal wind shift is the "monsoon." The most notable monsoon is that of southern and southeastern Asia.

Summer or Wet Monsoon Weather

During the summer, the low over central Asia draws warm, moist, unstable maritime air from the southwest over the continent. Strong surface heating coupled with rising of air flowing up the higher terrain produces extensive cloudiness, copious rain, and numerous thunderstorms. Rainfall at some stations in India exceeds 400 inches per year with highest amounts between June and October.

The monsoon is so pronounced that it influences circulation many miles out over the ocean. Note in figure 138 that in summer, prevailing winds from the Equator to the south Asian coast are southerly and southeasterly; without the monsoon influence, these areas would be dominated by northeasterly trades. Islands within the monsoon influence receive frequent showers.

Winter Monsoon Weather

Note in figure 139 how the winter flow has reversed from that shown in figure 138. Cold, dry air from the high plateau deep in the interior warms adiabatically as it flows down the southern slopes of the Himalayan Mountains. Virtually no rain falls in the interior in the dry winter monsoon. As the

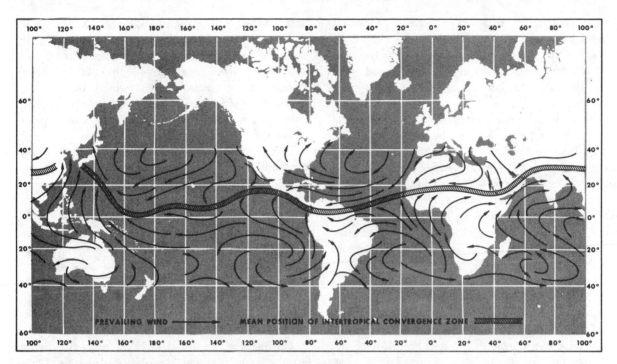

FIGURE 138. Prevailing winds throughout the Tropics in July. Remember that in the Southern Hemisphere, circulation around pressure centers is opposite that in the Northern Hemisphere.

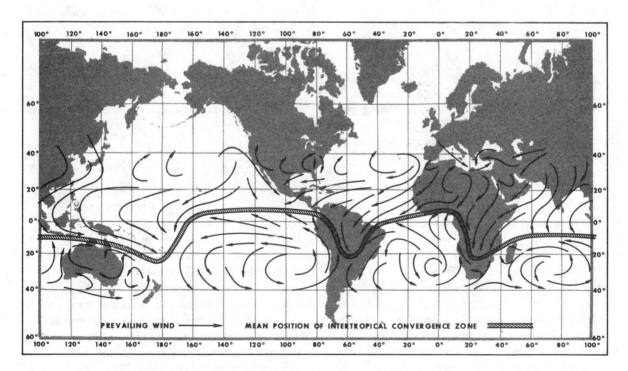

FIGURE 139. Prevailing winds in the Tropics in January.

dry air moves off shore over warmer water, it rapidly takes in more moisture, becomes warmer in low levels and, therefore, unstable. Rain is frequent over off-shore islands and even along coastal areas after the air has had a significant over-water trajectory.

The Philippine Islands are in an area of special interest. During the summer, they are definitely in southerly monsoon flow and are subjected to abundant rainfall. In the winter, wind over the Philippines is northeasterly—in the transition zone between the northeasterly trades and the monsoon flow. It is academic whether we call the phenomenon the trade winds or monsoon; in either case, it produces abundant rainfall. The Philippines have a year-round humid, tropical climate.

Other Monsoon Areas

Australia in July (Southern Hemisphere winter) is an area of high pressure with predominantly off-shore winds as shown in figure 138. Most of the continent is dry during the winter. In January, figure 139, winds are onshore into the continental low pressure. However, most of Australia is rimmed by mountains, coastal regions are wet where the onshore winds blow up the mountain slopes. The interior is arid where down-slope winds are warmed and dried.

Central Africa is known for its humid climate and jungles. Note in figures 138 and 139 that prevailing wind is onshore much of the year over these regions. Some regions are wet the year round; others have the seasonal monsoon shift and have a summer wet season and a winter dry season. Climate of Africa is so varied that only a detailed area-by-area study can explain the climate typical of each area.

In the Amazon Valley of South America during the Southern Hemisphere winter (July), southeast trades, as shown in figure 138, penetrate deep into the valley bringing abundant rainfall which contributes to the jungle climate. In January, the ITCZ moves south of the valley as shown in figure 139. The northeast trades are caught up in the monsoon, cross the Equator, and also penetrate the Amazon Valley. The jungles of the Amazon result largely from monsoon winds.

Flying Weather in Monsoons

During the winter monsoon, excellent flying weather prevails over dry interior regions. Over water, one must pick his way around showers and thunderstorms. In the summer monsoon, VFR flight over land is often restricted by low ceilings and heavy rain. IFR flight must cope with the hazards of thunderstorms. Freezing level in the Tropics is quite high—14,000 feet or higher—so icing is restricted to high levels.

TRANSITORY SYSTEMS

So far, we have concentrated on prevailing circulations. Now, let's turn to migrating tropical weather producers—the shear line, trough aloft, tropical wave, and tropical cyclone.

SHEAR LINE

A wind shear line found in the Tropics mainly results from midlatitude influences. In chapter 8 we stated that an air mass becomes modified when it flows from its source region. By the time a cold air mass originating in high latitudes reaches the Tropics, temperature and moisture are virtually the same on both sides of the front. A shear line, or wind shift, is all that remains. A shear line also results when a semi-permanent high splits into two cells inducing a trough as shown in figure 140.

These shear lines are zones of convergence creating forced upward motion. Consequently, consider-

able thunderstorm and rain shower activity occurs along a shear line.

TROUGH ALOFT

Troughs in the atmosphere, generally at or above 10,000 feet, move through the Tropics, especially along the poleward fringes. Figure 141 shows such a trough across the Hawaiian Island chain. As a trough moves to the southeast or east, it spreads middle and high cloudiness over extensive areas to the east of the trough line. Occasionally, a well-developed trough will extend deep into the Tropics, and a closed low forms at the equatorial end of the trough. The low then may separate from the trough and move westward producing a large amount of cloudiness and precipitation. If this occurs in the vicinity of a strong subtropical jet stream, extensive

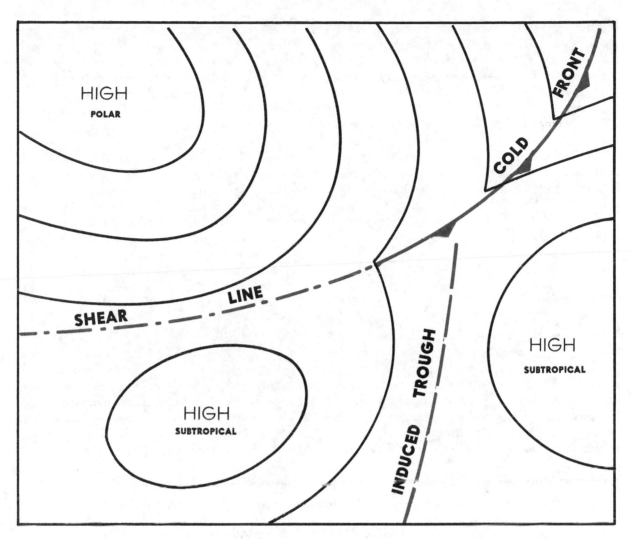

FIGURE 140. A shear line and an induced trough caused by a polar high pushing into the subtropics.

and sometimes dense cirrus and some convective and clear air turbulence often develop.

Troughs and lows aloft produce considerable amounts of rainfall in the Tropics, especially over land areas where mountains and surface heating lift air to saturation. Low pressure systems aloft contribute significantly to the record 460 inches average annual rainfall on Mt. Waialeale on Kauai, Hawaii. Other mountainous areas of the Tropics are also among the wettest spots on earth.

TROPICAL WAVE

Tropical waves (also called easterly waves) are common tropical weather disturbances, normally occurring in the trade wind belt. In the Northern Hemisphere, they usually develop in the southeast-

ern perimeter of the subtropical high pressure systems. They travel from east to west around the southern fringes of these highs in the prevailing easterly circulation of the Tropics. Surface winds in advance of a wave are somewhat more northerly than the usual trade wind direction. As the wave approaches, as shown in figure 142, pressure falls; as it passes, surface wind shifts to the east-southeast or southeast. The typical wave is preceded by very good weather but followed by extensive cloudiness, as shown in figure 143, and often by rain and thunderstorms. The weather activity is roughly in a north-south line.

Tropical waves occur in all seasons, but are more frequent and stronger during summer and early fall. Pacific waves frequently affect Hawaii; Atlan-

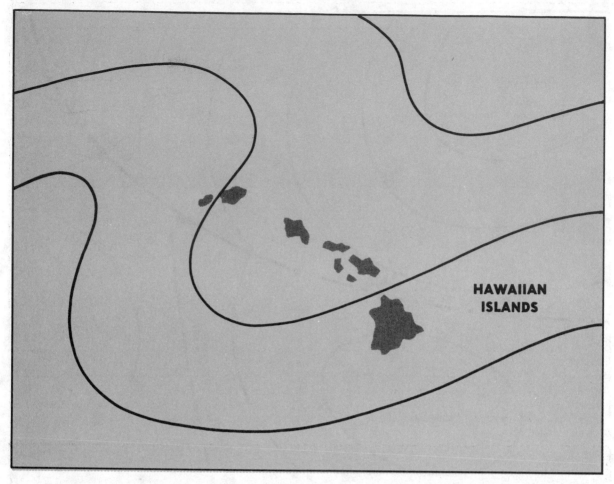

FIGURE 141. A trough aloft across the Hawaiian Islands. Extensive cloudiness develops east of the trough.

tic waves occasionally move into the Gulf of Mexico, reaching the U.S. coast.

TROPICAL CYCLONE

Tropical cyclone is a general term for any low that originates over tropical oceans. Tropical cyclones are classified according to their intensity based on average one-minute wind speeds. Wind gusts in these storms may be as much as 50 percent higher than the average one-minute wind speeds. Tropical cyclone international classifications are:

(1) Tropical Depression—highest sustained winds up to 34 knots (64 km/h),

(2) Tropical Storm—highest sustained winds of 35 through 64 knots (65 to 119 km/h), and

(3) Hurricane or Typhoon—highest sustained winds 65 knots (120 km/h) or more.

Strong tropical cyclones are known by different names in different regions of the world. A tropical cyclone in the Atlantic and eastern Pacific is a "hurricane"; in the western Pacific, "typhoon"; near Australia, "willy-willy"; and in the Indian Ocean, simply "cyclone." Regardless of the name, these tropical cyclones produce serious aviation hazards. Before we delve into these aspects, let's look at the development, movement, and decay of these cyclones.

Development

Prerequisite to tropical cyclone development are optimum sea surface temperature under weather systems that produce low-level convergence and cyclonic wind shear. Favored breeding grounds are tropical (easterly) waves, troughs aloft, and areas of converging northeast and southeast trade winds along the intertropical convergence zone.

The low level convergence associated with these systems, by itself, will not support development of a tropical cyclone. The system must also have

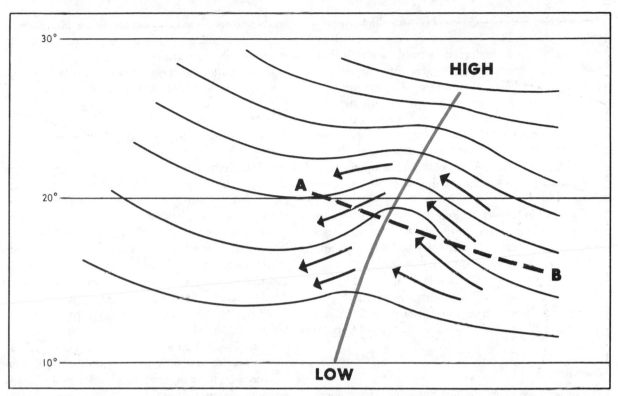

FIGURE 142. A Northern Hemisphere easterly wave. Progressing from (A) to (B), note that winds shift generally from northeasterly to southeasterly. The wave moves toward the west and is often preceded by good weather and followed by extensive cloudiness and precipitation.

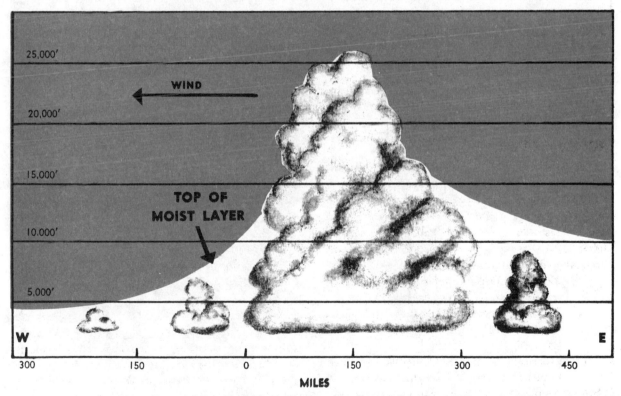

FIGURE 143. Vertical cross section along line A—B in figure 142.

horizontal outflow—divergence—at high tropospheric levels. This combination creates a "chimney," in which air is forced upward causing clouds and precipitation. Condensation releases large quantities of latent heat which raises the temperature of the system and accelerates the upward motion. The rise in temperature lowers the surface pressure which increases low-level convergence. This draws more moisture-laden air into the system. When these chain-reaction events continue, a huge vortex is generated which may culminate in hurricane force winds.

Figure 144 shows regions of the world where tropical cyclones frequently develop. Notice that they usually originate between latitudes 5° and 20°. Tropical cyclones are unlikely within 5° of the Equator because the Coriolis force is so small near the Equator that it will not turn the winds enough for them to flow around a low pressure area. Winds flow directly into an equatorial low and rapidly fill it.

Movement

Tropical cyclones in the Northern Hemisphere usually move in a direction between west and northwest while in low latitudes. As these storms move toward the midlatitudes, they come under the influence of the prevailing westerlies. At this time the storms are under the influence of two wind systems, i.e., the trade winds at low levels and prevailing westerlies aloft. Thus a storm may move very erratically and may even reverse course, or circle. Finally, the prevailing westerlies gain control and the storm recurves toward the north, then to the northeast, and finally to the east-northeast. By this time the storm is well into midlatitudes.

Decay

As the storm curves toward the north or east, it usually begins to lose its tropical characteristics and acquires characteristics of lows in middle latitudes. Cooler air flowing into the storm gradually weakens it. If the storm tracks along a coast line or over the open sea, it gives up slowly, carrying its fury to areas far removed from the Tropics. However, if the storm moves well inland, it loses its moisture source and weakens from starvation and increased surface friction, usually after leaving a trail of destruction and flooding.

When a storm takes on middle latitude characteristics, it is said to be "extratropical" meaning "outside the Tropics." Tropical cyclones produce weather conditions that differ somewhat from those produced by their higher latitude cousins and invite our investigation.

Weather in a Tropical Depression

While in its initial developing stage, the cyclone is characterized by a circular area of broken to overcast clouds in multiple layers. Embedded in these clouds are numerous showers and thunderstorms. Rain shower and thunderstorm coverage

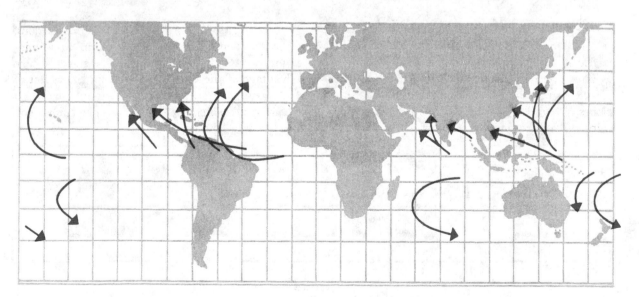

FIGURE 144.   Principal regions where tropical cyclones form and their favored directions of movement.

varies from scattered to almost solid. Diameter of the cloud pattern varies from less than 100 miles in small systems to well over 200 miles in large ones.

Weather in Tropical Storms and Hurricanes

As cyclonic flow increases, the thunderstorms and rain showers form into broken or solid lines paralleling the wind flow that is spiraling into the center of the storm. These lines are the spiral rain bands frequently seen on radar. These rain bands continually change as they rotate around the storm. Rainfall in the rain bands is very heavy, reducing ceiling and visibility to near zero. Winds are usually very strong and gusty and, consequently, generate violent turbulence. Between the rain bands, ceilings and visibilities are somewhat better, and turbulence generally is less intense.

The "eye" usually forms in the tropical storm stage and continues through the hurricane stage. In the eye, skies are free of turbulent cloudiness, and wind is comparatively light. The average diameter of the eye is between 15 and 20 miles, but sometimes is as small as 7 miles and rarely is more than 30 miles in diameter. Surrounding the eye is a wall of cloud that may extend above 50,000 feet. This "wall cloud" contains deluging rain and the strongest winds of the storm. Maximum wind speeds of 175 knots have been recorded in some storms. Figure 145 is a radar display and 146, a satellite photograph of a mature hurricane. Note the spiral rain bands and the circular eye. Notice the similarity between these two figures.

Detection and Warning

The National Weather Service has a specialized hurricane forecast and warning service center at Miami, Florida, which maintains constant watch for the formation and development of tropical cyclones. Weather information from land stations, ships at sea, reconnaissance aircraft, long range radars, and weather satellites is fed into the center. The center forecasts the development, movement, and intensity of tropical cyclones. Forecasts and warnings are issued to the public and aviation interests by field offices of the National Weather Service.

Flying

All pilots except those especially trained to explore tropical storms and hurricanes should AVOID THESE DANGEROUS STORMS. Occasionally, jet aircraft have been able to fly over small and less intense storms, but the experience of weather research aircraft shows hazards at all levels within them.

Tops of thunderstorms associated with tropical cyclones frequently exceed 50,000 feet. Winds in a typical hurricane are strongest at low levels, decreasing with altitude. However, research aircraft have frequently encountered winds in excess of 100 knots at 18,000 feet. Aircraft at low levels are exposed to sustained, pounding turbulence due to the surface friction of the fast-moving air. Turbulence increases in intensity in spiral rain bands and becomes most violent in the wall cloud surrounding the eye.

An additional hazard encountered in hurricanes is erroneous altitude readings from pressure altimeters. These errors are caused by the large pressure difference between the periphery of the storm and its center. One research aircraft lost almost 2,000 feet true altitude traversing a storm while the pressure altimeter indicated a constant altitude of 5,000 feet.

In short, tropical cyclones are very hazardous, so avoid them! To bypass the storm in a minimum of time, fly to the right of the storm to take advantage of the tailwind. If you fly to the left of the storm, you will encounter strong headwinds which may exhaust your fuel supply before you reach a safe landing area.

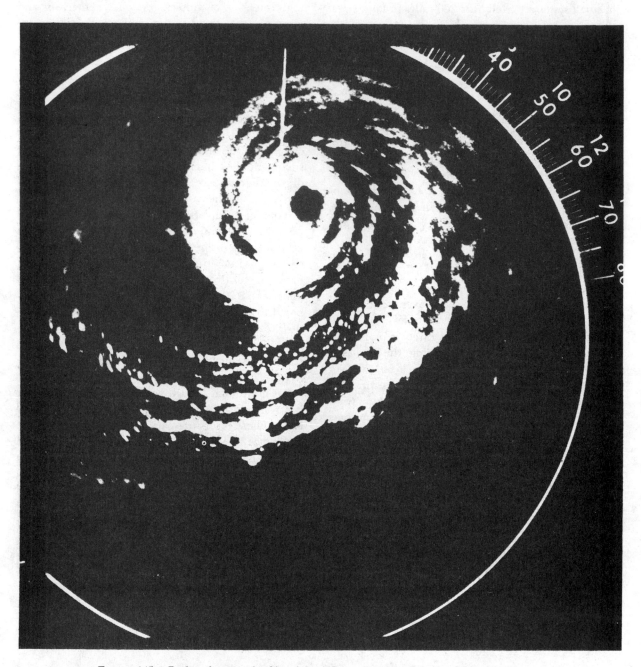

FIGURE 145.   Radar photograph of hurricane "Donna" observed at Key West, Florida.

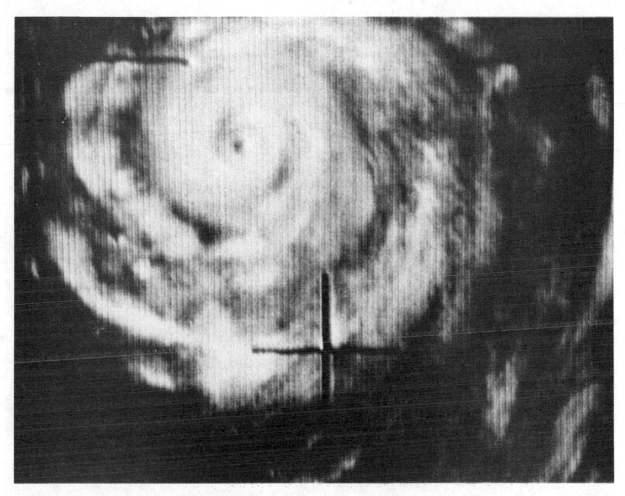

FIGURE 146.   A hurricane observed by satellite.

Chapter 16
SOARING WEATHER

While horse racing may be the "Sport of Kings," soaring may be considered the "King of Sports." Soaring bears the relationship to flying that sailing bears to power boating. Soaring has made notable contributions to meteorology. For example, soaring pilots have probed thunderstorms and mountain waves with findings that have made flying safer for all pilots. However, soaring is primarily recreational.

A sailplane must have auxiliary power to become airborne such as a winch, a ground tow, or a tow by a powered aircraft. Once the sailcraft is airborne and the tow cable released, performance of the craft depends on the weather and the skill of the pilot. Forward thrust comes from gliding downward relative to the air the same as thrust is developed in a power-off glide by a conventional aircraft. Therefore, to gain or maintain altitude, the soaring pilot must rely on upward motion of the air.

To a sailplane pilot, "lift" means the rate of climb he can achieve in an up-current, while "sink" denotes his rate of descent in a downdraft or in neutral air. "Zero sink" means that upward currents are just strong enough to enable him to hold altitude but not to climb. Sailplanes are highly efficient machines; a sink rate of a mere 2 feet per second provides an airspeed of about 40 knots, and a sink rate of 6 feet per second gives an airspeed of about 70 knots. Some two-place training craft have somewhat higher sink rates.

In lift, a sailplane pilot usually flies 35 to 40 knots with a sink rate of about 2 feet per second. Therefore, if he is to remain airborne, he must have an upward air current of at least 2 feet per second. There is no point in trying to soar until weather conditions favor vertical speeds greater than the minimum sink rate of the aircraft. These vertical currents develop from several sources, and these sources categorize soaring into five classes: (1) Thermal Soaring, (2) Frontal Soaring, (3) Sea Breeze Soaring, (4) Ridge or Hill Soaring, and (5) Mountain Wave Soaring.

THERMAL SOARING

Peter Dixon estimates that about 80 percent of all soaring in the U.S. depends on thermal lift.* What is a thermal? A thermal is simply the updraft in a small-scale convective current. Chapter 4 in the section "Convection," and chapter 9 in the section, "Convective Currents," explain the basic principle of convective circulation. The explanations are adequate for the pilot of a powered aircraft; but to the soaring pilot, they are only a beginning.

All pilots scan the weather pattern for convective activity. Remember that turbulence is proportional to the speed at which the aircraft penetrates adjacent updrafts and downdrafts. The fast moving powered aircraft experiences "pounding" and tries to avoid convective turbulence. The slower moving soaring pilot enjoys a gradual change from thermals to areas of sink. He chases after local convective cells using the thermals for lift.

A soaring aircraft is always sinking relative to the air. To maintain or gain altitude, therefore, the soaring pilot must spend sufficient time in thermals to overcome the normal sink of the aircraft as well as to regain altitude lost in downdrafts. He usually circles at a slow airspeed in a thermal and then darts on a beeline to the next thermal as shown in figure 147.

Low-level heating is prerequisite to thermals; and this heating is mostly from the sun, although

*Peter L. Dixon. SOARING, page 129; 1970; Ballantine Books, New York City.

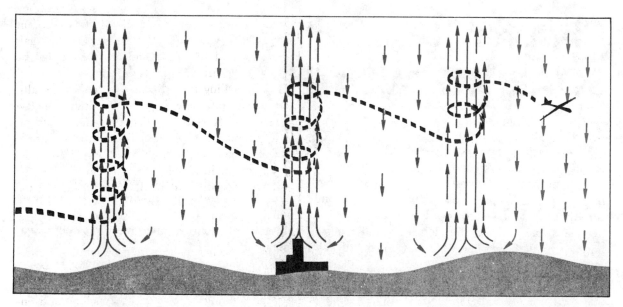

FIGURE 147. Thermals generally occur over a small portion of an area while downdrafts predominate. Updrafts in the thermals usually are considerably stronger than the downdrafts. Sailplane pilots gain altitude in thermals and hold altitude loss in downdrafts to a minimum.

it may be augmented by man-made heat sources such as chimneys, factories, and cities. Cool air must sink to force the warm air upward in thermals. Therefore, in small-scale convection, thermals and downdrafts coexist side by side. The net upward displacement of air must equal the net downward displacement. Fast rising thermals generally cover a small percentage of a convective area while slower downdrafts predominate over the remaining greater portion as diagrammed in figure 147.

Since thermals depend on solar heating, thermal soaring is restricted virtually to daylight hours with considerable sunshine. Air tends to become stable at night due to low-level cooling by terrestrial radiation, often resulting in an inversion at or near the surface (see chs. 3 and 6). Stable air suppresses convection, and thermals do not form until the inversion "burns off" or lifts sufficiently to allow soaring beneath the inversion. The earliest that soaring may begin varies from early forenoon to early afternoon, the time depending on the strength of the inversion and the amount of solar heating. Paramount to a pilot's soaring achievement is his skill in diagnosing and locating thermals.

LOCATING THERMALS

Since convective thermals develop from uneven heating at the surface, the most likely place for a thermal is above a surface that heats readily.

Types of Terrain Surfaces

When the sky is cloudless, the soaring pilot must look for those surfaces that heat most rapidly and seek thermals above those areas. Barren sandy or rocky surfaces, plowed fields, stubble fields surrounded by green vegetation, cities, factories, chimneys, etc., are good thermal sources. A pilot learns through experience the most favorable spots in his local area. But terrain features are only part of the story; time of day influences not only *when* thermals form but also *where*.

Sun Angle

Angle of the sun profoundly affects location of thermals over hilly landscapes. During early forenoon, the sun strikes eastern slopes more directly than other slopes; therefore, the most favorable areas for thermals are eastern slopes. The favorable areas move to southern slopes during midday. In the afternoon, they move to western slopes before they begin to weaken as the evening sun sinks toward the western horizon. For example, if a rocky knob protrudes above a grassy plain, the most likely area of thermals is over the eastern slope in the forenoon and the western slope in the afternoon. Once a pilot has sighted a likely surface, he may look for other visual cues.

Dust and Smoke

Surface winds must converge to feed a rising thermal; so when you sight a likely spot for a thermal, look for dust or smoke movement near the surface. If you can see dust or smoke "streamers" from two or more sources converging on the spot as shown in figure 148(A), you have chosen wisely. If, however, the streamers diverge as shown in figure 148(B), a downdraft most likely hovers over the spot and it's time to move on.

Rising columns of smoke from chimneys and factories mark thermals augmented by man-made sources. These rising columns are positive indication of thermals. They are good sources of lift if upward speed is great enough to support the aircraft and if they are broad enough to permit circling. Towns or cities may provide thermals; but to use a thermal over a populated area, the pilot must have sufficient altitude to glide clear of the area in event the thermal subsides.

Dust Devils

Dust devils occur under sunny skies over sandy or dusty, dry surfaces and are sure signs of strong thermals with lots of lift. To tackle this excellent source of lift, you must use caution. The thermals are strong and turbulent and are surrounded by areas of little lift or possibly of sink.

If approaching the dust devil at too low an altitude, an aircraft may sink to an altitude too low for recovery. A recommended procedure is to always approach the whirling vortex at an altitude 500 feet or more above the ground. At this altitude, you have enough airspace for maneuvering in the event you get into a downdraft or turbulence too great for comfort.

A dust devil may rotate either clockwise or counterclockwise. Before approaching the dusty column, determine its direction of rotation by observing dust and debris near the surface. Philip Wills* quotes R. H. Swinn, Chief Instructor of the Egyptian Gliding School, on approaching and en-

---

*Philip Wills. ON BEING A BIRD, page 79; 1953; Max Parrish and Co., Ltd.

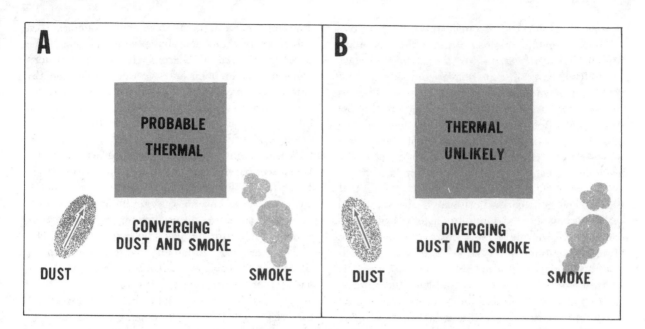

FIGURE 148. Using surface dust and smoke movement as indications of a thermal. When you have sighted an area which you think will heat rapidly (the red area), look for dust or smoke movement at the surface as an indicator of surface wind. Converging dust or smoke streamers (left) enhance the probability of a thermal. Diverging streamers reduce the likelihood of a thermal.

tering a dust devil: "... at around 500 feet; the pilot turns towards the dust devil and cuts his speed as he approaches it to the minimum consistent with the control of the glider. As he nears the whirling column of sand he makes a circle on the outside of the dust devil against the direction of rotation, care being taken to give it a wider berth on the downwind side. In light of the variometer reading on the initial circle, closer contact is made with the column or a hasty retreat is beat to a safer orbit."

FIGURE 149. Horizontal cross section of a dust devil rotating clockwise. If the aircraft approaches the dust devil with the direction of rotation as on the left, increasing tailwind reduces airspeed and may result in loss of altitude or even a stall. When the pilot regains equilibrium, his circling speed is the sum of his airspeed and the tangential speed of the vortex; his radius of turn may be too great to remain in the thermal. When approaching against the rotation, the aircraft gains airspeed; circling speed is slowed as the tangential speed of the vortex is subtracted from airspeed. The pilot has much more freedom and latitude for maneuvering. At the center is a core providing little or no lift. Immediately surrounding the core is a turbulent wall.

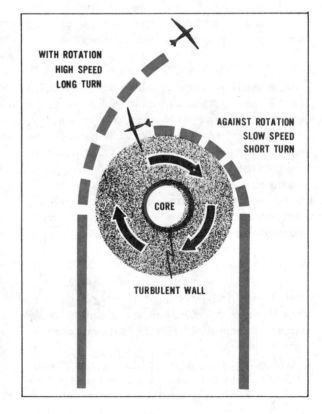

Why should you enter against the direction of rotation? Figure 149 diagrams a horizontal cross section of a clockwise rotating dust devil and ways of entering it. If you enter with the direction of rotation as on the left, the wind speed is added to your airspeed giving you a fast circling speed probably too great to remain in the thermal. Against the rotation as on the right, wind speed is subtracted from airspeed giving you a slow circling speed.

Why slow your airspeed to a minimum? As you approach the increasing headwinds, the inertia of the aircraft causes a surge in airspeed. If your approach is too fast, the surge could push the airspeed above the redline.

Stay out of the "eye" of the vortex. Centrifugal force in the center throws air outward, greatly reducing pressure within the hollow center. The rarified air in the center provides very little lift, and the wall of the hollow center is very turbulent. Further quoting Mr. Swinn,* "A too tight turn on the downwind side put a part of my inside wing into the vortex; the shock threw me into the straps and the wing bent in an alarming manner. This central area of greatly reduced pressure is something to be experienced to be believed. Closely following on this was the shock of hitting the area of greatest uplift just outside the central core. The net result was that the machine was thrown completely out of the column."

If you are 500 feet or more above the ground but having trouble finding lift, the dust devil is well worth a try. If the thermal is sufficiently broad to permit circling within it, you have it made. The dust column may be quite narrow, but this fact does not necessarily mean the thermal is narrow; the thermal may extend beyond the outer limits of visible dust. The way to find out is to try it. Approach the dusty column against the direction of rotation at minimum airspeed. Enter the column near the outer edge of the dust and stay away from the hollow vortex core. Remain alert; you are circling little more than a wing span away from violent turbulence.

Birds and Sailplanes

Soaring birds have an uncanny ability to locate thermals. When birds remain airborne without

*Ibid., page 80. Mr. Wills' book discusses at length the splendors and perils of dust devil flying by an experienced soaring pilot. It is recommended reading for a greater insight into this special aspect of soaring.

flapping their wings, they are riding a thermal. A climbing sailplane also shows the pilot's skill in locating thermals. When fishermen are scattered along a river bank or lake shore, the best place to cast your line is near the fisherman who is catching fish. So it is with soaring. Slip in below the successfully soaring aircraft and catch the thermal he is riding or cut in among or below soaring birds.

Wind causes a thermal to lean with altitude. When seeking the thermal supporting soaring birds or aircraft, you must make allowance for the wind. The thermal at lower levels usually is upwind from your high-level visual cue. A thermal may not be continuous from the surface upward to the soaring birds or sailplane; rather it may be in segments or bubbles. If you are unsuccessful in finding the thermal where you expect it, seek elsewhere.

Cumulus Clouds

When convective clouds develop, thermal soaring usually is at its best and the problem of locating thermals is greatly simplified. In chapter 6 we learned that upward moving air expands and cools as it rises. If the air is moist enough, expansional cooling lowers temperature to the dew point; a convective, or cumulus, cloud forms atop the thermal. Cumulus clouds are positive signs of thermals, but thermals grow and die. A cloud grows with a rising thermal; but when the thermal dies, the cloud slowly evaporates. Because the cloud dissipates *after* the thermal ceases, the pilot who can spot the difference between a growing and dying cumulus has enhanced his soaring skill.

The warmest and most rapidly rising air is in the center of the thermal. Therefore, the cloud base will be highest in the center giving a concave shape to the cloud base as shown in the left and center of figure 150. When the thermal ceases, the base assumes a convex shape as shown on the right. Another cue to look for is the outline of the cloud sides and top. Outline of the growing cumulus is firm and sharp. The dying cumulus has fragmentary sides and lacks the definite outline. These outlines are diagrammed also in figure 150. Figure 151 is a photograph of a dying cumulus.

You can expect to find a thermal beneath either of the growing cumuli in figure 150. On the average, the infant cumulus on the left would be the better choice because of its longer life expectancy. This is of course playing the probabilities since all cumuli do not grow to the same size.

As a cumulus cloud grows, it may shade the

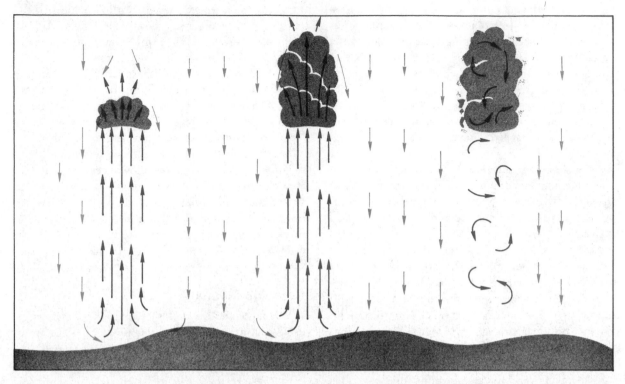

FIGURE 150. Cumulus clouds grow only with active thermals as shown left and center. On the right, the thermal has subsided and the cloud is decaying. Look for a thermal only under a cumulus with a concave base and sharp upper outlines. A cumulus with a convex base or fragmentary outline is dissipating; the thermal under it has subsided. Most often, a cloud just beginning to grow as on the left is the better choice because of its longer life expectancy.

surface that generated it. The surface cools, temporarily arresting the thermal. As the cloud dissipates or drifts away with the wind, the surface again warms and regenerates the thermal. This intermittent heating is one way in which thermals occur as segments or bubbles.

Cloud cover sometimes increases as surface heating increases until much of the sky is covered. Again, surface heating is cut off causing the thermals to weaken or cease entirely. The cloudiness may then decrease. If it is not too late in the day, thermals will regenerate. In the interim period of extensive cloud cover, you may have no choice but to land and wait for the clouds to move on or decrease in coverage.

The clouds may build upward to a high-level inversion and spread out at the base of the inversion to cover much of the sky. Solar heating is cut off and thermals weaken or die. This type of cloudiness can be persistent, often remaining until near sunset, and can halt thermal soaring until another day.

Although abundant convective cloud cover re-

duces thermal activity, we cannot quote a definite amount that renders thermals too weak for soaring. About 5/10 cover seems to be a good average approximation. Restriction of thermals by cumulus cloudiness first becomes noticeable at low levels. A sailplane may be unable to climb more than a few hundred feet at a low altitude while pilots at higher levels are maintaining height in or just beneath 6/10 to 8/10 convective cloud cover.

Towering Cumulus and Cumulonimbus

When air is highly unstable, the cumulus cloud can grow into a more ambitious towering cumulus or cumulonimbus. These clouds are a different breed. The energy released by copious condensation can increase buoyancy until the thermals become violent (see chs. 6, 7, and 11). Towering cumulus can produce showers. The cumulonimbus is the thunderstorm cloud producing heavy rain, hail, and icing. Well-developed *towering cumulus and cumulonimbus are for the experienced pilot only*. Some pilots find strong lift in or near convective precipitation, but they avoid hail which

FIGURE 151. Photograph of a dying cumulus. Note the indistinct edges and cloud fragments. The base appears to be convex. One would expect little or no lift beneath this cloud. In contrast, note the top of the cumulus in the lower left corner. Edges are more defined, and a thermal is more likely under this cloud.

can seriously batter the aircraft and ultimately deplete the wallet.

Violent thermals just beneath and within these highly developed clouds often are so strong that they will continue to carry a sailplane upward even with nose down and airspeed at the redline. The unwary pilot may find himself sucked into the cloud. The soaring pilot who inadvertently entered a thunderstorm and returned to tell about it never hankers for a repeat performance.

Middle and High Cloudiness

Dense, broken or overcast middle and high cloudiness shade the surface cutting off surface heating and convective thermals. On a generally warm bright day but with thin or patchy middle or high cloudiness, cumulus may develop, but the thermals are few and weak. The high-level cloudiness may drift by in patches. Thermals may surge and wane as the cloudiness decreases and increases. Never anticipate optimum thermal soaring when plagued by these mid- and high-level clouds.

Altocumulus castellanus clouds, middle-level convective clouds shown in figure 152, develop in updrafts at and just below the cloud levels. They do not extend upward from the surface. If a sailplane can reach levels near the cloud bases, the updrafts with altocumulus castellanus can be used in the same fashion as thermals formed by surface convection. The problem is reaching the convective level.

Wet Ground

Wet ground favors thermals less than dry ground since wet ground heats more slowly (see ch. 2,

FIGURE 152. Altocumulus castellanus clouds are middle level convective clouds. Most often, they develop in an unstable layer aloft, and thermals do not extend from the ground upward to these clouds. Convection with these clouds may be used for lift if the pilot is able to attain altitude to the base of the unstable layer. Smoke lying near the ground indicates stability in the lower levels.

"Heat and Temperature"). Some flat areas with wet soil such as swamps and tidewater areas have reputations for being poor thermal soaring areas. Convective clouds may be abundant but thermals generally are weak.

Showery precipitation from scattered cumulus or cumulonimbus is a sure sign of unstable air favorable for thermals. But when showers have soaked the ground in localized areas, downdrafts are almost certain over these wet surfaces. Avoid shower soaked areas when looking for lift.

So much for locating thermals. A pilot can also enhance his soaring skill by knowing what goes on within a thermal.

THERMAL STRUCTURE

Thermals are as varied as trees in a forest. No two are exactly alike. When surface heating is intense and continuous, a thermal, once begun, continues for a prolonged period in a steady column as in figure 153. Sometimes called the "chimney thermal," this type seems from experience to be most prevalent. In the chimney thermal, lift is available at any altitude below a climbing sailplane or soaring birds.

When heating is slow or intermittent, a "bubble" may be pinched off and forced upward; after an interval ranging from a few minutes to an hour or more, another bubble forms and rises as in figure 154. As explained earlier, intermittent shading by cumulus clouds forming atop a thermal is one reason for the bubble thermal. A sailplane or birds may be climbing in a bubble, but an aircraft attempting to enter the thermal at a lower altitude may find no lift.

A favored theoretical structure of some bubble thermals is the vortex shell which is much like a smoke ring blown upward as diagrammed in figure 155. Lift is strongest in the center of the ring; downdrafts may occur in the edges of the ring or

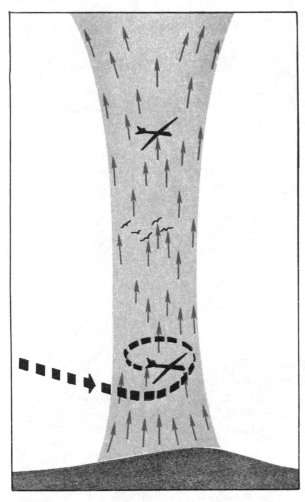

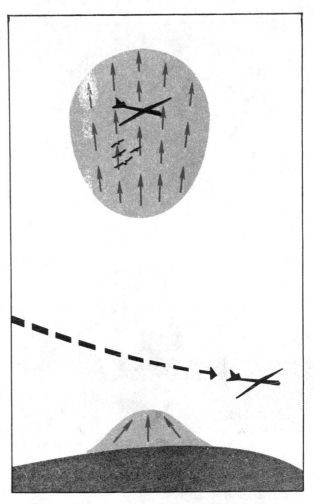

FIGURE 153. Experience indicates that the "chimney" thermal, which is continuous from the ground upward, is the most prevalent type. A sailplane can find lift in such a thermal beneath soaring birds or other soaring aircraft.

FIGURE 154. Thermals may be intermittent "bubbles." Frequency of the bubbles ranges from a few minutes to an hour or more. A soaring pilot will be disappointed when he seeks lift beneath birds or sailplanes soaring in this type thermal.

shell; and outside the shell, one would expect weak downdrafts.

Wind and Wind Shear

Thermals develop with a calm condition or with light, variable wind. However, it seems that a surface wind of 5 to 10 knots favors more organized thermals.

A surface wind in excess of 10 knots usually means stronger winds aloft resulting in vertical wind shear. This shear causes thermals to lean noticeably. When seeking a thermal under a climbing sailplane and you know or suspect that thermals are leaning in shear, look for lift upwind from the higher aircraft as shown in figure 156.

Effect of shear on thermals depends on the relative strength of the two. Strong thermals can remain fairly well organized with strong vertical wind shear; surface wind may even be at the maximum that will allow a safe launch. Weak thermals are disorganized and ripped to shreds by strong vertical wind shear; individual thermal elements become hard to find and often are too small to use for lift. A shear in excess of 3 knots per thousand feet distorts thermals to the extent that they are difficult to use.

No critical surface wind speed can tell us when to expect such a shear. However, shearing action often is visible in cumulus clouds. A cloud sometimes leans but shows a continuous chimney. At

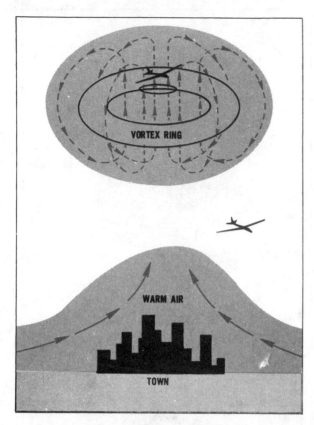

FIGURE 155. It is believed that a bubble thermal sometimes develops a vortex ring resembling a smoke ring blown straight upward. The center of the ring provides excellent lift. A pilot finds only weak lift or possibly sink in the fringes of the ring.

other times, the clouds are completely severed into segments by the shear as in figure 157. Remember, however, that this shearing action is at cloud level; thermals below the clouds may be well organized.

We must not overlook one other vital effect of the low-level wind shear. On final approach for landing, the aircraft is descending into decreasing headwind. Inertia of the aircraft into the decreasing wind causes a drop in airspeed. The decrease in airspeed may result in loss of control and perhaps a stall. The result can be an inelegant landing with possible injury and aircraft damage. A good rule is to add one knot airspeed to normal approach speed for each knot of surface wind.

Thermal Streets

Not infrequently, thermals become organized into "thermal streets." Generally, these streets are parallel to the wind; but on occasion they have

been observed at right angles to the wind. They form when wind direction changes little throughout the convective layer and the layer is capped by very stable air. The formation of a broad system of evenly spaced streets is enhanced when wind speed reaches a maximum within the convective layer; that is, wind increases with height from the surface upward to a maximum and then decreases with height to the top of the convective layer. Figure 158 diagrams conditions favorable for thermal streeting. Thermal streeting may occur either in clear air or with convective clouds.

The distance between streets in such a system is two to three times the general depth of the convective layer. If convective clouds are present, this distance is two to three times the height of the cloud tops. Downdrafts between these thermal streets are usually at least moderate and sometimes strong. Cumulus cloud streets frequently form in the United States behind cold fronts in the cold air of polar outbreaks in which relatively flat cumuli develop. A pilot can soar under a cloud street maintaining generally continuous flight and seldom, if ever, have to circle. Figure 159 is a photograph of bands of cumulus clouds marking thermal streets.

HEIGHT AND STRENGTH OF THERMALS

Since thermals are a product of instability, height of thermals depends on the depth of the unstable layer, and their strength depends on the degree of instability. If the idea of instability is not clear to you, now is the time to review chapter 6.

Most likely you will be soaring from an airport with considerable soaring activity—possibly the home base of a soaring club—and you are interested in a soaring forecast. Your airport may have an established source of a daily soaring weather forecast from the National Weather Service. If conditions are at all favorable for soaring, you will be specifically interested in the earliest time soaring can begin, how high the thermals will be, strength of the thermals, cloud amounts—both convective and higher cloudiness—visibility at the surface and at soaring altitudes, probability of showers, and winds both at the surface and aloft. The forecast may include such items as the thermal index (TI), the maximum temperature forecast, and the depth of the convective layer.

Many of these parameters the forecaster determines from upper air soundings plotted on a

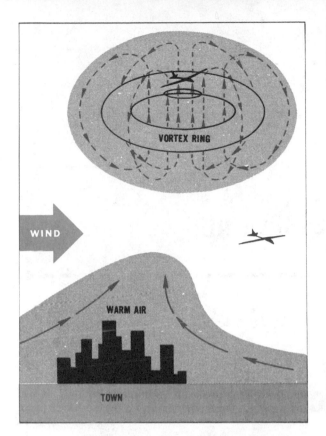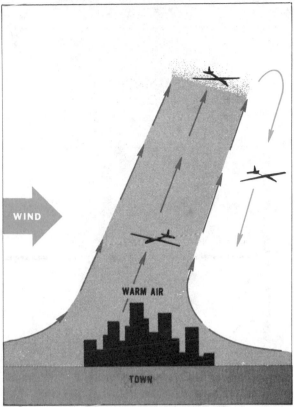

FIGURE 156.   Wind causes thermals to lean. A pilot seeking lift beneath soaring birds, other aircraft, or cumulus clouds should enter the thermal upwind from the higher level visual cue.

FIGURE 157.   Photograph of cumulus clouds severed by wind shear. Locating thermals and remaining in them under these clouds would be difficult.

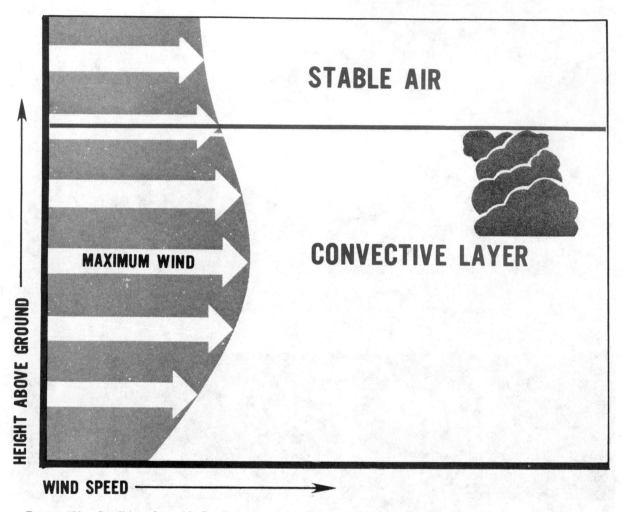

FIGURE 158. Conditions favorable for thermal streeting. A very stable layer caps the convective layer, and wind reaches a maximum within the convective layer. If cumulus clouds mark thermal streets, the top of the convective layer is about the height of the cloud tops.

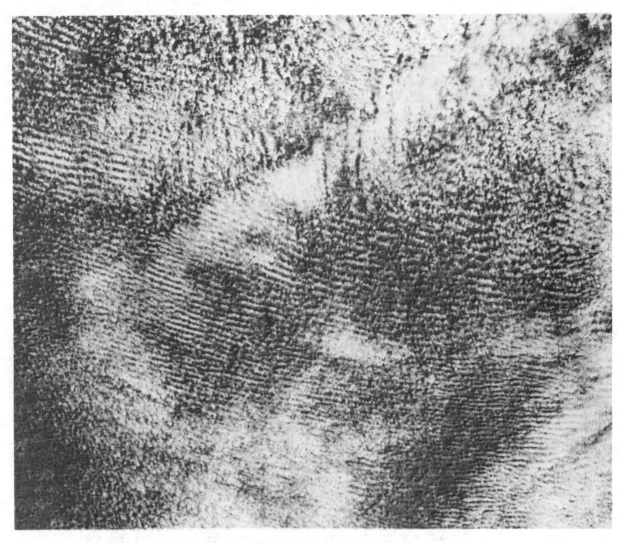

FIGURE 159.   Cumulus clouds in thermal streets photographed from a satellite by a high resolution camera. (Courtesy the National Environmental Satellite Service.)

pseudo-adiabatic chart. If you become familiar with this chart, you can better grasp the meanings of some of these forecast parameters; and you may try a little forecasting on your own.

The Pseudo-Adiabatic Chart

The pseudo-adiabatic chart is used to graphically compute adiabatic changes in vertically moving air and to determine stability. It has five sets of lines shown in figure 160. These lines are:

1. Pressure in millibars (horizontal lines),
2. Temperature in degrees Celsius (vertical lines),
3. Dry adiabats (sloping black lines),

4. Lines of constant water vapor or mixing ratio* (solid red lines), and
5. Moist adiabats (dashed red lines).

The chart also has an altitude scale in thousands of feet along the right margin and a Fahrenheit temperature scale across the bottom.

You might like to get one of these charts from a National Weather Service Office. The chart used in actual practice has a much finer grid than the one shown in figure 160. You can cover the chart with acetate and check examples given here along with others you can develop yourself. This procedure can greatly enhance your feel for processes occurring in a vertically moving atmosphere.

---

*Ratio of water vapor to dry air.

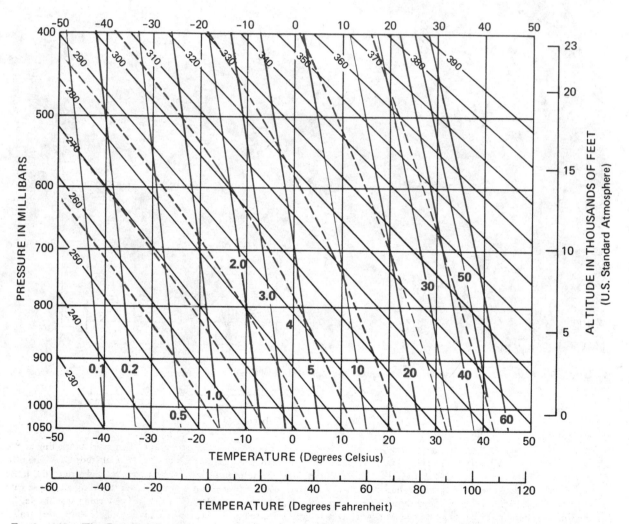

FIGURE 160. The Pseudo-Adiabatic Chart. Horizontal lines are pressure; vertical lines, temperature; sloping lines, dry adiabats graphing the rate of dry adiabatic cooling. Solid red lines are constant mixing ratio, and dashed red lines are moist adiabats graphing the saturated rate of cooling. Since red lines apply only to moist adiabatic changes, they are omitted from subsequent examples.

Examples shown here deal with dry thermals; and since the red lines in figure 160 concern moist adiabatic changes, they are omitted from the examples. If you care to delve deeper into use of the chart, you will find moist adiabatic processes even more intriguing than dry processes.

Plotted Sounding

An upper air observation, or sounding, is plotted on the pseudo-adiabatic chart as shown by the heavy, solid black line in figure 161. This plotting is the vertical temperature profile at the time the radiosonde observation was taken. It is the actual or existing lapse rate (see ch. 6). Blue lines are added to the illustration showing appropriate altitudes to aid you in interpreting the chart.

Depth of Convective Layer (Height of Thermals)

We know that for air to be unstable, the existing lapse rate must be equal to or greater than the dry adiabatic rate of cooling. In other words, in figure

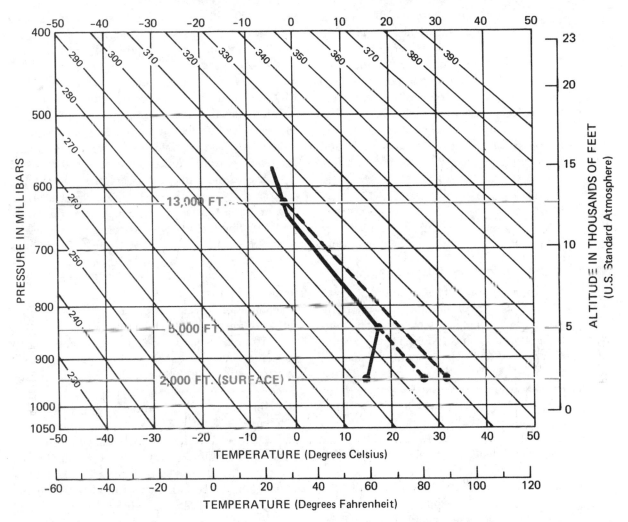

FIGURE 161. An early morning upper air observation plotted on the pseudo-adiabatic chart. The solid black line is the vertical temperature profile or existing lapse rate from the surface to about 15,000 feet ASL. Blue altitude lines are projected across the chart from the altitude scale on the right to aid in interpretation. If thermals are to develop, the lapse rate must become equal to or greater than the dry adiabatic rate of cooling—that is, the line representing the lapse rate must slope parallel to or slope more than the dry adiabats. Since it does not, the air in the early morning was stable. By the time the surface temperature reached 80° F, convection occurred to 5,000 feet; the existing lapse rate then was parallel to the dry adiabat following the dashed line from the surface to 5,000 feet; the air was unstable in the lower levels. By the time the temperature reached the afternoon maximum of 90° F, the air was unstable to 13,000 feet; the existing lapse rate in the heat of the day was dry adiabatic and the air unstable to 13,000 feet ASL. This is the maximum height you could expect thermals on this particular day.

161, the solid black line representing the plotted existing lapse rate would slope parallel to or slope more than the dry adiabats. Obviously it does not. Therefore, at the time the sounding was taken, the air was stable; there was no convective or unstable layer, and thermals were nonexistent. Thermal soaring was impossible.

Now assume that the sounding was made about the time of sunrise. Surface temperature was 59° F (15° C). As temperature rises near the surface during the day, air in the lower levels is warmed and forced upward, cooling at the dry adiabatic rate. Convection begins in the lowest levels. By the time the surface temperature reaches 80° F (about 27° C), convection lifts the air to the level at which it cools adiabatically to the temperature of the surrounding air at 5,000 feet. The existing lapse rate now becomes dry adiabatic from the surface to 5,000 feet and follows the dashed line from the surface to that level. Surface elevation is 2,000 feet ASL; so the convective layer is now 3,000 feet deep. Thermals exist to 3,000 feet above the surface, and low-level soaring is now possible. Above 5,000 feet the lapse rate still is essentially unchanged from the initial lapse rate.

Maximum Height of Thermals

Let's further assume that maximum temperature forecast for the day is 90° F (about 30° C). Plot 90° F at the surface elevation and draw a line (the dashed black line) parallel to the dry adiabats to the level at which it intersects the early morning sounding. This level is 13,000 feet ASL. The convective layer at time of maximum heating would be 11,000 feet deep and soaring should be possible to 13,000 feet ASL. The existing lapse rate in the heat of the day would follow the dashed line from the surface to 13,000 feet; above 13,000, the lapse rate would remain essentially unchanged.

Remember that we are talking about dry thermals. If convective clouds form below the indicated maximum thermal height, they will greatly distort the picture. However, if cumulus clouds do develop, thermals below the cloud base should be strengthened. If more higher clouds develop than were forecast, they will curtail surface heating, and most likely the maximum temperature will be cooler than forecast. Thermals will be weaker and will not reach as high an altitude.

Thermal Index (TI)

Since thermals depend on sinking cold air forcing warm air upward, strength of thermals depends on the temperature difference between the sinking air and the rising air—the greater the temperature difference the stronger the thermals. To arrive at an approximation of this difference, the forecaster computes a thermal index (TI).

A thermal index may be computed for any level; but ordinarily, indices are computed for the 850- and 700-millibar levels, or about 5,000 and 10,000 feet respectively. These levels are selected because they are in the altitude domain of routine soaring and because temperature data are routinely available for these two levels.

Three temperature values are needed—the observed 850-millibar and 700-millibar temperatures and the forecast maximum temperature. Let's assume a sounding as in figure 162 with an 850-millibar temperature of 15° C, a 700-millibar temperature of 10° C, and forecast maximum of 86° F (30° C). Plot the three temperatures using care to place the maximum temperature plot at field elevation (2,000 feet in figure 162). Now draw a line (the black dashed line) through the maximum temperature parallel to the dry adiabats. Note that the dashed line intersects the 850-millibar level at 20° C and the 700-millibar level at 4° C. Algebraically subtract these temperatures from actual sounding temperatures at corresponding levels. Note the difference is −5° C at 850 millibars (15 − 20 = −5) and +6 at 700 millibars (10 − 4 = +6). These values are the TI's at the two levels.

Strength of thermals is proportional to the magnitude of the negative value of the TI. A TI of −8 or −10 predicts very good lift and a long soaring day. Thermals with this high a negative value will be strong enough to hold together even on a windy day. A TI of −3 indicates a very good chance of sailplanes reaching the altitude of this temperature difference. A TI of −2 to zero leaves much doubt; and a positive TI offers even less hope of thermals reaching the altitude. Remember that the TI is a forecast value. A miss in the forecast maximum or a change in temperature aloft can alter the picture considerably. The example in figure 162 should promise fairly strong thermals to above 5,000 feet but no thermals to 10,000.

Figure 163 is another example showing an early morning sounding with a 3,000-foot surface temperature of 10° C (50° F), an 850-millibar temperature of 15° C, a 700-millibar temperature of 3° C, and a forecast maximum of 86° F (30° C). What are the TI's at 850 and 700 millibars? Would you expect thermals to 850 millibars? Would they

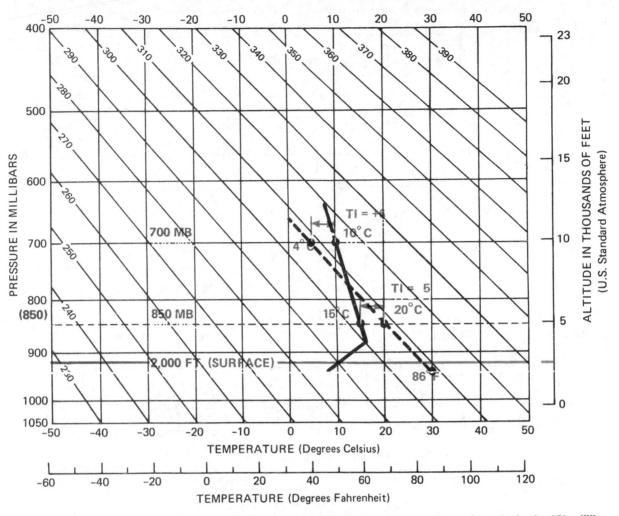

FIGURE 162. Computing the thermal index (TI). From an early morning upper air observation, obtain the 850-millibar and 700-millibar temperatures—15° C and 10° C respectively, in this example. Obtain a forecast maximum temperature, 86° F, and plot it at the surface elevation. Draw a dry adiabat, the dashed line, upward through the 700-millibar level. This dry adiabat is the temperature profile of a rising column of air. To find the TI at any level, subtract the temperature of the rising column at that level from the temperature of the original sounding at the same level. The TI at 850 millibars is −5 (15 − 20 = −5). At 700 millibars, the TI is +6 (10 − 4 = +6).

be moderate, strong, or weak? How about at 700 millibars? What is the maximum altitude you would expect thermals to reach? *Answers:* 850-millibar TI, −8; 700-millibar TI, −5; thermals would reach both levels, strong at 850, moderate at 700; maximum altitude of thermals, about 16,000 feet ASL.

Often the National Weather Service will have no upper air sounding taken near a soaring base. Forecasts must be based on a simulated sounding derived from distant observations. At other times, for some reason a forecast may not be available. Furthermore, you can often augment the forecast with local observations. You are never at a complete loss to apply some of the techniques just described.

Do It Yourself

The first step in determining height and strength of thermals is to obtain a local sounding. How do you get a local sounding? Send your tow aircraft aloft about sunrise and simply read outside air temperatures from the aircraft thermometer and altitudes from the altimeter. Read temperatures at 500-foot intervals for about the first 2,000 feet and at 1,000-foot intervals at higher altitudes. The information may be radioed back to the ground, or

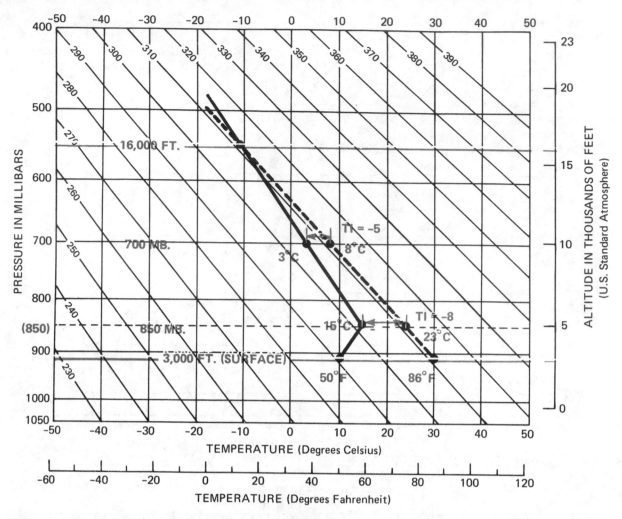

FIGURE 163. Another example of computing TI's and maximum height of thermals. See discussion in caption of figure 162. By the time of maximum heating, excellent lift should be available in lower levels and moderate lift above 10,000 feet. Although thermals should continue to 16,000 feet, you could expect weak lift above 12,000 or 13,000 feet because of the small difference between temperatures in the thermal and in the surrounding air.

may be recorded in flight and analyzed after landing. When using the latter method, read temperatures on both ascent and descent and average the temperatures at each level. This type of sounding is an airplane observation or APOB. Plot the sounding on the pseudo-adiabatic chart using the altitude scale rather than the pressure scale.

Next we need a forecast maximum temperature. Perhaps you can pick up this forecast temperature from the local forecast. If not, you can use your best judgment comparing today's weather with yesterday's.

Following is an APOB as taken by the tow aircraft from an airport elevation of 1,000 feet ASL:

Alt.	Temperatures °C		
	Ascent	Descent	Avg.
1000	17	19	18
1500	15	17	16
2000	20	20	20
2500	22	24	23
3000	22	22	22
4000	20	18	19
5000	18	18	18
6000	16	14	15
7000	13	13	13
8000	9	9	9
9000	7	5	6
10000	5	3	4
11000	1	1	1
12000	−3	−1	−2
13000	−5	−5	−5
14000	−6	−6	−6
15000	−7	..	−7

Plot the APOB on the pseudo-adiabatic chart using the average temperatures from the last column. Figure 164 shows the plotted APOB.

Next we need a forecast maximum temperature. Let's assume that a local forecast is not available and that weather today is essentially the same as it was yesterday. Yesterday's maximum was 95° F (35° C), so let's use the same maximum for today. We should not be too far wrong. Plot the maximum as shown and proceed to compute TI's and maximum height of thermals. Since our temperature data are for indicated altitudes rather than pressure levels, let's compute TI's for 5,000 feet and 10,000 feet rather than for pressure levels. What do you get for a TI at 5,000 feet? At 10,000 feet? What is the anticipated maximum altitude of thermals? *Answers:* TI at 5,000 feet, —4; TI at 10,000 feet, —3; maximum altitude of thermals, 14,000 feet.

Although these procedures are primarily for dry thermals, they work reasonably well for thermals below the bases of convective clouds.

Convective Cloud Bases

Soaring experience suggests a shallow, stable layer immediately below the general level of convective cloud bases through which it is difficult to soar. This layer is 200 to 600 feet thick and is known as the *sub-cloud layer*. The layer appears to act as a filter allowing only the strongest ther-

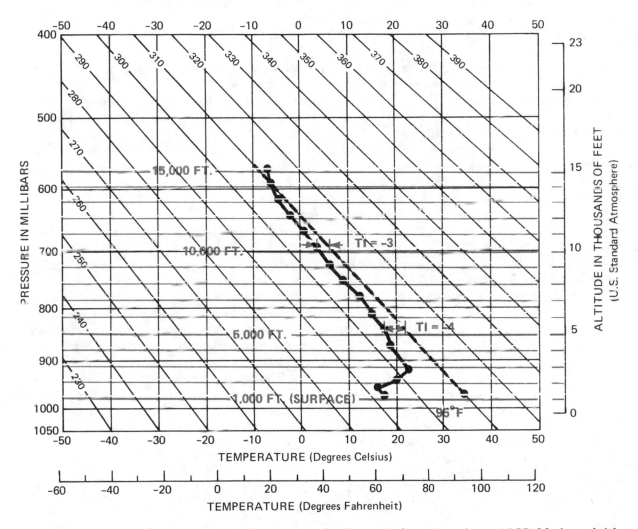

FIGURE 164.   An upper air observation made from an aircraft called an airplane observation or APOB. Maximum height of thermals and TI's are computed the same as in preceding examples except that TI's are for indicated altitudes instead of pressure levels. The APOB may be used in lieu of or as a supplement to the forecast.

mals to penetrate it and form convective clouds. Strongest thermals are beneath developing cumulus clouds.

Thermals intensify within a convective cloud; but evaporation cools the outer edges of the cloud causing a downdraft immediately surrounding it. Add to this the fact that downdrafts predominate between cumulus clouds, and you can see the slim chance of finding lift between clouds above the level of the cloud base. In general, thermal soaring during convective cloud activity is practical only at levels below the cloud base.

In chapter 6, we learned to estimate height in thousands of feet of a convective cloud base by dividing the surface temperature–dew point spread by 4. If the rising column were self-contained—that is, if no air were drawn into the sides of the thermal—the method would give a fairly accurate height of the base. However, this is not the case. Air *is* entrained or drawn into the sides of the thermal; and this entrained air lowers the water vapor content of the thermal allowing it to reach a somewhat higher level before condensation occurs. Bases of the clouds are generally 10 to 15 percent higher than the computed height.

Entrainment is a sticky problem; observers and forecasters can only estimate its effect. Until a positive technique is developed, heights of cumulus bases will tend to be reported and forecast too low. Currently, in the eastern United States, cumulus bases are seldom reported above 6,000 feet when the base may actually be 7,000 or 8,000 feet. In the western part of the country, cumulus bases have been observed by aircraft at 12,000 to 14,000 feet above the ground but seldom are reported above 10,000 feet.

CROSS-COUNTRY THERMAL SOARING

A pilot can soar cross-country using either isolated thermals or thermal streets. When using isolated thermals, he gains altitude circling in thermals and then proceeds toward the next thermal in the general direction of his cross-country. Under a thermal street, he may be able to proceed with little if any circling if his chosen course parallels the thermal streets. It goes without saying that he can obtain the greatest distance by flying in the direction of the wind.

In the central and eastern United States, the most favorable weather for cross-country soaring occurs behind a cold front. Lindsay* has found that about 82 percent of thermal cross-countrys in these areas were made after a cold front had passed and ahead of the following high pressure center. Four factors contribute to making this pattern ideal. (1) The cold polar air is usually dry, and thermals can build to relatively high altitudes. (2) The polar air is colder than the ground; and thus, the warm ground aids solar radiation in heating the air. Thermals begin earlier in the morning and last later in the evening. On occasions, soarable lift has been found at night. (3) Quite often, colder air at high altitudes moves over the cold, low-level outbreak intensifying the instability and strengthening the thermals. (4) The wind profile frequently favors thermal streeting—a real boon to speed and distance.

The same four factors may occur with cold frontal passages over mountainous regions in the western United States. However, rugged mountains break up the circulation; and homogeneous conditions extend over smaller areas than over the eastern parts of the country. The western mountain regions and particularly the desert southwest have one decided advantage. Air is predominantly dry with more abundant daytime thermal activity favoring cross-country soaring although it may be for shorter distances.

Among the world's most favorable tracks for long distance soaring is a high plains corridor along the east slope of the Rocky Mountains stretching from southwest Texas to Canada.** Many cross-country records have been set in this corridor. Southwest Texas is the chosen site for many national and international soaring meets. Terrain in the corridor is relatively flat and high with few trees; terrain surface ranges from barren to short grass. These surface features favor strong thermal activity. Prevailing wind is southerly and moderately strong giving an added boost to northbound cross-countrys.

---

*Charles V. Lindsay. "Types of Weather Favoring Cross-Country Soaring." *Soaring*, December 1964, pp. 6–9.

** For an in-depth discussion of this area, see "Thermal Soaring—Southwest Style," by David H. Owens, *Soaring*, May 1966, pp. 10–12.

FRONTAL SOARING

Warm air forced upward over cold air above a frontal surface can provide lift for soaring. However, good frontal lift is transitory, and it accounts for a very small portion of powerless flight. Seldom will you find a front parallel to your desired cross-country route, and seldom will it stay in position long enough to complete a flight. A slowly moving front provides only weak lift. A fast moving front often plagues the soaring pilot with cloudiness and turbulence.

A front can on occasion provide excellent lift for a short period. You may on a cross-country be riding wave or ridge lift and need to move over a flat area to take advantage of thermals. A front may offer lift during your transition.

Fronts often are marked by a change in cloud type or amount. However, the very presence of clouds may deter you from the front. Spotting a dry front is difficult. Knowing that a front is in the vicinity and studying your aircraft reaction can tell you when you are in the frontal lift. Staying in the lift is another problem. Observing ground indicators of surface wind helps.

An approaching front may enhance thermal or hill soaring. An approaching front or a frontal passage most likely will disrupt a sea breeze or mountain wave. Post frontal thermals in cold air were discussed earlier.

SEA BREEZE SOARING

In many coastal areas during the warm seasons, a pleasant breeze from the sea occurs almost daily. Caused by the heating of land on warm, sunny days, the sea breeze usually begins during early forenoon, reaches a maximum during the afternoon, and subsides around dusk after the land has cooled. The leading edge of the cool sea breeze forces warmer air inland to rise as shown in figure 165. Rising air from over land returns seaward at higher altitude to complete the convective cell.

A sailplane pilot operating in or near coastal areas often can find lift generated by this convective circulation. The transition zone between the cool, moist air from the sea and the warm, drier air inland is often narrow and is a shallow, ephemeral kind of pseudo-cold front.

SEA BREEZE FRONT

Sometimes the wedge of cool air is called a sea breeze front. If sufficient moisture is present, a line of cumuliform clouds just inland may mark the front. Whether marked by clouds or not, the upward moving air at the sea breeze front occasionally is strong enough to support soaring flight. Within the sea breeze, i.e., between the sea breeze front and the ocean, the air is usually stable, and normally, no lift may be expected at lower levels. However, once airborne, pilots occasionally have found lift at higher levels in the return flow aloft. A visual indication of this lift is cumulus extending seaward from the sea breeze front.

The properties of a sea breeze front and the extent of its penetration inland depend on factors such as the difference in land and sea water temperatures, general wind flow, moisture, and terrain.

Land vs Sea Water Temperature

A large difference in land and sea water temperature intensifies the convective cell generating a sea breeze. Where coastal waters are quite cool, such as along the California coast, and land temperatures warm rapidly in the daytime, the sea breeze becomes pronounced, penetrating perhaps 50 to 75 miles inland at times. Copious sunshine and cool sea waters favor a well-developed sea breeze front.

Strength and Direction of General Wind

The sea breeze is a local effect. Strong pressure gradients with a well-developed pressure system can overpower the sea breeze effect. Winds will follow the direction and speed dictated by the strong pressure gradient. Therefore, a sea breeze front is most likely when pressure gradient is weak and wind is light.

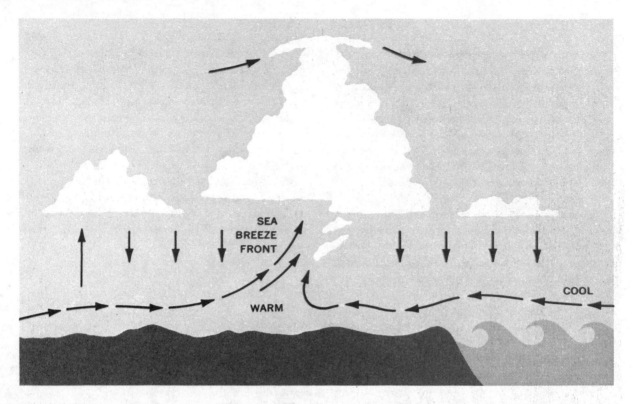

FIGURE 165. Schematic cross section through a sea breeze front. If the air inland is moist, cumulus often marks the front.

Moisture

When convection is very deep, the frontal effect of a sea breeze may sometimes trigger cumulonimbus clouds provided the lifted air over land contains sufficient moisture. More often, the cumulus are of limited vertical extent. Over vegetation where air is usually moist, sea breeze cumulus are the rule. Over arid regions, little or no cumulus development may be anticipated with a sea breeze front.

Terrain

Irregular or rough terrain in a coastal area may amplify the sea breeze front and cause convergence lines of sea breezes originating from different areas. Southern California and parts of the Hawaiian Islands are favorable for sea breeze soaring because orographic lift is added to the frontal convection. Sea breezes occasionally may extend to the leeward sides of hills and mountains unless the ranges are high and long without abrupt breaks. In either case, the sea breeze front converges on the windward slopes, and upslope winds augment the convection. Where terrain is fairly flat, sea breezes may

penetrate inland for surprising distances but with weaker lift along the sea breeze front. In the Tropics, sea breezes sometimes penetrate as much as 150 miles inland, while an average of closer to 50 miles inland is more usual in middle latitudes. Sea breezes reaching speeds of 15 to 25 knots are not uncommon.

VISUAL CLUES

When a sea breeze front develops, visual observations may provide clues to the extent of lift that you may anticipate, viz.:

1. Expect little or no lift on the seaward side of the front when the sea air is markedly void of convective clouds or when the sea breeze spreads low stratus inland. However, some lift may be present along the leading edge of the sea breeze or just ahead of it.
2. Expect little or no lift on the seaward side of the front when visibility decreases markedly in the sea breeze air. This is an indicator of stable air within the sea breeze.
3. A favorable visual indication of lift along the sea breeze front is a line of cumulus clouds marking the front; cumuli between

the sea breeze front and the ocean also indicate possible lift within the sea breeze air, especially at higher levels. Cumulus bases in the moist sea air often are lower than along the front.

4. When a sea breeze front is void of cumulus but converging streamers of dust or smoke are observed, expect convection and lift along the sea breeze front.

5. Probably the best combination to be sighted is cumuli and converging dust or smoke plumes along the sea breeze front as it moves upslope over hills or mountains. The upward motion is amplified by the upslope winds.

6. A difference in visibility between the sea air and the inland air often is a visual clue to the leading edge of the sea breeze. Visibility in the sea air may be restricted by haze while visibility inland is unrestricted. On the other hand, the sea air may be quite clear while visibility inland is restricted by dust or smoke.

LOCAL SEA BREEZE EXPLORATIONS

Unfortunately, a sea breeze front is not always easy to find, and it is likely that many an opportunity for sea breeze soaring goes unnoticed. As yet, little experience has been accrued in locating a belt of sea breeze lift without visual clues such as clouds, haze, or converging smoke or dust plumes. As the sport of soaring grows, so will the knowledge of sea breeze soaring expand and the peculiarities of more local areas come to light. In the United States, the area where the most experience probably has been gained is over the southern California high desert where the sea breeze moves eastward over the Los Angeles Coastal Plain into the Mojave Desert.

Los Angeles "Smoke Front"

The sea breeze front moving from the Los Angeles coastal plain into the Mojave Desert has been dubbed the "Smoke Front." It has intense thermal activity and offers excellent lift along the leading edge of the front. Associated with the sea breeze

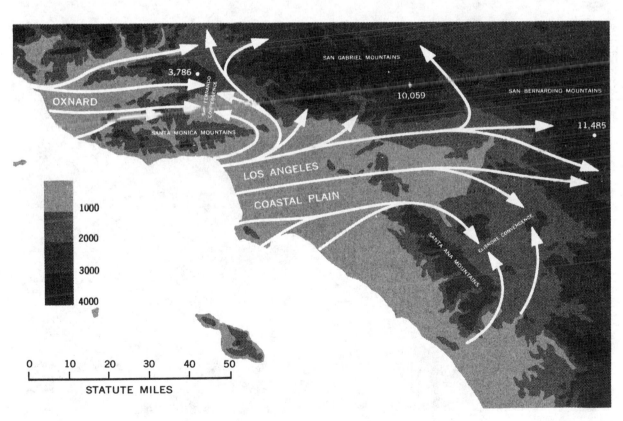

FIGURE 166. Sea breeze flow into the San Fernando Valley. Note the San Fernando convergence zone, upper left, and the Elsinore convergence zone, lower right.

193

that moves inland over the Los Angeles coastal plain are two important zones of convergence, shown in figure 166. Sea breezes of different origin meet in the convergence zones producing vertical currents capable of supporting sailplanes. One convergence line is the "San Fernando Convergence Zone;" a larger scale zone is in the Elsinore area, also shown in figure 166. This convergence zone apparently generates strong vertical currents since soaring pilots fly back and forth across the valley along the line separating smoky air to the north from relatively clear air to the south. Altitudes reached depend upon the stability, but usually fall within the 6,000 feet to 12,000 feet ASL range for the usual dry thermal type lift. Seaward, little or no lift is experienced in the sea breeze air marked by poor visibility.

Cape Cod Peninsula

Figure 167 shows converging air between sea breezes flowing inland from opposite coasts of the Cape Cod Peninsula. Later in the development of the converging sea breezes, the onset of convection is indicated by cumulus over the peninsula. Sailplane pilots flying over this area as well as over Long Island, New York, have found good lift in the convergence lines caused by sea breezes blowing inland from both coasts of the narrow land strips.

Great Lakes Area

Sea breeze fronts have been observed along the shore lines of the Great Lakes. Weather satellites have also photographed this sea breeze effect on the western shore of Lake Michigan. It is quite likely that conditions favorable for soaring occur at times.

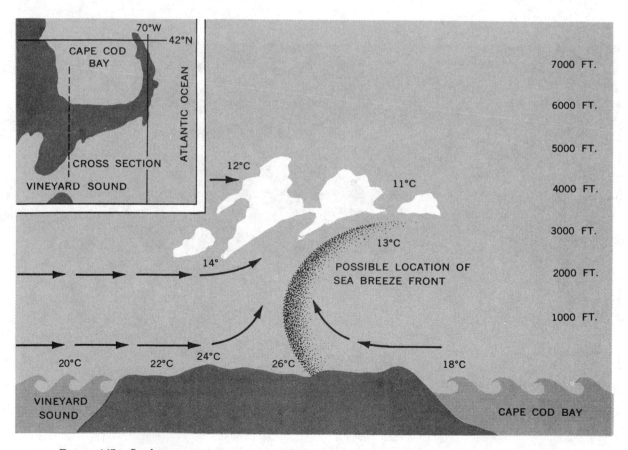

FIGURE 167. Sea breeze convergence zone, Cape Cod, Massachusetts. Sea breezes from opposite coasts converge over the cape.

194

RIDGE OR HILL SOARING

Wind blowing toward hills or ridges flows upward, over, and around the abrupt rises in terrain. The upward moving air creates lift which is sometimes excellent for soaring. Figure 168 is a schematic showing area of best lift. Ridge or hill soaring offers great sport to the sailplane pilot who accepts the challenge and can wait for proper wind and stability combinations.

WIND

To create lift over hills or ridges, wind direction should be within about 30 to 40 degrees normal to the ridge line. A sustained speed of 15 knots or more usually generates enough lift to support a sailplane. Height of the lift usually is two or three times the height of the rise from the valley floor to the ridge crest. Strong winds tend to increase turbulence and low-level eddies without an appreciable increase in the height of the lift.

STABILITY

Stability affects the continuity and extent of lift over hills or ridges. Stable air allows relatively streamlined upslope flow. A pilot experiences little or no turbulence in the steady, uniform area of best lift shown in figure 168. Since stable air tends to return to its original level, air spilling over the crest and downslope is churned into a snarl of leeside eddies, also shown in figure 168. Thus, stable air favors smooth lift but troublesome leeside low-altitude turbulence.

When the airstream is moist and unstable, upslope lift may release the instability generating strong convective currents and cumulus clouds over windward slopes and hill crests. The initially laminar flow is broken up into convective cells. While the updrafts produce good lift, strong downdrafts may compromise low altitude flight over rough terrain. As with thermals, the lift will be transitory rather than smooth and uniform.

STEEPNESS OF SLOPE

Very gentle slopes provide little or no lift. Most favorable for soaring is a smooth, moderate slope. An ideal slope is about 1 to 4 which with an upslope wind of 15 knots creates lift of about 6 feet

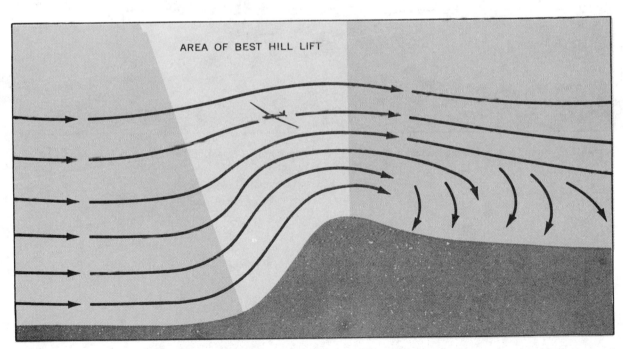

AREA OF BEST HILL LIFT

FIGURE 168. Schematic cross section of airflow over a ridge. Note the area of best lift. Downdrafts predominate leeward in the "wind shadow."

per second. With the same slope, a high-performance sailcraft with a sinking speed of 2 feet per second presumably could remain airborne with only a 5-knot wind!

Very steep escarpments or rugged slopes induce turbulent eddies. Strong winds extend these eddies to a considerable height usually disrupting any potential lift. The turbulent eddies also enhance the possibility of a low-altitude upset.

CONTINUITY OF RIDGES

Ridges extending for several miles without abrupt breaks tend to provide uniform lift through-

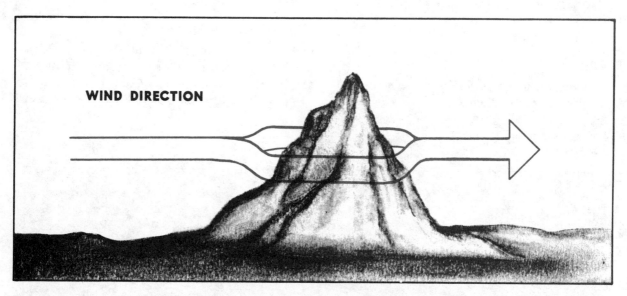

FIGURE 169.   Strong winds flowing around an isolated peak produce little lift. During light winds, sunlit slopes may be a favored location for thermals.

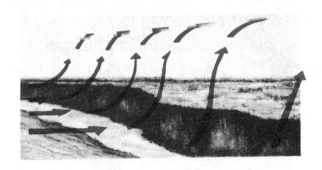

out their length. In contrast, a single peak diverts wind flow around the peak as well as over it and thus is less favorable for soaring. Figure 169 shows wind flow around an isolated peak.

Some wind flow patterns over ridges and hills are illustrated in figure 170. Deviations from these patterns depend on wind direction and speed, on stability, on slope profile, and on general terrain roughness.

SOARING IN UPSLOPE LIFT

The soaring pilot, always alert, must remain especially so in seeking or riding hill lift. You may be able to spot indicators of good lift. Other clues may mark areas to avoid.

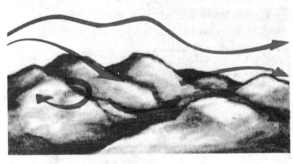

When air is unstable, do not venture too near the slope. You can identify unstable air either by the updrafts and downdrafts in dry thermals or by cumulus building over hills or ridges. Approaching at too low an altitude may suddenly put you in a downdraft, forcing an inadvertent landing.

When winds are strong, surface friction may create low-level eddies even over relatively smooth slopes. Also, friction may drastically reduce the effective wind speed near the surface. When climbing at low altitude toward a slope under these conditions, be prepared to turn quickly toward the valley in event you lose lift. Renew your attempt to climb farther from the hill.

If winds are weak, you may find lift only very near the sloping surface. Then you must "hug" the slope to find needed lift. However, avoid this procedure if there are indications of up and down drafts. In general, for any given slope, keep your distance from the slope proportional to wind speed.

Leeward of hills and ridges is an area where wind is blocked by the obstruction. Among soaring circles this area is called the "wind shadow." In the wind shadow, downdrafts predominate as shown in figure 168. If you stray into the wind shadow at an altitude near or below the altitude of the ridge crest, you may be embarrassed by an unscheduled and possibly rough landing. Try to stay within the area of best lift shown in figure 168.

FIGURE 170. Windflow over various types of terrain. The many deviations from these patterns depend on wind speed, slope profile, and terrain roughness.

MOUNTAIN WAVE SOARING

The great attraction of soaring in mountain waves stems from the continuous lift to great heights. Soaring flights to above 35,000 feet have frequently been made in mountain waves. Once a soaring pilot has reached the rising air of a mountain wave, he has every prospect of maintaining flight for several hours. While mountain wave soaring is related to ridge or hill soaring, the lift in a mountain wave is on a larger scale and is less transitory than lift over smaller rises in terrain. Figure 171 is a cross section of a typical mountain wave.

FORMATION

When strong winds blow across a mountain range, large "standing" waves occur downwind from the mountains and upward to the tropopause. The waves may develop singly; but more often, they occur as a series of waves downstream from the mountains. While the waves remain about stationary, strong winds are blowing through them.

You may compare a mountain wave to a series of waves formed downstream from a submerged rocky ridge in a fast flowing creek or river. Air dips sharply immediately to the lee of a ridge, then rises and falls in a wave motion downstream.

A strong mountain wave requires:

1. Marked stability in the airstream disturbed by the mountains. Rapidly building cumulus over the mountains visually marks the air unstable; convection, evidenced by the cumulus, tends to deter wave formation.

2. Wind speed at the level of the summit should exceed a minimum which varies from 15 to 25 knots depending on the height of the range. Upper winds should increase or at least remain constant with height up to the tropopause.

3. Wind direction should be within 30 degrees normal to the range. Lift diminishes as winds more nearly parallel the range.

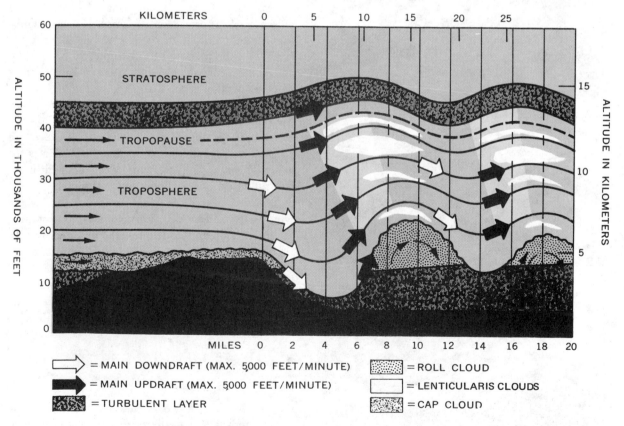

FIGURE 171. Schematic cross section of a mountain wave. Best lift is upwind from each wave crest for about one-third the distance to the preceding wave crest.

WAVE LENGTH AND AMPLITUDE

Wave length is the horizontal distance between crests of successive waves and is usually between 2 and 25 miles. In general, wave length is controlled by wind component perpendicular to the ridge and by stability of the upstream flow. Wave length is directly proportional to wind speed and inversely proportional to stability. Figure 172 illustrates wave length and also amplitude.

Amplitude of a wave is the vertical dimension and is half the altitude difference between the wave trough and crest. In a typical wave, amplitude varies with height above the ground. It is least near the surface and near the tropopause. Greatest amplitude is roughly 3,000 to 6,000 feet above the ridge crest. Wave amplitude is controlled by size and shape of the ridge as well as wind and stability. A shallow layer of great stability and moderate wind produces a greater wave amplitude than does a deep layer of moderate stability and strong winds. Also, the greater the amplitude, the shorter is the wave length. Waves offering the strongest and most consistent lift are those with great amplitude and short wave length.

VISUAL INDICATORS

If the air has sufficient moisture, lenticular (lens-shaped) clouds mark wave crests. Cooling of air ascending toward the wave crest saturates the air forming clouds. Warming of air descending beyond the wave crest evaporates the cloud. Thus, by continuous condensation windward of the wave crest and evaporation leeward, the cloud appears stationary although wind may be blowing through the wave at 50 knots or more. Lenticular clouds in successive bands downstream from the mountain mark a series of wave crests.

Spacing of lenticulars marks the wave length. Clearly identifiable lenticulars also suggest larger wave amplitude than clouds which barely exhibit lenticular form. These cloud types along with stratiform clouds on the windward slopes and along the mountain crest indicate the stability favorable to mountain wave soaring.

Thunderstorms or rapidly building cumulus over mountains mark the air unstable. As they reach maturity, the thunderstorms often drift downwind across leeward valleys and plains. Strong convective currents in the unstable air deter wave formation. If you sight numerous instability clouds, wait until another day for mountain wave soaring.

SOARING TURBULENCE

A mountain wave, in a manner similar to that in a thermal, means turbulence to powered aircraft, but to a slowly moving sailcraft, it produces lift

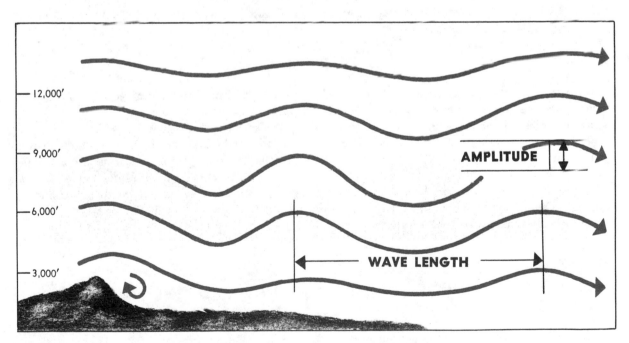

FIGURE 172. Wave length and amplitude.

and sink above the level of the mountain crest. But as air spills over the crest like a waterfall, it causes strong downdrafts. The violent overturning forms a series of "rotors" in the wind shadow of the mountain which are hazardous even to a sailplane (see ch. 9, figs. 81 through 84). Clouds resembling long bands of stratocumulus sometimes mark the area of overturning air. These "rotor clouds" appear to remain stationary, parallel the range, and stand a few miles leeward of the mountains. Turbulence is most frequent and most severe in the standing rotors just beneath the wave crests at or below mountain-top levels. This rotor turbulence is especially violent in waves generated by large mountains such as the Rockies. Rotor turbulence with lesser mountains is much less severe but is always present to some extent. The turbulence is greatest in well-developed waves.

FAVORED AREAS

Mountain waves occur most frequently along the central and northern Rockies and the northern Appalachians. Occasionally, waves form to the lee of mountains in Arkansas, Oklahoma, and southwestern Texas. Weather satellites have observed waves extending great distances downwind from the Rocky Mountains; one series extended for nearly 700 miles. The more usual distance is 150 to 300 miles. While Appalachian waves are not as strong as those over the Rockies, they occur frequently; and satellites have observed them at an average of 115 miles downwind. Wave length of these waves averages about 10 nautical miles.

RIDING THE WAVES

You often can detect a wave by the uncanny smoothness of your climb. On first locating a wave, turn into the wind and attempt to climb directly over the spot where you first detected lift *provided* you can remain at an altitude above the level of the mountain crest. *The lee side turbulent area is for the experienced pilot only.* After cautiously climbing well up into the wave, attempt to determine dimensions of the zone of lift. If the wave is over rugged terrain, it may be impossible and unnecessary to determine the wave length. Lift over such terrain is likely to be in patchy bands. Over more even terrain, the wave length may be easy to determine and use in planning the next stage of flight.

Wave clouds are a visual clue in your search for lift. The wave-like shape of lenticulars is usually more obvious from above than from below. Lift should prevail from the crest of the lenticulars upwind about one-third the wave length. When your course takes you across the waves, climb on the windward side of the wave and fly as quickly as possible to the windward side of the next wave. Wave lift of 300 to 1,200 feet per minute is not uncommon. Soaring pilots have encountered vertical currents exceeding 3,000 feet per minute, the strongest ever reported being 8,000 feet per minute.

IN CLOSING

Records are made to be broken. Altitude and distance records are a prime target of many sailplane enthusiasts. Distance records may be possible by flying a combination of lift sources such as thermal, frontal, ridge, or wave. Altitude records are set in mountain waves. Altitudes above 46,000 feet have been attained over the Rocky Mountains; soaring flights to more than 24,000 feet have been made in Appalachian waves; and flights to as high as 20,000 feet have been recorded from New England to North Carolina.

We sincerely hope that this chapter has given you an insight into the minute variations in weather that profoundly affect a soaring aircraft. When you have remained airborne for hours without power, you have met a unique challenge and experienced a singular thrill of flying.

GLOSSARY OF WEATHER TERMS

A

absolute instability—A state of a layer within the atmosphere in which the vertical distribution of temperature is such that an air parcel, if given an upward or downward push, will move away from its initial level without further outside force being applied.

absolute temperature scale—*See* Kelvin Temperature Scale.

absolute vorticity—*See* vorticity.

adiabatic process—The process by which fixed relationships are maintained during changes in temperature, volume, and pressure in a body of air without heat being added or removed from the body.

advection—The horizontal transport of air or atmospheric properties. In meteorology, sometimes referred to as the horizontal component of *convection*.

advection fog—Fog resulting from the transport of warm, humid air over a cold surface.

air density—The mass density of the air in terms of weight per unit volume.

air mass—In meteorology, an extensive body of air within which the conditions of temperature and moisture in a horizontal plane are essentially uniform.

air mass classification—A system used to identify and to characterize the different *air masses* according to a basic scheme. The system most commonly used classifies air masses primarily according to the thermal properties of their *source regions*: "tropical" (T); "polar" (P); and "Arctic" or "Antarctic" (A). They are further classified according to moisture characteristics as "continental" (c) or "maritime" (m).

air parcel—*See* parcel.

albedo—The ratio of the amount of electromagnetic *radiation* reflected by a body to the amount incident upon it, commonly expressed in percentage; in meteorology, usually used in reference to *insolation* (solar radiation); i.e., the albedo of wet sand is 9, meaning that about 9% of the incident insolation is reflected; albedoes of other surfaces range upward to 80–85 for fresh snow cover; average albedo for the earth and its atmosphere has been calculated to range from 35 to 43.

altimeter—An instrument which determines the altitude of an object with respect to a fixed level. *See* pressure altimeter.

altimeter setting—The value to which the scale of a *pressure altimeter* is set so as to read true altitude at field elevation.

altimeter setting indicator—A precision *aneroid barometer* calibrated to indicate directly the altimeter setting.

altitude—Height expressed in units of distance above a reference plane, usually above mean sea level or above ground.

(1) **corrected altitude**—Indicated altitude of an aircraft altimeter corrected for the temperature of the column of air below the aircraft, the correction being based on the estimated departure of existing temperature from standard atmospheric temperature; an approximation of true altitude.

(2) **density altitude**—The altitude in the standard atmosphere at which the air has the same density as the air at the point in question. An aircraft will have the same performance characteristics as it would have in a standard atmosphere at this altitude.

(3) **indicated altitude**—The altitude above mean sea level indicated on a *pressure altimeter* set at current local *altimeter setting*.

(4) **pressure altitude**—The altitude in the standard atmosphere at which the pressure is the same as at the point in question. Since an altimeter operates solely on pressure, this is the uncorrected altitude indicated by an altimeter set at standard sea level pressure of 29.92 inches or 1013 millibars.

(5) **radar altitude**—The altitude of an aircraft determined by radar-type radio altimeter; thus the actual distance from the nearest terrain or water feature encompassed by the downward directed radar beam. For all practical purposes, it is the "actual" distance above a ground or inland water surface or the true altitude above an ocean surface.

(6) **true altitude**—The exact distance above mean sea level.

altocumulus—White or gray layers or patches of cloud, often with a waved appearance; cloud elements appear as rounded masses or rolls; composed mostly of liquid water droplets which may be supercooled; may contain ice crystals at subfreezing temperatures.

altocumulus castellanus—A species of middle cloud of which at least a fraction of its upper part presents some vertically developed, cumuliform protuberances (some of which are taller than they are wide, as castles) and which give the cloud a crenelated or turreted appearance; especially evident when seen from the side; elements usually have a common base arranged in lines. This cloud indicates instability and turbulence at the altitudes of occurrence.

anemometer—An instrument for measuring *wind speed*.

aneroid barometer—A *barometer* which operates on the principle of having changing atmospheric pressure bend a metallic surface which, in turn, moves a pointer across a scale graduated in units of pressure.

angel—In radar meteorology, an *echo* caused by physical phenomena not discernible to the eye; they have been observed when abnormally strong temperature and/or moisture *gradients* were known to exist; sometimes attributed to insects or birds flying in the radar beam.

anomalous propagation (sometimes called AP)—In radar meteorology, the greater than normal bending of the radar beam such that *echoes* are received from ground *targets* at distances greater than normal *ground clutter*.

anticyclone—An area of high atmospheric pressure which has a closed circulation that is anticyclonic, i.e., as viewed from above, the circulation is clockwise in the Northern Hemisphere, counterclockwise in the Southern Hemisphere, undefined at the Equator.

anvil cloud—Popular name given to the top portion of a *cumulonimbus* cloud having an anvil-like form.

APOB—A *sounding* made by an aircraft.

Arctic air—An air mass with characteristics developed mostly in winter over Arctic surfaces of ice and snow. Arctic air extends to great heights, and the surface temperatures are basically, but not always, lower than those of *polar air*.

Arctic front—The surface of discontinuity between very cold (Arctic) air flowing directly from the Arctic region and another less cold and, consequently, less dense air mass.

astronomical twilight—*See* twilight.

atmosphere—The mass of air surrounding the Earth.

atmospheric pressure (also called barometric pressure)—The pressure exerted by the atmosphere as a consequence of gravitational attraction exerted upon the "column" of air lying directly above the point in question.

atmospherics—Disturbing effects produced in radio receiving apparatus by atmospheric electrical phenomena such as an electrical storm. Static.

aurora—A luminous, radiant emission over middle and high latitudes confined to the thin air of high altitudes and centered over the earth's magnetic poles. Called "aurora borealis" (northern lights) or "aurora australis" according to its occurrence in the Northern or Southern Hemisphere, respectively.

attenuation—In radar meteorology, any process which reduces power density in radar signals.

(1) **precipitation attenuation**—Reduction of power density because of absorption or reflection of energy by precipitation.

(2) **range attenuation**—Reduction of radar power density because of distance from the antenna. It occurs in the outgoing beam at a rate proportional to 1/range². The return signal is also attenuated at the same rate.

B

backing—Shifting of the wind in a counterclockwise direction with respect to either space or time; opposite of *veering*. Commonly used by meteorologists to refer to a cyclonic shift (counterclockwise in the Northern Hemisphere and clockwise in the Southern Hemisphere).

backscatter—Pertaining to radar, the energy reflected or scattered by a *target*; an *echo*.

banner cloud (also called cloud banner)—A banner-like cloud streaming off from a mountain peak.

barograph—A continuous-recording *barometer*.

barometer—An instrument for measuring the pressure of the atmosphere; the two principle types are *mercurial* and *aneroid*.

barometric altimeter—*See* pressure altimeter.

barometric pressure—Same as *atmospheric pressure*.

barometric tendency—The change of barometric pressure within a specified period of time. In aviation weather observations, routinely determined periodically, usually for a 3-hour period.

beam resolution—*See* resolution.

Beaufort scale—A scale of wind speeds.

black blizzard—Same as *duststorm*.

blizzard—A severe weather condition characterized by low temperatures and strong winds bearing a great amount of snow, either falling or picked up from the ground.

blowing dust—A type of *lithometeor* composed of dust particles picked up locally from the surface and blown about in clouds or sheets.

blowing sand—A type of *lithometeor* composed of sand picked up locally from the surface and blown about in clouds or sheets.

blowing snow—A type of *hydrometeor* composed of snow picked up from the surface by the wind and carried to a height of 6 feet or more.

blowing spray—A type of *hydrometeor* composed of water particles picked up by the wind from the surface of a large body of water.

bright band—In radar meteorology, a narrow, intense *echo* on the *range-height indicator* scope resulting from water-covered ice particles of high reflectivity at the melting level.

Buys Ballot's law—If an observer in the Northern Hemisphere stands with his back to the wind, lower pressure is to his left.

C

calm—The absence of wind or of apparent motion of the air.

cap cloud (also called cloud cap)—A standing or stationary cap-like cloud crowning a mountain summit.

ceiling—In meteorology in the U.S., (1) the height above the surface of the base of the lowest layer of clouds or *obscuring phenomena* aloft that hides more than half of the sky, or (2) the *vertical visibility* into an *obscuration*. See summation principle.

ceiling balloon—A small balloon used to determine the height of a cloud base or the extent of vertical visibility.

ceiling light—An instrument which projects a vertical light beam onto the base of a cloud or into surface-based obscuring phenomena; used at night in conjunction with a *clinometer* to determine the height of the cloud base or as an aid in estimating the vertical visibility.

ceilometer—A cloud-height measuring system. It projects light on the cloud, detects the reflection by a photoelectric cell, and determines height by triangulation.

Celsius temperature scale (abbreviated C)—A temperature scale with zero degrees as the melting point of pure ice and 100 degrees as the boiling point of pure water at standard sea level atmospheric pressure.

Centigrade temperature scale—Same as *Celsius temperature scale.*

chaff—Pertaining to radar, (1) short, fine strips of metallic foil dropped from aircraft, usually by military forces, specifically for the purpose of jamming radar; (2) applied loosely to *echoes* resulting from chaff.

change of state—In meteorology, the transformation of water from one form, i.e., solid (ice), liquid, or gaseous (water vapor), to any other form. There are six possible transformations designated by the five terms following:

(1) **condensation**—The change of water vapor to liquid water.

(2) **evaporation**—The change of liquid water to water vapor.

(3) **freezing**—The change of liquid water to ice.

(4) **melting**—The change of ice to liquid water.

(5) **sublimation**—The change of (a) ice to water vapor or (b) water vapor to ice. *See* latent heat.

Chinook—A warm, dry *foehn* wind blowing down the eastern slopes of the Rocky Mountains over the adjacent plains in the U.S. and Canada.

cirriform—All species and varieties of *cirrus, cirrocumulus,* and *cirrostratus* clouds; descriptive of clouds composed mostly or entirely of small ice crystals, usually transparent and white; often producing *halo* phenomena not observed with other cloud forms. Average height ranges upward from 20,000 feet in middle latitudes.

cirrocumulus—A *cirriform* cloud appearing as a thin sheet of small white puffs resembling flakes or patches of cotton without shadows; sometimes confused with *altocumulus.*

cirrostratus—A *cirriform* cloud appearing as a whitish veil, usually fibrous, sometimes smooth; often produces *halo* phenomena; may totally cover the sky.

cirrus—A *cirriform* cloud in the form of thin, white feather-like clouds in patches or narrow bands; have a fibrous and/or silky sheen; large ice crystals often trail downward a considerable vertical distance in fibrous, slanted, or irregularly curved wisps called mares' tails.

civil twilight—*See* twilight.

clear air turbulence (abbreviated CAT)—Turbulence encountered in air where no clouds are present; more popularly applied to high level turbulence associated with *wind shear.*

clear icing (or clear ice)—Generally, the formation of a layer or mass of ice which is relatively transparent because of its homogeneous structure and small number and size of air spaces; used commonly as synonymous with *glaze*, particularly with respect to aircraft icing. Compare with *rime icing.* Factors which favor clear icing are large drop size, such as those found in *cumuliform* clouds, rapid accretion of supercooled water, and slow dissipation of *latent heat* of fusion.

climate—The statistical collective of the weather conditions of a point or area during a specified interval of time (usually several decades); may be expressed in a variety of ways.

climatology—The study of *climate.*

clinometer—An instrument used in weather observing for measuring angles of inclination; it is used in conjunction with a *ceiling light* to determine cloud height at night.

cloud bank—Generally, a fairly well-defined mass of cloud observed at a distance; it covers an appreciable portion of the horizon sky, but does not extend overhead.

cloudburst—In popular teminology, any sudden and heavy fall of *rain*, almost always of the *shower* type.

cloud cap—*See* cap cloud.

cloud detection radar—A vertically directed radar to detect cloud bases and tops.

cold front—Any non-occluded *front* which moves in such a way that colder air replaces warmer air.

condensation—*See* change of state.

condensation level—The height at which a rising *parcel* or layer of air would become saturated if lifted adiabatically.

condensation nuclei—Small particles in the air on which water vapor condenses or sublimates.

condensation trail (or contrail) (also called vapor trail)—A cloud-like streamer frequently observed to form behind aircraft flying in clear, cold, humid air.

conditionally unstable air—Unsaturated air that will become unstable on the condition it becomes saturated. *See* instability.

conduction—The transfer of heat by molecular action through a substance or from one substance in contact with another; transfer is always from warmer to colder temperature.

constant pressure chart—A chart of a constant pressure surface; may contain analyses of height, wind, temperature, humidity, and/or other elements.

continental polar air—*See* polar air.

continental tropical air—*See* tropical air.

contour—In meteorology, (1) a line of equal height on a constant pressure chart; analogous to contours on a relief map; (2) in radar meteorology, a line on a radar scope of equal *echo* intensity.

contouring circuit—On weather radar, a circuit which displays multiple contours of *echo* intensity simultaneously on the *plan position indicator* or *range-height indicator* scope. *See* contour (2).

contrail—Contraction for *condensation trail*.

convection—(1) In general, mass motions within a fluid resulting in transport and mixing of the properties of that fluid. (2) In meteorology, atmospheric motions that are predominantly vertical, resulting in vertical transport and mixing of atmospheric properties; distinguished from *advection*.

convective cloud—*See* cumuliform.

convective condensation level (abbreviated CCL)—The lowest level at which condensation will occur as a result of *convection* due to surface heating. When condensation occurs at this level, the layer between the surface and the CCL will be thoroughly mixed, temperature *lapse rate* will be dry adiabatic, and *mixing ratio* will be constant.

convective instability—The state of an unsaturated layer of air whose *lapse rates* of temperature and moisture are such that when lifted adiabatically until the layer becomes saturated, convection is spontaneous.

convergence—The condition that exists when the distribution of winds within a given area is such that there is a net horizontal inflow of air into the area. In convergence at lower levels, the removal of the resulting excess is accomplished by an upward movement of air; consequently, areas of low-level convergent winds are regions favorable to the occurrence of clouds and precipitation. Compare with *divergence*.

Coriolis force—A deflective force resulting from earth's rotation; it acts to the right of wind direction in the Northern Hemisphere and to the left in the Southern Hemisphere.

corona—A prismatically colored circle or arcs of a circle with the sun or moon at its center; coloration is from blue inside to red outside (opposite that of a *halo*); varies in size (much smaller) as opposed to the fixed diameter of the halo; characteristic of clouds composed of water droplets and valuable in differentiating between middle and cirriform clouds.

corposant—*See* St. Elmo's Fire.

corrected altitude (approximation of true altitude)—*See* altitude.

cumuliform—A term descriptive of all convective clouds exhibiting vertical development in contrast to the horizontally extended *stratiform* types.

cumulonimbus—A cumuliform cloud type; it is heavy and dense, with considerable vertical extent in the form of massive towers; often with tops in the shape of an *anvil* or massive plume; under the base of cumulonimbus, which often is very dark, there frequently exists *virga*, precipitation and low ragged clouds (*scud*), either merged with it or not; frequently accompanied by lightning, thunder, and sometimes hail; occasionally produces a tornado or a waterspout; the ultimate manifestation of the growth of a cumulus cloud, occasionally extending well into the stratosphere.

cumulonimbus mamma—A *cumulonimbus* cloud having hanging protuberances, like pouches, festoons, or udders, on the under side of the cloud; usually indicative of severe turbulence.

cumulus—A cloud in the form of individual detached domes or towers which are usually dense and well defined; develops vertically in the form of rising mounds of which the bulging upper part often resembles a cauliflower; the sunlit parts of these clouds are mostly brilliant white; their bases are relatively dark and nearly horizontal.

cumulus fractus—*See* fractus.

cyclogenesis—Any development or strengthening of cyclonic circulation in the atmosphere.

cyclone—(1) An area of low atmospheric pressure which has a closed circulation that is cyclonic, i.e., as viewed from above, the circulation is counterclockwise in the Northern Hemisphere, clockwise in the Southern Hemisphere, undefined at the Equator. Because cyclonic circulation and relatively low atmospheric pressure usually co-exist, in common practice the terms cyclone and low are used interchangeably. Also, because cyclones often are accompanied by inclement (sometimes destructive) weather, they are frequently referred to simply as storms. (2) Frequently misused to denote a *tornado*. (3) In the Indian Ocean, a *tropical cyclone* of hurricane or typhoon force.

D

deepening—A decrease in the central pressure of a pressure system; usually applied to a *low* rather than to a *high*, although technically, it is acceptable in either sense.

density—(1) The ratio of the mass of any substance to the volume it occupies—weight per unit volume. (2) The ratio of any quantity to the volume or area it occupies, i.e., population per unit area, *power density*.

density altitude—*See* altitude.

depression—In meteorology, an area of low pressure; a *low* or *trough*. This is usually applied to a certain stage in the development of a *tropical cyclone*, to migratory lows and troughs, and to upper-level lows and troughs that are only weakly developed.

dew—Water condensed onto grass and other objects near the ground, the temperatures of which have fallen below the initial dew point temperature of the surface air, but is still above freezing. Compare with *frost*.

dew point (or dew-point temperature)—The temperature to which a sample of air must be cooled, while the *mixing ratio* and barometric pressure remain constant, in order to attain saturation with respect to water.

discontinuity—A zone with comparatively rapid transition of one or more meteorological elements.

disturbance—In meteorology, applied rather loosely: (1) any low pressure or cyclone, but usually one that is relatively small in size; (2) an area where weather, wind, pressure, etc., show signs of cyclonic development; (3) any deviation in flow or pressure that is associated with a disturbed state of the weather, i.e., cloudiness and precipitation; and (4) any individual circulatory system within the primary circulation of the atmosphere.

diurnal—Daily, especially pertaining to a cycle completed within a 24-hour period, and which recurs every 24 hours.

divergence—The condition that exists when the distribution of winds within a given area is such that there is a net horizontal flow of air outward from the region. In divergence at lower levels, the resulting deficit is compensated for by subsidence of air from aloft; consequently the air is heated and the relative humidity lowered making divergence a warming and drying process. Low-level divergent regions are areas unfavorable to the occurrence of clouds and precipitation. The opposite of *convergence*.

doldrums—The equatorial belt of calm or light and variable winds between the two tradewind belts. Compare *intertropical convergence zone*.

downdraft—A relative small scale downward current of air; often observed on the lee side of large objects restricting the smooth flow of the air or in precipitation areas in or near *cumuliform* clouds.

drifting snow—A type of *hydrometeor* composed of snow particles picked up from the surface, but carried to a height of less than 6 feet.

drizzle—A form of *precipitation*. Very small water drops that appear to float with the air currents while falling in an irregular path (unlike *rain*, which falls in a comparatively straight path, and unlike *fog* droplets which remain suspended in the air).

dropsonde—A *radiosonde* dropped by parachute from an aircraft to obtain *soundings* (measurements) of the atmosphere below.

dry adiabatic lapse rate—The rate of decrease of temperature with height when unsaturated air is lifted adiabatically (due to expansion as it is lifted to lower pressure). *See* adiabatic process.

dry bulb—A name given to an ordinary thermometer used to determine temperature of the air; also used as a contraction for *dry-bulb temperature*. Compare *wet bulb*.

dry-bulb temperature—The temperature of the air.

dust—A type of *lithometeor* composed of small earthen particles suspended in the atmosphere.

dust devil—A small, vigorous *whirlwind*, usually of short duration, rendered visible by dust, sand, and debris picked up from the ground.

duster—Same as *duststorm*.

duststorm (also called duster, black blizzard)—An unusual, frequently severe weather condition characterized by strong winds and dust-filled air over an extensive area.

D-value—Departure of true altitude from pressure altitude (*see* altitude); obtained by algebraically subtracting true altitude from pressure altitude; thus it may be plus or minus. On a constant pressure chart, the difference between actual height and *standard atmospheric* height of a constant pressure surface.

E

echo—In radar, (1) the energy reflected or scattered by a *target;* (2) the radar scope presentation of the return from a target.

eddy—A local irregularity of wind in a larger scale wind flow. Small scale eddies produce turbulent conditions.

estimated ceiling—A ceiling classification applied when the ceiling height has been estimated by the observer or has been determined by some other method; but, because of the specified limits of time, distance, or precipitation conditions, a more descriptive classification cannot be applied.

evaporation—*See* change of state.

extratropical low (sometimes called extratropical cyclone, extratropical storm)—Any *cyclone* that is not a *tropical cyclone*, usually referring to the migratory frontal cyclones of middle and high latitudes.

eye—The roughly circular area of calm or relatively light winds and comparatively fair weather at the center of a well-developed *tropical cyclone*. A *wall cloud* marks the outer boundary of the eye.

F

Fahrenheit temperature scale (abbreviated F)—A temperature scale with 32 degrees as the melting point of pure ice and 212 degrees as the boiling point of pure water at standard sea level atmospheric pressure (29.92 inches or 1013.2 millibars).

Fall wind—A cold wind blowing downslope. Fall wind differs from *foehn* in that the air is initially cold enough to remain relatively cold despite compressional heating during descent.

filling—An increase in the central pressure of a pressure system; opposite of *deepening;* more commonly applied to a low rather than a high.

first gust—The leading edge of the spreading downdraft, *plow wind*, from an approaching thunderstorm.

flow line—A *streamline*.

foehn—A warm, dry downslope wind; the warmness and dryness being due to adiabatic compression upon descent; characteristic of mountainous regions. *See* adiabatic process, Chinook, Santa Ana.

fog—A *hydrometeor* consisting of numerous minute water droplets and based at the surface; droplets are small enough to be suspended in the earth's atmosphere indefinitely. (Unlike *drizzle*, it does not fall to the surface; differs from cloud only in that a cloud is not based at the surface; distinguished from haze by its wetness and gray color.)

fractus—Clouds in the form of irregular shreds, appearing as if torn; have a clearly ragged appearance; applies only to stratus and cumulus, i.e., *cumulus* fractus and *stratus* fractus.

freezing—*See* change of state.

freezing level—A level in the atmosphere at which the temperature is 0° C (32° F).

front—A surface, interface, or transition zone of discontinuity between two adjacent *air masses* of different densities; more simply the boundary between two different air masses. *See* frontal zone.

frontal zone—A *front* or zone with a marked increase of density gradient; used to denote that fronts are not truly a "surface" of discontinuity but rather a "zone" of rapid transition of meteorological elements.

frontogenesis—The initial formation of a *front* or *frontal zone*.

frontolysis—The dissipation of a *front*.

frost (also hoarfrost)—Ice crystal deposits formed by sublimation when temperature and dew point are below freezing.

funnel cloud—A *tornado* cloud or *vortex* cloud extending downward from the parent cloud but not reaching the ground.

G

glaze—A coating of ice, generally clear and smooth, formed by freezing of supercooled water on a surface. *See* clear icing.

gradient—In meteorology, a horizontal decrease in value per unit distance of a parameter in the direction of maximum decrease; most commonly used with pressure, temperature, and moisture.

ground clutter—Pertaining to radar, a cluster of *echoes*, generally at short range, reflected from ground *targets*.

ground fog—In the United States, a *fog* that conceals less than 0.6 of the sky and is not contiguous with the base of clouds.

gust—A sudden brief increase in wind; according to U.S. weather observing practice, gusts are reported when the variation in wind speed between peaks and lulls is at least 10 knots.

H

hail—A form of *precipitation* composed of balls or irregular lumps of ice, always produced by convective clouds which are nearly always *cumulonimbus*.

halo—A prismatically colored or whitish circle or arcs of a circle with the sun or moon at its center; coloration, if not white, is from red inside to blue outside (opposite

that of a *corona*); fixed in size with an angular diameter of 22° (common) or 46° (rare); characteristic of clouds composed of ice crystals; valuable in differentiating between *cirriform* and forms of lower clouds.

haze—A type of *lithometeor* composed of fine dust or salt particles dispersed through a portion of the atmosphere; particles are so small they cannot be felt or individually seen with the naked eye (as compared with the larger particles of *dust*), but diminish the visibility; distinguished from *fog* by its bluish or yellowish tinge.

high—An area of high barometric pressure, with its attendant system of winds; an *anticyclone*. Also high pressure system.

hoar frost—*See* frost.

humidity—Water vapor content of the air; may be expressed as *specific humidity*, *relative humidity*, or *mixing ratio*.

hurricane—A *tropical cyclone* in the Western Hemisphere with winds in excess of 65 knots or 120 km/h.

hydrometeor—A general term for particles of liquid water or ice such as rain, fog, frost, etc., formed by modification of water vapor in the atmosphere; also water or ice particles lifted from the earth by the wind such as sea spray or blowing snow.

hygrograph—The record produced by a continuous-recording *hygrometer*.

hygrometer—An instrument for measuring the water vapor content of the air.

I

ice crystals—A type of *precipitation* composed of unbranched crystals in the form of needles, columns, or plates; usually having a very slight downward motion, may fall from a cloudless sky.

ice fog—A type of fog composed of minute suspended particles of ice; occurs at very low temperatures and may cause *halo* phenomena.

ice needles—A form of *ice crystals*.

ice pellets—Small, transparent or translucent, round or irregularly shaped pellets of ice. They may be (1) hard grains that rebound on striking a hard surface or (2) pellets of snow encased in ice.

icing—In general, any deposit of ice forming on an object. *See* clear icing, rime icing, glaze.

indefinite ceiling—A ceiling classification denoting *vertical visibility* into a surface based obscuration.

indicated altitude—*See* altitude.

insolation—Incoming solar *radiation* falling upon the earth and its atmosphere.

instability—A general term to indicate various states of the atmosphere in which spontaneous *convection* will occur when prescribed criteria are met; indicative of turbulence. *See* absolute instability, conditionally unstable air, convective instability.

intertropical convergence zone—The boundary zone between the trade wind system of the Northern and Southern Hemispheres; it is characterized in maritime climates by showery precipitation with cumulonimbus clouds sometimes extending to great heights.

inversion—An increase in temperature with height—a reversal of the normal decrease with height in the *troposphere;* may also be applied to other meteorological properties.

isobar—A line of equal or constant barometric pressure.

iso echo—In radar circuitry, a circuit that reverses signal strength above a specified intensity level, thus causing a void on the scope in the most intense portion of an echo when maximum intensity is greater than the specified level.

isoheight—On a weather chart, a line of equal height; same as *contour* (1).

isoline—A line of equal value of a variable quantity, i.e., an isoline of temperature is an *isotherm*, etc. *See* isobar, isotach, etc.

isoshear—A line of equal *wind shear.*

isotach—A line of equal or constant wind speed.

isotherm—A line of equal or constant temperature.

isothermal—Of equal or constant temperature, with respect to either space or time; more commonly, temperature with height; a zero *lapse rate.*

J

jet stream—A quasi-horizontal stream of winds 50 knots or more concentrated within a narrow band embedded in the westerlies in the high *troposphere.*

K

katabatic wind—Any wind blowing downslope. *See* fall wind, foehn.

Kelvin temperature scale (abbreviated K)—A temperature scale with zero degrees equal to the temperature at which all molecular motion ceases, i.e., absolute zero (0° K = −273° C); the Kelvin degree is identical to the Celsius degree; hence at standard sea level pressure, the melting point is 273° K and the boiling point 373° K.

knot—A unit of speed equal to one nautical mile per hour.

L

land breeze—A coastal breeze blowing from land to sea, caused by temperature difference when the sea surface is warmer than the adjacent land. Therefore, it usually blows at night and alternates with a *sea breeze*, which blows in the opposite direction by day.

lapse rate—The rate of decrease of an atmospheric variable with height; commonly refers to decrease of temperature with height.

latent heat—The amount of heat absorbed (converted to kinetic energy) during the processes of change of liquid water to water vapor, ice to water vapor, or ice to liquid water; or the amount released during the reverse processes. Four basic classifications are:

(1) **latent heat of condensation**—Heat released during change of water vapor to water.

(2) **latent heat of fusion**—Heat released during change of water to ice or the amount absorbed in change of ice to water.

(3) **latent heat of sublimation**—Heat released during change of water vapor to ice or the amount absorbed in the change of ice to water vapor.

(4) **latent heat of vaporization**—Heat absorbed in the change of water to water vapor; the negative of latent heat of condensation.

layer—In reference to sky cover, clouds or other obscuring phenomena whose bases are approximately at the same level. The layer may be continuous or composed of detached elements. The term "layer" does not imply that a clear space exists between the layers or that the clouds or *obscuring phenomena* composing them are of the same type.

lee wave—Any stationary wave disturbance caused by a barrier in a fluid flow. In the atmosphere when sufficient moisture is present, this wave will be evidenced by *lenticular clouds* to the lee of mountain barriers; also called *mountain wave* or *standing wave.*

lenticular cloud (or lenticularis)—A species of cloud whose elements have the form of more or less isolated, generally smooth lenses or almonds. These clouds appear most often in formations of orographic origin, the result of *lee waves*, in which case they remain nearly stationary with respect to the terrain (standing cloud), but they also occur in regions without marked orography.

level of free convection (abbreviated LFC)—The level at which a *parcel* of air lifted dry-adiabatically until saturated and moist-adiabatically thereafter would become warmer than its surroundings in a conditionally unstable atmosphere. *See.* conditional instability and adiabatic process.

lifting condensation level (abbreviated LCL)—The level at which a *parcel* of unsaturated air lifted dry-adiabatically would become saturated. Compare *level of free convection* and *convective condensation level.*

lightning—Generally, any and all forms of visible electrical discharge produced by a *thunderstorm.*

lithometeor—The general term for dry particles suspended in the atmosphere such as dust, haze, smoke, and sand.

low—An area of low barometric pressure, with its attendant system of winds. Also called a barometric depression or *cyclone.*

M

mammato cumulus—Obsolete. *See* cumulonimbus mamma.

mare's tail—*See* cirrus.

maritime polar air (abbreviated mP)—*See* polar air.

maritime tropical air (abbreviated mT)—*See* tropical air.

maximum wind axis—On a constant pressure chart, a line denoting the axis of maximum wind speeds at that constant pressure surface.

mean sea level—The average height of the surface of the sea for all stages of tide; used as reference for elevations throughout the U.S.

measured ceiling—A ceiling classification applied when the ceiling value has been determined by instruments or the known heights of unobscured portions of objects, other than natural landmarks.

melting—*See* change of state.

mercurial barometer—A *barometer* in which pressure is determined by balancing air pressure against the weight of a column of mercury in an evacuated glass tube.

meteorological visibility—In U.S. observing practice, a main category of *visibility* which includes the subcategories of *prevailing visibility* and *runway visibility*. Meteorological visibility is a measure of horizontal visibility near the earth's surface, based on sighting of objects in the daytime or unfocused lights of moderate intensity at night. Compare *slant visibility*, *runway visual range*, *vertical visibility*. *See* surface visibility, tower visibility, and sector visibility.

meteorology—The science of the *atmosphere*.

microbarograph—An aneroid *barograph* designed to record atmospheric pressure changes of very small magnitudes.

millibar (abbreviated mb.)—An internationally used unit of pressure equal to 1,000 dynes per square centimeter. It is convenient for reporting *atmospheric pressure*.

mist—A popular expression for drizzle or heavy fog.

mixing ratio—The ratio by weight of the amount of water vapor in a volume of air to the amount of dry air; usually expressed as grams per kilogram (g/kg).

moist-adiabatic lapse rate—*See* saturated-adiabatic lapse rate.

moisture—An all-inclusive term denoting water in any or all of its three states.

monsoon—A wind that in summer blows from sea to a continental interior, bringing copious rain, and in winter blows from the interior to the sea, resulting in sustained dry weather.

mountain wave—A *standing wave* or *lee wave* to the lee of a mountain barrier.

N

nautical twilight—*See* twilight.

negative vorticity—*See* vorticity.

nimbostratus—A principal cloud type, gray colored, often dark, the appearance of which is rendered diffuse by more or less continuously falling rain or snow, which in most cases reaches the ground. It is thick enough throughout to blot out the sun.

noctilucent clouds—Clouds of unknown composition which occur at great heights, probably around 75 to 90 kilometers. They resemble thin *cirrus*, but usually with a bluish or silverish color, although sometimes orange to red, standing out against a dark night sky. Rarely observed.

normal—In meteorology, the value of an element averaged for a given location over a period of years and recognized as a standard.

numerical forecasting—*See* numerical weather prediction.

numerical weather prediction—Forecasting by digital computers solving mathematical equations; used extensively in weather services throughout the world.

O

obscuration—Denotes sky hidden by surface-based *obscuring phenomena* and *vertical visibility* restricted overhead.

obscuring phenomena—Any *hydrometeor* or *lithometeor* other than clouds; may be surface based or aloft.

occlusion—Same as *occluded front*.

occluded front (commonly called occlusion, also called frontal occlusion)—A composite of two fronts as a *cold front* overtakes a *warm front* or *quasi-stationary front*.

orographic—Of, pertaining to, or caused by mountains as in orographic clouds, orographic lift, or orographic precipitation.

ozone—An unstable form of oxygen; heaviest concentrations are in the stratosphere; corrosive to some metals; absorbs most ultraviolet solar radiation.

P

parcel—A small volume of air, small enough to contain uniform distribution of its meteorological properties, and large enough to remain relatively self-contained and respond to all meteorological processes. No specific dimensions have been defined, however, the order of magnitude of 1 cubic foot has been suggested.

partial obscuration—A designation of sky cover when part of the sky is hidden by surface based *obscuring phenomena*.

pilot balloon—A small free-lift balloon used to determine the speed and direction of winds in the upper air.

pilot balloon observation (commonly called PIBAL)—A method of winds-aloft observation by visually tracking a *pilot balloon*.

plan position indicator (PPI) scope—A radar indicator scope displaying range and azimuth of *targets* in polar coordinates.

plow wind—The spreading downdraft of a *thunderstorm;* a strong, straight-line wind in advance of the storm. *See* first gust.

polar air—An air mass with characteristics developed over high latitudes, especially within the subpolar highs. Continental polar air (cP) has cold surface temperatures, low moisture content, and, especially in its source regions, has great stability in the lower layers. It is shallow in comparison with *Arctic air*. Maritime polar (mP) initially possesses similar properties to those of continental polar air, but in passing over warmer water it becomes unstable with a higher moisture content. Compare *tropical air*.

polar front—The semipermanent, semicontinuous *front* separating air masses of tropical and polar origins.

positive vorticity—*See* vorticity.

power density—In radar meteorology the amount of radiated energy per unit cross sectional area in the radar beam.

precipitation—Any or all forms of water particles, whether liquid or solid, that fall from the atmosphere and reach the surface. It is a major class of *hydrometeor*, distinguished from cloud and *virga* in that it must reach the surface.

precipitation attenuation—*See* attenuation.

pressure—*See* atmospheric pressure.

pressure altimeter—An *aneroid barometer* with a scale graduated in altitude instead of pressure using *standard atmospheric* pressure-height relationships; shows indicated altitude (not necessarily true altitude); may be set to measure altitude (indicated) from any arbitrarily chosen level. *See* altimeter setting, altitude.

pressure altitude—*See* altitude.

pressure gradient—The rate of decrease of pressure per unit distance at a fixed time.

pressure jump—A sudden, significant increase in *station pressure*.

pressure tendency—*See* barometric tendency.

prevailing easterlies—The broad current or pattern of persistent easterly winds in the Tropics and in polar regions.

prevailing visibility—In the U.S., the greatest horizontal visibility which is equaled or exceeded throughout half of the horizon circle; it need not be a continuous half.

prevailing westerlies—The dominant west-to-east motion of the atmosphere, centered over middle latitudes of both hemispheres.

prevailing wind—Direction from which the wind blows most frequently.

prognostic chart (contracted PROG)—A chart of expected or forecast conditions.

pseudo-adiabatic lapse rate—*See* saturated-adiabatic lapse rate.

psychrometer—An instrument consisting of a *wet-bulb* and a *dry-bulb* thermometer for measuring wet-bulb and dry-bulb temperature; used to determine water vapor content of the air.

pulse—Pertaining to radar, a brief burst of electromagnetic radiation emitted by the radar; of very short time duration. *See* pulse length.

pulse length—Pertaining to radar, the dimension of a radar pulse; may be expressed as the time duration or the length in linear units. Linear dimension is equal to time duration multiplied by the speed of propagation (approximately the speed of light).

Q

quasi-stationary front (commonly called stationary front)—A *front* which is stationary or nearly so; conventionally, a front which is moving at a speed of less than 5 knots is generally considered to be quasi-stationary.

R

RADAR (contraction for radio detection and ranging)—An electronic instrument used for the detection and ranging of distant objects of such composition that they scatter or reflect radio energy. Since *hydrometeors* can scatter radio energy, *weather radars*, operating on certain frequency bands, can detect the presence of precipitation, clouds, or both.

radar altitude—*See* altitude.

radar beam—The focused energy radiated by radar similar to a flashlight or searchlight beam.

radar echo—*See* echo.

radarsonde observation—A *rawinsonde observation* in which winds are determined by radar tracking a balloon-borne target.

radiation—The emission of energy by a medium and transferred, either through free space or another medium, in the form of electromagnetic waves.

radiation fog—*Fog* characteristically resulting when radiational cooling of the earth's surface lowers the air temperature near the ground to or below its initial dew point on calm, clear nights.

radiosonde—A balloon-borne instrument for measuring pressure, temperature, and humidity aloft. Radiosonde observation—a *sounding* made by the instrument.

rain—A form of *precipitation*; drops are larger than *drizzle* and fall in relatively straight, although not necessarily vertical, paths as compared to *drizzle* which falls in irregular paths.

rain shower—*See* shower.

range attenuation—*See* attenuation.

range-height indicator (RHI) scope—A radar indicator scope displaying a vertical cross section of *targets* along a selected azimuth.

range resolution—*See* resolution.

RAOB—A *radiosonde* observation.

rawin—A *rawinsonde* observation.

rawinsonde observation—A combined winds aloft and radiosonde observation. Winds are determined by tracking the *radiosonde* by radio direction finder or radar.

refraction—In radar, bending of the *radar beam* by variations in atmospheric density, water vapor content, and temperature.

(1) **normal refraction**—Refraction of the radar beam under normal atmospheric conditions; normal radius of curvature of the beam is about 4 times the radius of curvature of the Earth.

(2) **superrefraction**—More than normal bending of the radar beam resulting from abnormal vertical gradients of temperature and/or water vapor.

(3) **subrefraction**—Less than normal bending of the radar beam resulting from abnormal vertical gradients of temperature and/or water vapor.

relative humidity—The ratio of the existing amount of water vapor in the air at a given temperature to the maximum amount that could exist at that temperature; usually expressed in percent.

relative vorticity—*See* vorticity.

remote scope—In radar meteorology a "slave" scope remoted from weather *radar.*

resolution—Pertaining to radar, the ability of radar to show discrete *targets* separately, i.e., the better the resolution, the closer two targets can be to each other, and still be detected as separate targets.

(1) **beam resolution**—The ability of radar to distinguish between targets at approximately the same range but at different azimuths.

(2) **range resolution**—The ability of radar to distinguish between targets on the same azimuth but at different ranges.

ridge (also called ridge line)—In meteorology, an elongated area of relatively high atmospheric pressure; usually associated with and most clearly identified as an area of maximum anticyclonic curvature of the wind flow (*isobars, contours,* or *streamlines*).

rime icing (or rime ice)—The formation of a white or milky and opaque granular deposit of ice formed by the rapid freezing of supercooled water droplets as they impinge upon an exposed aircraft.

rocketsonde—A type of *radiosonde* launched by a rocket and making its measurements during a parachute descent; capable of obtaining *soundings* to a much greater height than possible by balloon or aircraft.

roll cloud (sometimes improperly called rotor cloud)—A dense and horizontal roll-shaped accessory cloud located on the lower leading edge of a *cumulonimbus* or less often, a rapidly developing *cumulus;* indicative of turbulence.

rotor cloud (sometimes improperly called *roll cloud*)—A turbulent cloud formation found in the lee of some large mountain barriers, the air in the cloud rotates around an axis parallel to the range; indicative of possible violent turbulence.

runway temperature—The temperature of the air just above a runway, ideally at engine and/or wing height, used in the determination of density *altitude;* useful at airports when critical values of density altitude prevail.

runway visibility—The *meteorological visibility* along an identified runway determined from a specified point on the runway; may be determined by a *transmissometer* or by an observer.

runway visual range—An instrumentally derived horizontal distance a pilot should see down the runway from the approach end; based on either the sighting of high intensity runway lights or on the visual contrast of other objects, whichever yields the greatest visual range.

S

St. Elmo's Fire (also called corposant)—A luminous brush discharge of electricity from protruding objects, such as masts and yardarms of ships, aircraft, lightning rods, steeples, etc., occurring in stormy weather.

Santa Ana—A hot, dry, *foehn* wind, generally from the northeast or east, occurring west of the Sierra Nevada Mountains especially in the pass and river valley near Santa Ana, California.

saturated adiabatic lapse rate—The rate of decrease of temperature with height as saturated air is lifted with no gain or loss of heat from outside sources; varies with temperature, being greatest at low temperatures. *See* adiabatic process and dry-adiabatic lapse rate.

saturation—The condition of the atmosphere when actual *water vapor* present is the maximum possible at existing temperature.

scud—Small detached masses of stratus *fractus* clouds below a layer of higher clouds, usually *nimbostratus.*

sea breeze—A coastal breeze blowing from sea to land, caused by the temperature difference when the land surface is warmer than the sea surface. Compare *land breeze.*

sea fog—A type of *advection fog* formed when air that has been lying over a warm surface is transported over a colder water surface.

sea level pressure—The *atmospheric pressure* at mean sea level, either directly measured by stations at sea level or empirically determined from the *station pressure* and temperature by stations not at sea level; used as a common reference for analyses of surface pressure patterns.

sea smoke—Same as *steam fog.*

sector visibility—*Meteorological visibility* within a specified sector of the horizon circle.

sensitivity time control—A radar circuit designed to correct for range *attenuation* so that echo intensity on the scope is proportional to reflectivity of the *target* regardless of range.

shear—*See* wind shear.

shower—*Precipitation* from a *cumuliform* cloud; characterized by the suddenness of beginning and ending, by the rapid change of intensity, and usually by rapid change in the appearance of the sky; showery precipitation may be in the form of rain, ice pellets, or snow.

slant visibility—For an airborne observer, the distance at which he can see and distinguish objects on the ground.

sleet—*See* ice pellets.

smog—A mixture of *smoke* and *fog*.

smoke—A restriction to visibility resulting from combustion.

snow—Precipitation composed of white or translucent ice crystals, chiefly in complex branched hexagonal form.

snow flurry—Popular term for snow *shower*, particularly of a very light and brief nature.

snow grains—*Precipitation* of very small, white opaque grains of ice, similar in structure to *snow* crystals. The grains are fairly flat or elongated, with diameters generally less than 0.04 inch (1 mm.).

snow pellets—*Precipitation* consisting of white, opaque approximately round (sometimes conical) ice particles having a snow-like structure, and about 0.08 to 0.2 inch in diameter; crisp and easily crushed, differing in this respect from *snow grains;* rebound from a hard surface and often break up.

snow shower—*See* shower.

solar radiation—The total electromagnetic *radiation* emitted by the sun. *See* insolation.

sounding—In meteorology, an upper-air observation; a *radiosonde* observation.

source region—An extensive area of the earth's surface characterized by relatively uniform surface conditions where large masses of air remain long enough to take on characteristic temperature and moisture properties imparted by that surface.

specific humidity—The ratio by weight of *water vapor* in a sample of air to the combined weight of water vapor and dry air. Compare *mixing ratio*.

squall—A sudden increase in wind speed by at least 15 knots to a peak of 20 knots or more and lasting for at least one minute. Essential difference between a *gust* and a squall is the duration of the peak speed.

squall line—Any nonfrontal line or narrow band of active *thunderstorms* (with or without *squalls*).

stability—A state of the atmosphere in which the vertical distribution of temperature is such that a *parcel* will resist displacement from its initial level. (*See also* instability.)

standard atmosphere—A hypothetical atmosphere based on climatological averages comprised of numerous physical constants of which the most important are:

(1) A surface *temperature* of 59° F (15° C) and a surface pressure of 29.92 inches of mercury (1013.2 millibars) at sea level;

(2) A *lapse rate* in the troposphere of 6.5° C per kilometer (approximately 2° C per 1,000 feet);

(3) A *tropopause* of 11 kilometers (approximately 36,000 feet) with a temperature of −56.5° C; and

(4) An *isothermal* lapse rate in the stratosphere to an altitude of 24 kilometers (approximately 80,000 feet).

standing cloud (standing lenticular altocumulus)—*See* lenticular cloud.

standing wave—A wave that remains stationary in a moving fluid. In aviation operations it is used most commonly to refer to a *lee wave* or *mountain wave*.

stationary front—Same as *quasi-stationary front*.

station pressure—The actual *atmospheric pressure* at the observing station.

steam fog—Fog formed when cold air moves over relatively warm water or wet ground.

storm detection radar—A weather radar designed to detect *hydrometeors* of precipitation size; used primarily to detect storms with large drops or hailstones as opposed to clouds and light precipitation of small drop size.

stratiform—Descriptive of clouds of extensive horizontal development, as contrasted to vertically developed *cumuliform* clouds; characteristic of stable air and, therefore, composed of small water droplets.

stratocumulus—A low cloud, predominantly *stratiform* in gray and/or whitish patches or layers, may or may not merge; elements are tessellated, rounded, or roll-shaped with relatively flat tops.

stratosphere—The atmospheric layer above the tropopause, average altitude of base and top, 7 and 22 miles respectively; characterized by a slight average increase of temperature from base to top and is very stable; also characterized by low moisture content and absence of clouds.

stratus—A low, gray cloud layer or sheet with a fairly uniform base; sometimes appears in ragged patches; seldom produces precipitation but may produce *drizzle* or *snow grains*. A *stratiform* cloud.

stratus fractus—*See* fractus.

streamline—In meteorology, a line whose tangent is the wind direction at any point along the line. A flowline.

sublimation—*See* change of state.

subrefraction—*See* refraction.

subsidence—A descending motion of air in the atmosphere over a rather broad area; usually associated with *divergence*.

summation principle—The principle states that the cover assigned to a layer is equal to the summation of the sky cover of the lowest layer plus the additional coverage at all successively higher layers up to and including the layer in question. Thus, no layer can be assigned a sky cover less than a lower layer, and no sky cover can be greater than 1.0 (10/10).

superadiabatic lapse rate—A *lapse rate* greater than the *dry-adiabatic lapse rate*. *See* absolute instability.

supercooled water—Liquid water at temperatures colder than freezing.

superrefraction—*See* refraction.

surface inversion—An *inversion* with its base at the surface, often caused by cooling of the air near the surface as a result of *terrestrial radiation*, especially at night.

surface visibility—Visibility observed from eye-level above the ground.

synoptic chart—A chart, such as the familiar weather map, which depicts the distribution of meteorological conditions over an area at a given time.

T

target—In radar, any of the many types of objects detected by radar.

temperature—In general, the degree of hotness or coldness as measured on some definite temperature scale by means of any of various types of thermometers.

temperature inversion—*See* inversion.

terrestrial radiation—The total infrared *radiation* emitted by the Earth and its atmosphere.

thermograph—A continuous-recording *thermometer*.

thermometer—An instrument for measuring *temperature*.

theodolite—An optical instrument which, in meteorology, is used principally to observe the motion of a *pilot balloon*.

thunderstorm—In general, a local storm invariably produced by a *cumulonimbus* cloud, and always accompanied by lightning and thunder.

tornado (sometimes called cyclone, twister)—A violently rotating column of air, pendant from a cumulonimbus cloud, and nearly always observable as "funnel-shaped." It is the most destructive of all small-scale atmospheric phenomena.

towering cumulus—A rapidly growing *cumulus* in which height exceeds width.

tower visibility—*Prevailing visibility* determined from the control tower.

trade winds—Prevailing, almost continuous winds blowing with an easterly component from the subtropical high pressure belts toward the *intertropical convergence zone;* northeast in the Northern Hemisphere, southeast in the Southern Hemisphere.

transmissometer—An instrument system which shows the transmissivity of light through the atmosphere. Transmissivity may be translated either automatically or manually into *visibility* and/or *runway visual range*.

tropical air—An air mass with characteristics developed over low latitudes. Maritime tropical air (mT), the principal type, is produced over the tropical and subtropical seas; very warm and humid. Continental tropical (cT) is produced over subtropical arid regions and is hot and very dry. Compare *polar air*.

tropical cyclone—A general term for a *cyclone* that originates over tropical oceans. By international agreement, tropical cyclones have been classified according to their intensity, as follows:

(1) **tropical depression**—winds up to 34 knots (64 km/h);

(2) **tropical storm**—winds of 35 to 64 knots (65 to 119 km/h);

(3) **hurricane or typhoon**—winds of 65 knots or higher (120 km/h).

tropical depression—*See* tropical cyclone.

tropical storm—*See* tropical cyclone.

tropopause—The transition zone between the *troposphere* and *stratosphere*, usually characterized by an abrupt change of *lapse rate*.

troposphere—That portion of the *atmosphere* from the earth's surface to the *tropopause;* that is, the lowest 10 to 20 kilometers of the atmosphere. The troposphere is characterized by decreasing temperature with height, and by appreciable water vapor.

trough (also called trough line)—In meteorology, an elongated area of relatively low atmospheric pressure; usually associated with and most clearly identified as an area of maximum cyclonic curvature of the wind flow (*isobars*, *contours*, or *streamlines*); compare with *ridge*.

true altitude—*See* altitude.

true wind direction—The direction, with respect to true north, from which the wind is blowing.

turbulence—In meteorology, any irregular or disturbed flow in the atmosphere.

twilight—The intervals of incomplete darkness following sunset and preceding sunrise. The time at which evening twilight ends or morning twilight begins is determined by arbitrary convention, and several kinds of twilight have been defined and used; most commonly civil, nautical, and astronomical twilight.

(1) **Civil Twilight**—The period of time before sunrise and after sunset when the sun is not more than 6° below the horizon.

(2) **Nautical Twilight**—The period of time before sunrise and after sunset when the sun is not more than 12° below the horizon.

(3) **Astronomical Twilight**—The period of time before sunrise and after sunset when the sun is not more than 18° below the horizon.

twister—In the United States, a colloquial term for *tornado*.

typhoon—A *tropical cyclone* in the Eastern Hemisphere with winds in excess of 65 knots (120 km/h).

U

undercast—A cloud *layer* of ten-tenths (1.0) coverage (to the nearest tenth) as viewed from an observation point above the layer.

unlimited ceiling—A clear sky or a sky cover that does not meet the criteria for a *ceiling*.

unstable—*See* instability.

updraft—A localized upward current of air.

upper front—A *front* aloft not extending to the earth's surface.

upslope fog—Fog formed when air flows upward over rising terrain and is, consequently, adiabatically cooled to or below its initial *dew point*.

V

vapor pressure—In meteorology, the pressure of water vapor in the atmosphere. Vapor pressure is that part of the total atmospheric pressure due to water vapor and is independent of the other atmospheric gases or vapors.

vapor trail—Same as *condensation trail*.

veering—Shifting of the wind in a clockwise direction with respect to either space or time; opposite of backing. Commonly used by meteorologists to refer to an anticyclonic shift (clockwise in the Northern Hemisphere and counterclockwise in the Southern Hemisphere).

vertical visibility—The distance one can see upward into a surface based *obscuration;* or the maximum height from which a pilot in flight can recognize the ground through a surface based obscuration.

virga—Water or ice particles falling from a cloud, usually in wisps or streaks, and evaporating before reaching the ground.

visibility—The greatest distance one can see and identify prominent objects.

visual range—*See* runway visual range.

vortex—In meteorology, any rotary flow in the atmosphere.

vorticity—Turning of the atmosphere. Vorticity may be imbedded in the total flow and not readily identified by a flow pattern.

    (a) **absolute vorticity**—the rotation of the Earth imparts vorticity to the atmosphere; absolute vorticity is the combined vorticity due to this rotation and vorticity due to circulation relative to the Earth (relative vorticity).

    (b) **negative vorticity**—vorticity caused by anticyclonic turning; it is associated with downward motion of the air.

    (c) **positive vorticity**—vorticity caused by cyclonic turning; it is associated with upward motion of the air.

    (d) **relative vorticity**—vorticity of the air relative to the Earth, disregarding the component of vorticity resulting from Earth's rotation.

W

wake turbulence—*Turbulence* found to the rear of a solid body in motion relative to a fluid. In aviation terminology, the turbulence caused by a moving aircraft.

wall cloud—The well-defined bank of vertically developed clouds having a wall-like appearance which form the outer boundary of the *eye* of a well-developed *tropical cyclone*.

warm front—Any non-occluded *front* which moves in such a way that warmer air replaces colder air.

warm sector—The area covered by warm air at the surface and bounded by the *warm front* and *cold front* of a *wave cyclone*.

water equivalent—The depth of water that would result from the melting of snow or ice.

waterspout—*See* tornado.

water vapor—Water in the invisible gaseous form.

wave cyclone—A *cyclone* which forms and moves along a front. The circulation about the cyclone center tends to produce a wavelike deformation of the front.

weather—The state of the *atmosphere*, mainly with respect to its effects on life and human activities; refers to instantaneous conditions or short term changes as opposed to *climate*.

weather radar—Radar specifically designed for observing weather. *See* cloud detection radar and storm detection radar.

weather vane—A *wind vane*.

wedge—Same as *ridge*.

wet bulb—Contraction of either *wet-bulb temperature* or *wet-bulb thermometer*.

wet-bulb temperature—The lowest *temperature* that can be obtained on a *wet-bulb thermometer* in any given sample of air, by evaporation of water (or ice) from the muslin wick; used in computing *dew point* and *relative humidity*.

wet-bulb thermometer—A thermometer with a muslin-covered bulb used to measure wet-bulb temperature.

whirlwind—A small, rotating column of air; may be visible as a dust devil.

willy-willy—A *tropical cyclone* of hurricane strength near Australia.

wind—Air in motion relative to the surface of the earth; generally used to denote horizontal movement.

wind direction—The direction **from** which wind is blowing.

wind speed—Rate of wind movement in distance per unit time.

wind vane—An instrument to indicate wind direction.

wind velocity—A vector term to include both *wind direction* and *wind speed*.

wind shear—The rate of change of *wind velocity* (direction and/or speed) per unit distance; conventionally expressed as vertical or horizontal wind shear.

X–Y–Z

zonal wind—A west wind; the westerly component of a wind. Conventionally used to describe large-scale flow that is neither cyclonic nor anticyclonic.

INDEX